WHAT IS
OPUS DEI?

Conspiracy Books is a topical range of titles dedicated to publishing the truth about all conspiracies - whether ancient or modern, theoretical or real. The series is informative, entertaining, subjective and incisive, and will endeavour to bring the reader closer than ever before to the reality of the conspiracies that surround us.

WHAT IS
OPUS DEI?

NOAM FRIEDLANDER

COLLINS & BROWN

First published in the United Kingdom in 2005 by
Collins & Brown
151 Freston Road
London W10 6TH

An imprint of Anova Books Company Ltd

Produced by Conspiracy Books
PO Box 51726, London NW1 9ZH, UK

ISBN 1 84340 288 2

A CIP catalogue record for this book is available from
the British Library.

The author and publishers have made every
reasonable effort to contact copyright holders. Any
errors that may have occurred are inadvertent and
anyone who has not been contacted is invited to
write to the publishers so that full acknowledgement
may be made in subsequent editions of this work.

10 9 8 7 6 5 4 3 2

Printed and bound in Great Britain by
Creative Print & Design (Wales), Ebbw Vale

This book can be ordered direct from the publisher.
Contact the marketing department, but try your
bookshop first.

www.anovabooks.com

Contents

Introduction

Opus Dei and its origins

These days a trip to New York usually involves sightseeing and shopping. It's a magnet for rampaging tourists keen to pick up the cheapest bargains or the latest fashions, while taking in the imposing architecture of the skyscraper-filled city. Head to Murray Hill, a smart neighborhood near midtown Manhattan, and you will find the Empire State and Chrysler Buildings nearby, as well as fashionista's favorite haunts, Jimmy Choo, and the department store Lord & Taylor. In 2001, a newcomer moved into the district: Opus Dei.

"New York is a center of work and activity in the United States," says Brian Finnerty, National Director of Communications for the Prelature of the Holy Cross and Opus Dei. "Much of what goes on in the United States flows through New York. It's appropriate for us to be there."

Appropriate? An interesting choice of words as New York is in fact a strange choice for the Roman Catholic organization, which is known for its secretive profile. There is no escaping this latest venture. The 17-storey building commands the corner of Lexington Avenue and 34th Street and, at a cost of around $47 million, is Opus Dei's US national headquarters. Hardly discreet, the building is around 12,369m² (133,000ft²), with six floors of the building set aside for the national organization. It seems Opus Dei has a statement to make.

If you are lucky enough to be invited inside the nerve center, you will discover a self-sufficient building kitted out for a Catholic army of sorts, which combines residences for both women and men, along with a conference, educational, and instructional center for Opus Dei members. Tired? Weary Catholics can spend the night in one of the 100 bedrooms. Fancy a bite to eat? There are six dining rooms. Alongside that, visitors can enjoy the libraries, living rooms, meeting rooms, and offices. Prayer, naturally, is not ignored, with chapels on the second, eighth and sixteenth floors, ornamented with finished woodwork and marble. Yet, strangely, for a modern construction it appears old-fashioned and dated in style—a red brick edifice rather than the more traditional millenniumesque building materials such as glass and metal. A reflection of their traditional beliefs perhaps?

Stand on the opposite street corner, and you will see people constantly bustling in and out of the headquarters; wander around the outside of the premises and you will notice two separate entrances on separate streets, one for the women's residence and another for the men's residence. There is also separate on-site parking for men and women. Segregation of the sexes is just one aspect of Opus Dei, and one of the few things immediately visible to the outside world.

Father Vladimir Feltzman, ex-Opus Dei member and a respected Roman Catholic priest who now works for the diocese of London's Westminster, explains the segregation issue: "It's just a very male sort of thing," he says in interview. "Women are women; they are seen as, sort of, not quite human in the sense that they are emotional, they can't control themselves in the same way men can. Their role traditionally is that of rearing children and supporting the man."

So, while the women and men separately enter this grand, formidable and highly public structure, little is actually known about the movement. What is Opus Dei? Who belongs to Opus Dei? Where, and, more importantly, how has the movement amassed the kind of wealth necessary to buy a 57m (186ft) high building in the center of Manhattan? Should we be afraid of Opus Dei?

A brief investigation of the movement shows that, despite being small in numbers, its global presence is phenomenal. Many of its members hold influential positions of power across the globe. Opus Dei members and senior officials have frequently come out publicly to state that their aim is not world domination nor is it to gain political influence across the globe. Instead, claims Opus Dei, its aim is to contribute to the evangelizing mission of the Church. This role was previously taken on by the Church's former all-conquering global power, the Jesuit movement, whose influence and evangelizing missions has diminished over the centuries, leaving Opus Dei as the beating heart of the Church and proving to be the most dynamic force within the Catholic Church over the last 50 years of the 20th century.

Opus Dei has gained papal approval because not only has it proved to be a successful evangelizing mission, but also its work all over the world has resulted in schools, universities, and residences, which are all founded on Opus Dei principles. Yet conspiracy theories concerning Opus Dei abound, most of them loaded and unproven.

Critics also comment that Opus Dei appears to go only for the "elite", which again adds fuel to conspiracy theories. Opus Dei would deny this claim, as many of its early members were ordinary Christians. As for targeting an "elite", there is a simple explanation. When the organization was first conceived, self-preservation was all-important. What better way to ensure the ongoing existence of an organization than to target those in positions of influence and power? However, to understand the origin of these theories, it is important to appreciate the origins of the movement itself.

Say the words "Opus Dei," and you will get a variety of responses. A scholar will tell you it means "God's Work". Those who have read Dan Brown's book, *The Da Vinci Code*, will know it as a holy Mafia, filled with self-flagellating angry monks. Some Catholics think it is a cult or sect, while others recognize that it has a place in the Catholic Church. Most, however, agree that Opus Dei is one of the most controversial groups within the Catholic Church today. It was this supposed sense of mystery and controversy that drew Brown's attention to the organization for *The Da Vinci Code*, but he claims he worked hard to create a fair and balanced depiction of the organization.

Considering the images Brown created, including that of a murderous albino monk, Opus Dei is naturally affronted at Brown's creation. Opus Dei is a devout organization and one of its greatest devotions is to secrecy. It is a policy held by Opus Dei, and it refers to its secrecy as "holy discretion". Ex-members contend that this "holy Omerta" is backed up by its own constitution. The old constitutions of 1950, superseded since 1982, cited an obligation to "conceal the number of members from outsiders" and "to always maintain prudent silence about the names of other members, and not reveal to anyone one's own membership in Opus Dei." By blocking information to non-members, it immediately creates suspicion and resentment. However, times change. Opus Dei's press offices—across the globe from Africa, Oceania, and Asia to America (North and South) and Europe—are only too helpful to provide stats and data about the organization, as well as answer the criticisms and charges levelled against them. Yet despite this openness, there are still detractors.

"To its critics it [Opus Dei] is a powerful, even dangerous, cult-like organization that uses secrecy and manipulation to advance its agenda," writes Rev James Martin, a Jesuit priest and author of a 1995 article "Opus Dei In the United States", which appeared in a Jesuit magazine criticizing Opus Dei.

Opus Dei founder Josemaría Escrivá de Balaguer, however, takes a different view: "We are not religious. We bear no resemblance to a religion nor is there any authority on earth which could require us to be religious. Yet in Opus Dei we venerate and love the religious state. Misunderstandings, if they should occur, would show a lack of Christian spirit, for our Faith calls for unity, not for rivalries or divisions."

There are still some ex-members of Opus Dei who, having left the movement, have spoken out against it. "Before I joined, I was not shown the Opus Dei statutes or rules," says an ex-Opus Dei member who wishes to remain unnamed, "and I did not know that any were in existence. When I lived in the Center of Studies, we took classes on them and were encouraged to memorize them because we were not allowed to take notes on them. They were in Spanish, so some-one had to translate them for us. The bishops of each archdiocese where Opus Dei operates has a copy in Latin. ODAN (a website for the Opus Dei Awareness Network) has just published an English transla-tion for the first time ever."

"I respect their experience," says Andrew Soane, communications officer for Opus Dei in London, "but I think it's atypical. I also think that when someone leaves Opus Dei, it's a bit like a marriage breaking up. You've committed yourself to Opus Dei and then you leave. It can be quite traumatic for people, and it seems to me that some of them have suffered. But, I think it's useful to remember that most people who leave Opus Dei stay on good terms, and, over the years, about half of them come back and start attending meetings again. We stay on good terms with ex-members and they stay on good terms with us."

Yet, the theories and the conspiracies about the movement abound. "Members lead a kind of double life," says Paul Baumann, a columnist for the liberal Catholic magazine *Commonweal*. "To the world, they are successful doctors or lawyers, distinguished only by their professional skills and autonomy; off the job they must not only engage in an intense life of prayer (all to the good) but be strictly accountable to those above them in 'the Work' (more problematic)."

The reason for some of this suspicion could be due to the fact that Opus Dei publishes no financial statements or membership lists. Its internal structure is kept private, while business ventures controlled by its members are also not revealed. The organization also reports, once every five years, only to the Pope, thanks to its unique prelature stature. This was granted to the movement by Pope John Paul II in 1982 and allows Opus Dei to be given its own bishop, the Prelate, who has worldwide jurisdiction over the spiritual work and organization of its members.

The organization, however, denies all allegations of secrecy. "It's not secret," says Bill Schmitt, a former communications director of Opus Dei. "It's private. Big difference." In a 1967 interview, the founder Escrivá concurred: "The members detest secrecy."

Schmitt's defense is backed up by Marc Carroggio, Opus Dei's information officer in Rome: "We have 84,000 members. These include 'numeraries', like myself, and 'supernumeraries'. Numeraries commit themselves to chastity, poverty, obedience, and to living Christian virtues according to the teaching of the Opus Dei. We live together in houses, or Pastoral Centers, of which there are 1,654. Each center has a director. Supernumeraries are active members who are allowed to marry and have children. In addition, there are 'cooperators', or active supporters. There are at least several hundred thousand of these. There are also about 1,500 Opus Dei priests." Carroggio says lists of numeraries and supernumeraries are not secret, but they are "confidential" because religious commitment is a "personal affair".

Despite Opus Dei's protestations, the secrecy allegations continue and the movement's constitutions are not readily available to the general public but solely to the elite or high-ranking members within the movement. Opus Dei's excuse? Since the organization received the blessing of Pope John Paul II, the constitutions have been given to the bishops of every single diocese where Opus Dei operates. That, the movement feels, is enough. The organization also has an internal magazine *Crónica*, which is not easily available outside the movement.

Ultimately, Opus Dei is a holy organization, which, according to its many critics, has broken bread with the century's most notorious dictators. A fierce ambition has taken it from one of the most private of organizations to a commanding presence at the heart of one of the world's biggest religions, and all this has been achieved since 1928. Now, it remains answerable to one person and one person only, his Holiness the Pope. Just how and where did Opus Dei, as well as all the allegations and criticisms that surround the movement, originate?

Where Did it all Begin?

Escrivá always said he was interested in the aristocracy, for blood, intelligence, and money. Because, for God, only the best is good enough. The lamb must be pure, perfect, without the blot. This goes back to something that's always been there. Only the best can be given to God. First born. Not the second born. And not women.

Father Vladimir Feltzman, ex-Opus Dei member, on Opus Dei, September 2004

Josemaría Escrivá de Balaguer, a devout Catholic, founded Opus Dei in Spain in 1928. He had been born at the turn of the 20th century in Barbastro, which lies in the northern corner of Spain in Aragon.

Significantly, Spain was a country that was divided into numerous regions, which led to a fragmented and insular State. A strategic stronghold, thanks to Spain's positioning between Europe and Africa with borders on both the Mediterranean and the Atlantic, the country had been invaded through the centuries by Phoenicians, Greeks, Carthaginians, Romans, Goths, Arabs, French, Portuguese, and the English, with each invader making its own impression on Spanish society.

The industrial revolutions sweeping Europe during the 19th century had passed over most of Spain, which, along with Portugal, was one of the poorest countries in Europe at the beginning of the 20th. The Spanish people were suffering. Food was scarce, education minimal, and healthcare poor: infant mortality stood at 128,395 deaths in 1900 out of a total population of 18.6 million (compared with 11,590 deaths in 1976 and a total population of around 36 million).

Furthermore, regions across Spain differed wildly in terms of economic developments and technological advancements. The regions of Catalonia and the Basque provinces had a firm foothold in the 20th century but, during the early 1900s, areas such as Aragon, New Castile, and Andalusia were still stuck in the 18th century. In these regions, peasants lived off the harsh (and often infertile) land, which was controlled by the aristocrats or wealthy bourgeois. Employment for these peasants rarely lasted throughout the whole year, leaving them in a state of near-starvation when they weren't working.

Within Spain there was a lack of social mobility—people stayed within their family trades and rarely moved up the social ladder. If you were born poor in Spain then you stayed poor, while the rich remained wealthy. Spain was not on the regular tourist route—unlike today, when the Costa del Sol and Costa Brava are regular bustling haunts for European travellers.

In addition, the country had lost the last of her overseas colonies—Cuba, Puerto Rico, and the Philippines—in the American-Spanish war of 1898. Her overseas empire gone, and separated from the rest of Europe by the great wall of the Pyrenees, Spain turned in on herself and as she did, the Catholic Church strengthened its already powerful grip on the national psyche. It was practically the only institution that could claim to have unified the country in the past.

Spain, in the early 1920s then, was made up of half a dozen "kingdoms" and each one had its own administration, laws, and Cortes (government)—only the King of Spain linked these various kingdoms and his power, at this time, was incredibly limited. Furthermore, voting within Spain for the Cortes was limited to men alone—it wasn't until a new law in the 1931 Constitution that women won the right to vote and also the right to be elected to any public office. There was, however, the one common thread running throughout Spain—the Church, a powerful force, whose word was rarely questioned. It had been in the name of the Church and of evangalization that Spain had embarked on its conquests of the New World. So for some people the Church was the true Spain.

But evidence of dissatisfaction among the poor was growing. There were significant rumblings of dissent at the nation's shaky economic situation and some popular fury at the stagnant, repressive nature of the social situation. Antonio Maura, a Conservative prime minister who came to power in 1907, legalized strikes, reformed the judiciary system, and tried to regulate rural rents, and make elections fairer. His efforts backfired, however. In attempting to bring in liberal reforms he distanced himself further from the anarchists who had begun gaining ground among the disenfranchized of Spain. Combined with the alliance of the Liberal and the Republican parties, Maura's alienating of the left led to anarchist uprisings in several regions, especially among the farm laborers of Andalusia and industrial workers in Barcelona. Spain's parliamentary monarchy lost stability amid growing dissidence throughout Spanish society, and political groups resorted to violence. One such group involved in the fighting were the Carlists.

The Carlists, a royalist faction of the 19th and 20th centuries, originated in the 1830s and were followers of Don Carlos de Borbón (they believed Don Carlos was the rightful king following King Fernando VII's death in 1833; however his daughter Princess Isabel was named as heir). The Carlist movement grew, founded on the ideas of absolute monarchy and a return to the Inquisition. By 1909, during riots in Barcelona, there were tales of the Carlists massing for an uprising as well as convents around the city collecting arms. A split across the country was becoming ever more apparent.

Republican movements pressing for greater democracy demanded constitutional reforms. The first basis of a small, yet strong, socialist movement started growing in the factories and mines of the Basque provinces and Asturias. Elsewhere, the regionalist sentiments in Catalonia became grumbles of dissatisfaction as they demanded autonomy. King Alfonso XIII tried to interfere and, as a result, lost prestige—his subjects viewing him as a meddler with too much personal ambition.

These voices of dissent were to lead to a growing radical movement arguing for change—and, eventually, to the election in 1931 of Spain's Republican government. The new government was set up quickly and relatively smoothly, as its ministers had been preparing for years. Niceto Alcalá Zamora was chosen as the Head of State, and he selected Manuel Azaña to be Head of War. The Republic set out to fix all the above-mentioned sources of fragmentation and disarray—separatists, the relationship between Church and State, social values, agrarian reform, the role of the military, and the disputes between landowners, merchants, and peasants.

At this stage, Catalonia's capital Barcelona was the largest supporter of the new republic—possibly why it proved so successful, since Catalonia was the industrial center of Spain during the 1930s, with

70 percent of all industry and 50 percent of industrial workers. Barcelona was also the largest voice in the separatist movement—it supported and elected a government it hoped would free it.

It was into this world that Escrivá was born in 1902. His family were comfortably well off. He was one of six children, of whom only two others survived—Carmen (who was born in 1899 and died in 1957) and their brother Santiago (who was born much later, in 1919, and who died in 1994). Like many children of that era, young Josemaría Escrivá fell ill while a baby. As a result, his mother Dolores, a Barbastro native, took him to a small shrine dedicated to the Virgin Mary at Torreciudad, a local place of pilgrimage, and the prayers to save her child's life were answered. Escrivá recovered, and it was later recorded by Opus Dei followers to be a favour of Our Lady, especially as his three sisters later died—Rosario, when she was only one, Dolores at five, and finally, Asunción (known as Chon), who died shortly after her eighth birthday.

Possibly as a result of "the miracle", Escrivá was educated by the Piarists, a Roman Catholic order of men, whose aim is to administer free education and instruction, especially to poor boys. Yet, according to historians, Escrivá's family were moderately wealthy. Dolores had the assistance of a cook, a maid, and a nanny to look after the house, and a manservant was employed to do the heavy work, while his father José had his own textile business.

This period of relative prosperity was not to last, however. When Josemaría was 13, his father textile business collapsed. The region of Aragon (and thus Barbastro) found life difficult in the years leading up to World War I. The agricultural economy on which Barbastro's commerce depended was failing, and the region lacked banks and other financial institutions to give businesses the credit they needed to survive the bad times.

With Don José declared bankrupt, the family was forced to sell its house, release its servants (something practically unheard of in middle-class Spain during this era), and relocate. The Escrivás moved to Logroño, a town in the same region, in 1915, where José found some work by going into partnership in a clothes shop called "La Gran Ciudad de Londres" ("The Great City of London").

It was a time of change for the Escrivá family, now lacking in funds. The young Escrivá attended Logroño's state *instituto* in the mornings, as well as a "tutorial college" run by laymen, St Anthony's, in the afternoon.

Logroño was a provincial capital at the time with about 25,000 inhabitants and, although the town itself was prosperous, the Escrivás lived in a 7m² (75ft²), fourth-floor, walk-up apartment with no heating. It was a cramped environment, and certainly a change from the early days in Barbastro when Don José's family had lived among the upper middle-class sector of society. Here in Logroño, with Don José working as a salaried clerk, the family had to "make do" with Dona Dolores and her daughter Carmen doing all the household chores.

It was soon after his move to Logroño, according to Opus Dei legend, that Escrivá received his spiritual calling. In the winter of 1918, Escrivá was walking through the snow-covered streets of Logroño when he spotted tracks left in the snow belonging to a Carmelite brother, who was walking in bare feet. It was at this point, we are told, that Escrivá felt he had a personal calling from God, which proved the spark that started his interest in Christianity. "He interpreted the footprints as a sign that God wanted something of him," writes Michael Clark, author of *Reason To Believe*.

"God is calling you to serve Him," explained Escrivá later, "and from the ordinary...there is something holy, something divine, hidden in the most ordinary situations..."

As a result of his "calling" Escrivá began his ecclesiastical studies in Logroño, which would lead to his entering the diocesan seminary of Zaragoza in 1920. While studying, Escrivá also pursued studies in civil law with his superiors' permission. During that time Escrivá's spiritual life became deeply rooted in the Eucharist, visiting the Basilica of Our Lady of Pilar every day to seek inspiration.

As Escrivá later recalled: "Since I felt those inklings of God's love, I sought to carry out, within the limits of my smallness, what He expected from this poor instrument...And, with those yearnings, I prayed and prayed and prayed, in constant prayer. I kept on repeating: *'Domine, ut sit. Domine, ut videam'*, like the poor fellow in the Gospel, who shouted out because God can do everything: 'Lord, that I may see! Lord, that it may come to be!'"

Escrivá was a hard worker and considered a conscientious student, but again his life was about to change. His father died in 1924, just three weeks before Escrivá was due to be ordained a deacon, and it was now up to the son to support his family. The only remaining siblings in the family were his sister Carmen, who was twenty-five, and his young brother Santiago, who was only five.

In early 1925, Escrivá's mother brought Carmen and Santiago to live in Zaragoza, not far from the seminary and, on March 28th, 1925, Escrivá was ordained a priest. The young Escrivá moved to Perdiguera, a small rural parish, for a brief stay of only two months before returning to Zaragoza. In 1927, Escrivá's bishop gave him permission to move to Madrid to obtain his doctorate in law. At the same time, he supported himself and his family with other jobs, including teaching law courses.

"He was an energetic person," said Bishop Javier Echevarría, the Opus Dei Prelate, in 2002 at the celebration of the centenary of Escrivá's birth. "He was strong, understanding, and optimistic. He always acted responsibly, was generous, and was full of zeal for souls."

His zeal saw him, on September 30th, 1928, set up a retreat in Madrid at the Residence of the Missionaries of Saint Vincente de Paul, which was due to last five days. It was at this retreat, only two days in, that Escrivá says he received his "inspiration from God". On October 2nd, Escrivá was in his room studying, reading through some notes and meditating when he received his vision.

"I received the vision about the Work while I was reading those notes," Escrivá later wrote. "Deeply moved, I kneeled down—I was alone in my room—and gave thanks to the Lord, and I remember the emotion the sound of the church bells of Our Lady of the Angels [brought to me]...If others sacrifice so much for God and their neighbor, couldn't I do something too? I began to have an inkling of what Love is, to realize that my heart was yearning for something great, for love." A movement was born—though the name "Opus Dei" was not used until the early 1930s.

"He says he had an inspiration," explains Father Vladimir Feltzman, former Opus Dei member, who lived with Escrivá in Rome. "That told him that everybody, not just nuns and monks or 'professionals' who were totally committed, but outside, normal-life Christians—everybody (a) is a child of God, as St Paul says, and (b) that they're all called and are capable of striving for affection in wherever they are, through whatever they're doing. In other words they don't have to become nuns or monks or rabbis or do something special. You can be a first-class professional, and by being as good a human being as you can you can still fulfil your vocation."

"Your duty is to sanctify yourself," said Escrivá. "Yes, even you. Who thinks that task is only for priests and the religious? To everyone, without exception, our Lord said: 'Be perfect, as my heavenly Father is perfect'."

Cardinal Luciani, Patriarch of Venice, and later Pope John Paul I, said of Escrivá, just before his elevation to papal status in 1978: "If an idea or a significant phrase occurred to him, even in the midst of a conversation, he would pull a notepad out of his pocket and jot down a word or half a line, to be used later in his writing. Apart from writing books (which are very widely read, even today), he dedicated himself energetically and tenaciously to promoting his great project of spirituality: organizing the association of Opus Dei. There's a proverb, which says: 'Give a man from Aragon a nail and he'll hammer it in with his own head.' Well, Msgr Escrivá has written: 'I'm from Aragon. I'm very stubborn.' He did not waste a minute."

Escrivá spent the next few years studying at the University of Madrid, making contacts and meeting new people, while continuing to teach—he still had to support his mother and siblings after all. Working quietly, Escrivá began to spread his ideal to people with whom he came into contact. An important source of new members came from the Cicuéndez Academy, where he taught canon and Roman law. (Cicuéndez was a private academy, similar to the Amado Institute where Escrivá had taught in Zaragoza; law students who could not attend regular classes at the university registered here as "unofficial" students, and they made up the large majority of the intake.)

During this period there are reports that Escrivá also spent his time serving as a chaplain to a charitable organization known as the Foundation for the Sick, which had been started in Madrid by a group of Catholic women. This work involved visits to public hospitals, but also gave Escrivá the chance to keep a lookout for potential recruits who would devote their lives to Opus Dei. As it happened, sick people in hospital, some of them critically ill, proved easy recruits to pray and offer their sufferings for Opus Dei. "Opus Dei grew among the sick and poor of Madrid hospitals," wrote Escrivá, referring to the "energy" generated for him by the prayers of the sick he often visited. Escrivá also wrote about the hours he spent in the slums of Madrid, listening to children's confessions, reporting: "I used to go to bed dead tired".

As time went on, Escrivá gathered about him a group of loyal university students and recent graduates, including José Romeo, the younger brother of one of Escrivá's fellow law students in Zaragoza. A second group was made up of priests, while a third comprised workmen and clerks whom Escrivá met during a talk he had given for a mission organized by the Foundation for the Sick in June 1930.

There are differing opinions about the young Escrivá. While Bishop Javier Echevarría, the present Prelate of Opus Dei, naturally praises the movement's founder, there are others who doubt his talent. One of them, Manuel Mindán, who claims to have known Escrivá during his early years, describes him as: "an obscure man, introvert and with a very serious lack of keenness...I do not understand how a man with so short an intelligence could go so far." Taking Mindán's points on board—just how original were Escrivá's thoughts and beliefs? Had Escrivá stumbled on something new? According to Feltzman, Opus Dei was actually "part of a movement that was going on all over Europe".

"A woman would ask the bishop: 'What would you like me to do?' And he would say: 'I'd like you to be a journalist' [or] 'I'd like you to be a mother' or 'I'd like you to be whatever', and she'd get on with it," explains Feltzman. "So Opus Dei was within that context. It's along the lines of John Henry Newman [the British Anglo-Catholic who was one of the founders of the 19th-century Oxford Movement, who believed that the Church should be active in the community] saying, 'We're all called to holiness'. It's not just professionals, in that sort of movement, but everyone. But, when Escrivá said it, in Spain, it was a fantastically sort of novel idea."

Furthermore, according to John Martin, writing in *The Remnant* newspaper: "In fact, such an organization already existed, and it was right there in Spain. This was the Parochial Cooperators of Christ the King, founded in 1922 by a zealous Spanish Jesuit with the French name of François de Paule Vallet." According to Martin, Father Vallet, who died in 1947, was a follower of the 30-day Ignatian exercises, which, he discovered, led to a remarkable faith-regeneration of power. He condensed these exercises into a five-day format and they proved so popular that his discovery made an impact across France (leading to "La Cité Catholique", a network of Catholic lay groups that studied Catholic doctrine and tried to restore Christ as king over society). Martin also reports that Vallet had been banished from Spain but, it appears, his influence and teachings remained. His banishment, as Martin points out, took place in 1928, the very year that Escrivá's work on Opus Dei began.

From the outset, Escrivá felt that it was important to create an organization within the Catholic Church that emphasized lay people, instead of focusing solely on the spirituality of the clergy—so making Catholics (and non-Catholics) more aware of the importance of sanctity in daily living and of serving God in ordinary work and everyday tasks. The basic principle was simple: anyone could achieve holiness by offering their daily work to God. The idea that the work of a lay person was just as important (in God's eyes) as that of a priest was a new concept in Spain. This tenet is still held by members today.

Escrivá later wrote in his book *Camino* (*The Way*, published in Spanish in 1934 under the title of *Consideraciones Espirituales*, before being expanded in 1939 to become *The Way*): "If you want to give yourself to God in the world, rather than being scholarly (women needn't be scholars: it's enough for them to be prudent) you must be spiritual, closely united to our Lord by prayer..."

On the surface, Escrivá's ideas were innovative and democratic—it was a radical ideology. Before the creation of Opus Dei, the way to "holiness" was commonly observed as something for only the clergy or other religious workers. The belief that people who were not part of the clergy were now holy, too, was an exciting philosophy. However, scratch the surface of Escrivá's beliefs and the antiquated doctrines of Spain could be found in abundance underneath. Spanish society didn't treat women as equals (like many other European nations during this era), little tolerance was shown to members of other faiths, and as for homosexuality, forget it. This was 1930s Spain. While there have been changes across the country since then, little has changed within Opus Dei. It sees itself as a bastion of preserving tradition and faith—and remains locked in its antiquated, traditional world.

Having established a new ideology, the next logical step for Escrivá was to win new recruits to his task quickly. *Crónica*, Opus Dei's internal magazine, carried a statement from Escrivá regarding recruitment: "This holy coercion is necessary".

Escrivá was looking for men—women didn't feature in the initial stages of Opus Dei—but these weren't just any men. He had a firm idea of the type of people he wanted to enlist, right from the start. It is at this point that the idea of a democratic faith starts to fall apart. The people he needed had to be bright, well-connected, well-educated, potential leaders and decision makers.

The world of academia was (and still is) the obvious place to start. Initiating university students and ingratiating himself with the middle classes as well as the upper echelons of society was a key factor for Escrivá. As Feltzman says: "He wanted the best. Escrivá always said he was interested in the aristocracy, for blood, intelligence, and money. Because, for God, only the best is good enough." To this day Opus Dei residential centers are often located near universities or in prosperous neighborhoods.

The logic in recruiting well-educated, well-connected candidates is nothing new. It goes back to the Renaissance and the theory of *Cuius regio, eius religio*—meaning, literally, "whose the rule; his the religion". You start from the head of a group and work downwards. An anachronistic belief, it had worked for the Christian evangelists. By converting tribal leaders, early Roman Catholic missionaries had converted entire tribes, at least nominally, for they frequently continued also to worship their local gods.

Supporters of Opus Dei, however, deny that this was their sole means of recruitment—to take on the "head of a group". Instead, they are keen to stress that Escrivá sought converts from across the social spectrum.

When Opus Dei started out, Escrivá utilized his contacts from his student days in Logroño and Zaragoza, as well as seeking support from the priests who had shared his lodging house when he lived in Madrid. Networking was (and remains) a key factor for Opus Dei members and for Escrivá when he was starting out.

Escrivá spent time in the late 1920s walking through the Madrid streets or visiting the small cafés often frequented by students, explaining the theories of his beliefs. He ensured that they understood the meaning of seeking holiness in the world (one of Opus Dei's main principles), and showed them how to keep in contact with God at every moment of their day, whether they were studying, working, travelling, relaxing at home, or with friends. Escrivá also frequently brought students to his mother's home, where they spent time in a welcoming family atmosphere.

One of the more prominent members was Isidoro Zorzano, an engineer with the Andalusian railways in Malaga and one of Escrivá's former classmates, whom Escrivá had met by chance on the street when Zorzano was looking for some spiritual guidance in 1930. "I remember Isidoro Zorzano," wrote Santiago Escrivá, Josemaría's younger brother. "A classmate of Josemaría's in the last three years of high school at Logroño Institute. He used to say he was struck by how my brother could earn top grades with a normal amount of study, without seeming to make any great effort, while he (Zorzano) had to spend hours and hours studying just to get decent grades."

With Zorzano signed up, Escrivá wrote letters to everyone he knew, both inside and outside the Spanish capital, as well as asking acquaintances and members of his congregation (Escrivá still worked as a chaplain) whether they knew of any suitable male candidates. Before long, Escrivá had made a number of influential friends among both the clerical and lay communities, as he began to develop Opus Dei through letters, while cultivating the aristocracy and slowly, but surely, beginning to collect a few disciples.

One such disciple was trainee architect Miguel Fisac, who later played a large part in helping to establish Opus Dei. "Pedro Casciaro took me to the DYA residence [Opus Dei's first center, which opened in Madrid in 1933 and became the first college student residence—a rented flat at first, to which students could go for extra tuition in certain subjects] and presented me to Josemaría Escrivá... Like me, Pedro Casciaro and Francisco Botella also studied architecture and they lived in the residency. They had joined Opus Dei and began to pester me relentlessly to join as well. A young and likeable priest [Escrivá], we had a pleasant conversation and he invited me to join them."

Opus Dei targeted men, but in 1930, two years after the movement's foundation, Escrivá claims to have received his second "inspiration" and became more inclusive as the movement began to recruit both men and women. Soon after this, Escrivá established separate branches of Opus Dei for men and women, which was the beginning of the frequent separation of the sexes within the organization. However, in a contemporary context, such male/female discrimination was entirely characteristic of Spanish society in the 1920s.

Today there are still two separate branches within Opus Dei—one for men and the other for women—and the sexes are still rigidly segregated, with separate Opus Dei residence centers.

"His attitude to women was terribly Edwardian," explains Feltzman. "There are two types of female numerary members [within Opus Dei]. There's the ordinary numerary and there's the auxiliary numerary. The numerary dresses in white, while the auxiliary dresses in green and you can't change from one to the other. The middle-class, feminine ordinary numeraries have to sleep on a board, not on a mattress, and they can't cuddle babies because they might be lured to get broody. But the auxiliary numeraries, because they're 'rough' and 'insensitive', can sleep on a bed and can cuddle babies because they won't be affected. Now that's an Edwardian mindset. It's all upstairs-downstairs."

In 1932, Escrivá went on a retreat for a week. During this time he set himself a rigorous plan, and created a demanding list of sacrifices for himself. He had a complete fast one day a week, would not eat sweets, and decided not to drink water except during Mass. It was at this time that he also practiced the traditional mortifications of using the *disciplines*—a whip of cords—and the *cilice*, a spiked chain, which can be worn around the upper thigh (it is considered to be a modern version of the traditional hairshirt). He also slept on the floor three nights a week and resolved not to complain about life or issues to anyone, "unless it is to seek spiritual direction".

Following this retreat, Escrivá wrote to Father Sánchez, his spiritual director, in 1934 saying: "Our Lord is undoubtedly asking me, Father, to step up my penance. When I am faithful to him in this matter, the Work seems to take on new impetus." As with many religious men, he saw that a vigorous and dedicated approach to his faith brought him the results he was looking for—namely, further clarity when trying to define Opus Dei.

During this period, Escrivá was struggling financially. He had to support his family and had the chance to walk away from the foundations of Opus Dei, which was, during this time, still in its embryonic stage. According to John Coverdale in his book *Uncommon Faith*, it was at this point in Escrivá's career that he was offered a lifeline. He reports that Angel Herrera, the National President of Catholic Action and editor of *El Debate*, wanted to open a center in Madrid to train young priests. Escrivá was invited to be the spiritual director of the center, which would have given him considerable influence as well as power in directing Catholic Action in Spain. Instead, Escrivá chose to continue working on Opus Dei, saying: "I appreciate the offer, but I can't accept. I have to follow the path...to which God calls me."

It was a decision Escrivá had to make as the two movements differ wildly and, if he was to have any success with Opus Dei, then he had to turn his back on this opportunity. Catholic Action, a movement that had begun in the early 1930s, involved lay people taking part in (and supporting) the official apostolic activities of the hierarchy. In fact, in 1932, the Spanish Catholic Action group, a group of single men ranging in age from 16 to 30, began planning a pilgrimage to the Shrine of St James the Apostle in Spain for the year 1937. Their goal at that time was to evangelize the Spanish-speaking world. Opus Dei envisions laymen (and eventually women) carrying out apostolate primarily in the world, with no special mandate from the hierarchy.

As stated, by 1934 Escrivá had published the first draft of his book *The Way*, under the title of *Spiritual Considerations*. Later that year, it was evident that the first flat Escrivá had rented for the DYA Academy had become too small. In the autumn of 1934 he transferred it to a larger one, and offered not only teaching and study activities but also accommodation for a small number of university students.

Escrivá's work took time to establish itself within Spanish society, but, only five years after his vision, his strategies were all in place: recruit the best, harvest the best, and then send them out to sow more seeds. However, the next ten years of the movement were uncertain years for Opus Dei. Like many other Catholics, many members of Opus Dei (though not all) considered there was only one side to support when the Republican army swept across the country during the Spanish Civil War and that was General Franco. Not only was he battling for Spain, but, in many Catholics' eyes, he was also fighting for the freedom of Christianity. In backing Franco, Opus Dei turned its back on the Republicans. If Franco lost, Opus Dei, and indeed Catholicism, would suffer. If the general succeeded, however, Opus Dei and many other Catholics would hold prime positions under Franco's rule. It was a time of hiding, persecution, and fear—as well as hope and belief in Franco. Opus Dei and the majority of Catholics across Spain just had to hope that Franco would win.

A Historic Crusade

The Communists were terrible; massacring, persecuting, torturing, raping. And then along comes Franco, with his invasion from the south, and he eventually wins thanks to Hitler, Mussolini. So who are the saviors of Christianity? Hitler, Mussolini. Nobody as yet in Spain knows about concentration camps, so 1936, 1937, 1938, the savior of Christianity is Hitler. That is there. Like it or not, it's understandable. If you've been in hiding because you've been persecuted and suddenly along comes Franco with his coal-scuttle helmets and the German *Luftwaffe* supporting him, you say 'Thank God we've been liberated'.

Father Vladimir Feltzman, ex-Opus Dei member, on Opus Dei, September 2004

On July 22nd, 1936, at the start of the Spanish Civil War, 18 nuns of the Monastery of St Joseph were scattered throughout the Madrid streets disguised in secular clothes. Some found shelter with Catholic families, while others hid in the basement of the Hibernia Hotel. Two days later, five nuns ventured out of the hotel. Two went to a nearby boarding house while three of them made their way up the street. The three nuns were spotted by a soldier eating his lunch in a parked jeep. Dropping his food, a soldier shouted across to his colleagues: "Shoot them. They're nuns." The three women had nowhere to run, they were trapped and knew that death was imminent.

The Republican militiamen shot the three Carmelite nuns in the middle of the street. Reports after the shooting state that one died instantly, another was then refused transport to a nearby hospital by a bus driver. Instead, he wanted to finish her off, while the third nun wandered around in a daze until another band of militiamen executed her. A bloody end, but this was a typical event that surrounded priests, monks, and nuns during the 1930s.

A month later, Escrivá himself was nearly caught by anti-Catholic forces. According to Escrivá's biographers, on August 30th, 1936, the priest was hiding at a friend's house. At around two o'clock in the afternoon, a group of soldiers were sweeping the neighborhood for Catholics—enemies of the state. The soldiers rang the bell, and while an elderly maid went to open the door, Escrivá and his two companions disappeared up the service stairway to hide in an attic.

Escrivá had a close escape—the soldiers came close to finding their soot-filled, poorly ventilated bolt hole—and he and his companions had to stay hidden away until nine o'clock that evening until they were sure they were safe from capture.

Such near misses for Escrivá and his followers and, indeed, for other Catholic priests, meant that Opus Dei continued to be discreet about its operations. Since the proclamation of the Republic in Spain in 1931 these were dangerous times for any Catholic movement. Many Spaniards felt the Church had too much political power and wealth. For centuries, Roman Catholicism had been the official religion of Spain and the Church had been an important force in Spanish government, exercising considerable influence over education and freedom of expression. Some members of the clergy even held seats in the senate, a division of Spain's parliament, the Cortes.

As the Republican government grew in power from the early 1930s there was a chance for revenge against Catholics. After all, the complete Church catechism, republished in 1927, had branded Liberalism "a most grievous sin...Generally a mortal sin". A multiparty coalition of socialists and middle-class republicans now dominated the government, and the largest coalition parties wanted sweeping changes in Spain's social, political, and economic institutions. In order to do this the Republic reforms in place wanted to restructure the military and reduce the Church's power—two major institutions that had enjoyed privileged positions in Spanish society.

Soon after the Republic was proclaimed, the Ministry for Justice published a statement that criticized the wealth of the Catholic Church. Further reforms included legalizing divorce, which had been illegal under Catholic Spain, ending the Church's role in education, and reducing the size of the officer corps. Naturally, all this had a devastating effect on the Church. By 1933, the Church Rule had ordered the separation of Church and State, withdrawing the influence of the Church on many schools.

"We learned with great sorrow that therein, at the beginning, it is openly declared that the State has no official religion, thus reaffirming that separation of State from Church which was, alas, decreed in the new Spanish Constitution," wrote Pope Pius XI to a group of leading Spanish archbishops in 1933. "We shall not delay here to repeat that it is a serious error to affirm that this separation is licit and good in itself, especially in a nation almost totally Catholic. Separation, well considered, is only the baneful consequence—as We often have declared, especially in the encyclical *Quas Primas*—of laicism, or rather the apostasy of society that today feigns to alienate itself from God and therefore from the Church."

Thus, the hatred for Catholics was spreading, and times were dangerous for priests and religious leaders. Priests were targets for assassination by street patrols, independent militia groups, or just anyone who felt like being a hero for the day. Ultimately, when the final figures were collated, it was revealed that 13 bishops, 4,184 secular priests, 2,365 religious (all male members of religious orders) and 283 nuns were killed during the conflict—Pope John Paul II later canonized several of these Spanish Civil War martyrs.

Naturally, the Catholic Church was hostile to the government's attempts to reduce its power and its obvious antipathy towards the faith. Furthermore, because of the persecutions endured by many Catholics, Franco Francisco's rebellion received open support from the Church. His Nationalists were hailed as the defenders of religion while the Republicans were the opponents of the Church.

After the army revolted against the Republican government in 1936, Franco quickly rose to be the leader of the insurrection. A letter entitled "The Two Cities", written by the Bishop of Salamanca, Enrique Pli y Deniel, was sent to Franco to show the bishop's (as well as the Catholics') support. The letter quoted St Augustine, as the bishop distinguished between the earthly city (the Republican zone) where hatred, anarchy, and Communism prevailed, and the celestial city (the Nationalist zone) where the love of God, heroism, and martyrdom were the rule. The Salamancan bishop wasn't alone in his support of Franco—all the Catholic world rallied around the Spanish dictator.

"I look upon you as the great defender of the true Spain," wrote the Archbishop of Westminster to Franco, "the country of Catholic principles where Catholic social justice and charity will be applied for the common good under a firm, peace-loving government."

In August 1936, German bishops issued a pastoral letter congratulating Hitler on his decision to aid Franco. The Pope's decision to make murdered Catholics into martyrs was followed by an official recognition of the Franco government on August 28th, 1937.

Franco had support throughout Europe. His army was supported by troops from Nazi Germany (Legion Condor) and Fascist Italy (Corpo Truppe Volontari), while Salazar's Portugal also openly assisted the Nationalists from the start. Franco's battle in Spain was viewed as a holy war, a crusade. While Pli y Deniel referred to the "satanic enemies of Spain", the Archbishop of Valladolid called the war "the most heroic crusade recorded in history", and a dozen cardinals, bishops, and priests, did likewise. Cardinal Goma, Archbishop of Toledo and Primate of Spain, several months later, issued a pastoral letter (El Caso Espana, November 24th, 1936) calling it "a true crusade for the Catholic religion. Christ versus Anti-Christ are engaged in battle for our souls."

Franco was held up as a protector of the faith—a modern-day crusader, fighting for justice. Pope Pius XI also helped Franco's cause by blessing a group of exiled Spaniards, and clearly distinguished between the Christian heroism of the Nationalists and the savage barbarism of the Republic.

"The Spanish Civil War", said Pope Pius XI on Christmas Day, 1936, "is a foretaste of what is being prepared for Europe and the World unless the nations take appropriate measures against it."

After Pius XI's death in 1939, his successor, Pius XII, continued to give Franco papal support: "The nation selected by God," wrote Pius XII, "as the principal instrument for the evangelization of the New World and an unconquerable bulwark of the Catholic faith, has given to the proselytizers of materialistic atheism in our century the highest proof that above all there remains the eternal values of religion and of the spirit...The people of Spain...[who] came to the defense of the faith and of Christian civilization...and aided by God, who does not abandon those who believe in Him...against the provocation of atheism. God in his compassion will lead Spain on the safe road of your traditional and Catholic greatness."

The two Popes felt that support for the Spanish Civil War was paramount. Catholics continued to be persecuted—churches were raised to the ground or defaced, priests were murdered (usually after being taken for midnight car rides known as *Paseos*, where they would be strung up at the roadside), nuns were raped, and ordinary Catholics were forced underground. After the war, it is estimated that 12 percent of Spanish monks, 13 percent of priests, and 20 percent of bishops were killed, while many others fled abroad.

One such priest, Father Juan María de la Cruz, was travelling from the train station to a friend's house when he passed the church of "de Los Juanes". The priest saw men ripping apart the church interior and getting ready to burn it down, so he raced over to the scene to express his disgust. On telling the men he was a priest, he was taken to Modelo di Valencia jail. In August 1936, together with nine other prisoners, de la Cruz was taken south of Valencia to be shot and killed. Testimonies like de la Cruz's litter the history of the Spanish Civil War.

Escrivá was one of the "lucky ones" who survived. During 1936, Escrivá was forced into hiding at the home of his mother, who had moved to Madrid with her son, and his organization was forced underground.

The next few months, according to Escrivá's official biographers, saw Escrivá seeking a temporary haven in a psychiatric clinic, as he feigned madness and was helped by the clinic's director Dr Suils. Suils was a former classmate of Escrivá's from Logroño, and had given refuge to several people in his private asylum in Madrid. However, Opus Dei detractors claim that Escrivá was indeed mad, and use Escrivá's incarceration as a means to attack the movement by claiming Opus Dei's leader was, according to their evidence, insane. His supporters argue that he merely feigned his madness in order to escape the Communist forces intent on killing him and priests like him. Furthermore, Escrivá's brother, Santiago, joined him in the asylum, as well as other Opus Dei members such as Gonzalez Barredo and Jimenez Vargas.

The asylum, however, was not a totally safe hiding place, as the militia suspected that some of the patients were political refugees and, at one point, turned up at the asylum and took away one of the patients. As a result, after some months Escrivá left the sanatorium and he and some companions were able to gain access to the consulate of Honduras.

During the Spanish Civil War, the Honduran consulate became a regular haunt for refugees—consequently, food was scarce and the atmosphere fraught with fear. Escrivá and his companions felt they could not stay there and so, in October 1937, an expanded group made its escape, leaving Madrid for Valencia. Escrivá, José María Albareda, Sainz, and Tomás Alvira found a car and enough petrol to reach their destination, where they were due to meet up with Pedro Casciaro and Francisco Botella. After Valencia, Escrivá, Albareda, Jimenez Vargas, Alvira, and Sainz took a night train to Barcelona, before making arrangements to cross the border to their next destination nearly a month later.

"During October 1937," remembers Miguel Fisac, one of Escrivá's companions who fled from Madrid to join him, "Juan Jimenez Vargas, a doctor from the Work [Opus Dei], turned up at my house. He picked me up and gave me a false ID. That night, we left by train with money my father had managed to collect for us. After an eventful journey, we joined up with Casciaro and Botella in Valencia, and we arrived in Barcelona where Escrivá and three others were all waiting. After a month in Barcelona, as well as another month hiding in the Pyrenees, we went to Andorra and France, and from there we reached San Sebastián—the so-called 'National Zone'."

The group had split into three—one with Escrivá, Albareda,and Jimenez Vargas, who took a bus from Barcelona to Oliana, nearly 40km (25 miles) from Andorra. The second group consisted of Casciaro, Botella, and Fisac, and they headed cross-country to avoid the military checkpoint at Basella (all three were likely to attract attention, being close to military age). The third group, meanwhile, consisted of Sainz and Alvira, who were also of military age. The men regrouped in the Rialp forest, and had an arduous trek over rough terrain, which included looping north over the French border before heading back south to Pamplona in Spain, in December 1937.

By January 1938, the group had finally taken up residence in Burgos, in the state of Castilla-León, in northern Spain. The journey had certainly proved difficult but left an impression on all of Escrivá's travelling companions—especially as, according to Opus Dei's internal tradition, the Virgin Mary is meant to have confirmed Escrivá in his mission during the passage through the forest.

Burgos, Escrivá's final destination, is an old city lying on the lower slopes of a castle-crowned hill overlooking the Arlanzón River. In July 1936, it had become the official seat of General Franco's Nationalist government and was used as a base for campaigns towards Madrid and the Basque states. As Burgos was a Nationalist zone, Escrivá was (relatively) free to exercise his beliefs.

"We used to go for walks along the banks of the River Arlanzón," said Escrivá later. "There we would talk, and while they opened their hearts, I tried to guide them with suitable advice to confirm their decisions or open up new horizons in their interior lives. And always, with God's help, I would do all I could to encourage them and stir up in their hearts the desire to live genuinely Christian lives. Our walks would sometimes take us as far as the abbey of Las Huelgas. On other occasions we would find our way to the cathedral."

Burgos proved a creative outlet for Escrivá, as it was during his time in the Nationalist stronghold that he finished his major work that was to become *The Way*. Burgos also proved a useful networking center, and Escrivá made some well-connected friends, who would have approved of the "national Catholicism" he was developing in his book. In *Camino* Escrivá sums up his view of "national Catholicism" as well as taking his inspiration from the doctrine of the Council of Trent, which canonized the union between Church and State. Maxim 525 of *Camino* begins: "to be 'Catholic' means to love your country and be second to none in that love."

Despite the fact that Escrivá was working and writing in his hideaway, there were constant rumors circulating back in Madrid that he had been killed. It was at this time that Escrivá would write a circular newsletter to Opus Dei members in various places serving on both sides of the conflict, carefully phrasing them so their meaning was obscured to possibly hostile readers (during the conflict the mail was screened by the authorities on both sides). It was a traumatic time for the early disciples as Opus Dei members (of whom there were only a few) were being hunted down by anti-religious forces. It was also a hard time for Escrivá's mother—one report tells of how Republicans caught a man they mistakenly thought was her son, killed him, and then strung up the dead body outside her house.

Escrivá continued to write to fellow Opus Dei members while in Burgos, as communication was a key factor for Opus Dei. When the war ended, he needed to have allies he could count on, especially as times were hard while they lived in exile in the north. Escrivá and his followers pooled resources as they had little to live on, but managed to survive by working together while Escrivá prayed and carried out various penances and fasts.

The civil war was nearly over, and in March 1939, with Franco victorious, Escrivá and his followers were told they could return to Madrid. They returned to their home city on March 28th, 1939—just two days before the end of the war was declared.

It wasn't the most welcome of homecomings. Despite the celebrations taking place all over Madrid—some 200,000 troops had been brought into the city to take part in a grand victory parade for Franco's triumph—Opus Dei had work to do. Its student academy/residence had been completely destroyed, and the group needed to rebuild and quickly. Still, as the majority of Opus Dei members had backed Franco throughout the civil war, at least the group could celebrate the Spanish leader's success—it was also a victory for the Church.

"Our fight is a crusade," said Franco in a statement in July 1938, "in which Europe's fate is at stake...No difficulties have prevented the rescue of over three million Spaniards from Red barbarism during the second triumphal year."

Following Franco's entry into Madrid on March 27th, 1939, the Italian Foreign Minister, Galleazo Ciano, Mussolini's son-in-law, wrote in his diary: "Madrid has fallen and with the capital all the other cities of Red Spain. The war is over. It is a new, formidable victory for Fascism, perhaps the greatest one so far." By March 31st, all of Spain was in Nationalist hands. Franco's headquarters issued a final bulletin on April 1st, 1939. Handwritten by Franco, it reads: "Today, with the Red Army captive and disarmed, our victorious troops have achieved their final military objectives. The war is over."

Franco also received a telegram from the Pope, thanking him for the immense joy that Spain's "Catholic victory" had brought him. Victory gave substance to Franco's carefully constructed self-image as medieval crusader, defender of the faith, and restorer of Spanish national greatness, with his relationship with the Church as an important element of his new regime.

While Franco was celebrating his victory, his people were recovering from the shock of the civil war itself. Those who'd lived through the trauma of the war had experienced hate and violence, and had seen their country divided—with many of them going hungry and losing their homes during the conflict. Following the war, there was a desire among many of those who'd survived to fulfil their own personal, political, and religious aspirations to rebuild their damaged country.

"The Communists were terrible; massacring, persecuting, torturing, raping," explains Father Vladimir Feltzman. "And then along comes Franco...and he eventually wins thanks to Hitler, Mussolini. So who are the saviors of Christianity? Hitler, Mussolini. Nobody as yet in Spain knows about concentration camps, so 1936, 1937, 1938, the savior of Christianity is Hitler. That is there. Like it or not, it's understandable. If you've been in hiding because you've been persecuted and suddenly along comes Franco with his coal-scuttle helmets and the German *Luftwaffe* supporting him, you say 'Thank God we've been liberated'."

Today, many of Escrivá's followers deny that he was an out-and-out follower of Franco and Hitler. However, as stated, the enemy of Catholicism was Communism and, as such, both Franco and Hitler were seen as saviors of the faith. Feltzman claimed in a 1987 interview that "For Escrivá it was a not a matter of Hitler against the Jews, or Hitler against the Slavs, it was Hitler against Communism." However, there is some dispute as regards this statement between Opus Dei and one ex-Opus Dei member. Naturally, Opus Dei members do not believe that Escrivá could ever have held such views; yet Feltzman asserts that he did.

Across Europe, in the early 1930s, the enemy within was Communism. "Those thoughts continued across the world," continues Feltzman. "Under Reagan in the US, and now, the 'Axis of Evil' was Communism and, therefore, anything that was against Communism was pro-Christianity. That's the reason why Hitler was supported by Christians, and by members of Opus Dei. Now there were 70 of them, who volunteered to go and fight in what's called the Blue Brigade on the Eastern Front. None of them were accepted. They were all academics and not very fit, but that was how people saw them."

George Orwell, in his *Homage to Catalonia*, also comments on how, at the start of Franco's regime, the Spanish dictator was not "strictly" comparable with Hitler or Mussolini. When Franco first rose to prominence, his *coup* was seen as a military mutiny, which was backed by both the aristocracy and the Church, and was not an attempt to impose Fascism, argues Orwell. Instead, Franco's aim was to "restore Feudalism"—Communism was the enemy and even one British newspaper, the *Daily Mail*, represented Franco as a patriot, delivering his country from "fiendish Reds".

For Spain, the immediate war was over as of April 1st, 1939—although guerrilla resistance to Franco continued into the late 1940s, meaning that Spanish participation in World War II was largely limited to declarations, treaties, and politics rather than fighting beyond Spain's own borders. Though sympathetic to the Fascist powers of Germany and Italy, and prepared to provide them with assistance, Franco kept Spain out of direct involvement in the conflict, apart from sending a division of troops to fight alongside the Germans on the Eastern Front.

He later moved the country to a more neutral stance, but by the end of the war Franco was still viewed as the last surviving Fascist dictator. With the country in disarray, Franco needed able, bright and supportive followers to implement his new regime. Opus Dei proved up to the task. The movement became influential in Spanish policy, legal reforms, and education.

In order to realize the success of Opus Dei, it is important to understand how it flourished under Franco. Following the Spanish Civil War, there were just 15 members left in the Opus Dei movement. One member, José Isasa, had died in combat, while three others had left Opus Dei just before the war. Yet, although the organization was small in numbers in 1939, just under 20 years later, three of its recruits were the core men responsible for leading the team that revitalized the Spanish economy. This, possibly, could account for the reasons behind the persistent conspiracies concerning Opus Dei—how did it achieve so much within such a small space of time?

Franco Wins—and Opus Dei Expands

Unfortunately, in many journalists' minds, Opus Dei is filed under 'F' for Franco...It's not as though Escrivá was a Francoist as such. He just ended up on that side.

Andrew Soane, Opus Dei's communications officer in London, March 2005

Franco's victory saw the restoration of the Church's privileges. During the Franco years, Roman Catholicism was the only religion to have legal status; other worship services could not be advertised and only the Roman Catholic Church could own property or publish books. The government not only continued to pay priests' salaries and to subsidize the Church, but it also assisted in the reconstruction of church buildings damaged by the war. Laws were passed abolishing divorce and banning the sale of contraceptives. Catholic religious instruction became mandatory in all schools. Franco secured in return the right to name Roman Catholic bishops in Spain, as well as wield power over appointments of clergy down to the parish priest level.

Yet, while the Catholics prospered, the country wasn't without suffering, especially for those on the losing side. Martha Gellhorn, in her book *The Undefeated*, points out that there were around 300,000 executions in the six years following Franco's ascent to power. She argues that, by 1941, many members of the Spanish Republicans were fleeing the country and joining up with the Maquis (the French resistance). As a result, from the mid-1940s onwards, there was a close relationship between the Maquis and Spanish resistance bands throughout France.

Despite these pockets of insurgence, Franco was in control, and due to Escrivá's belief in "national Catholicism", where religious faith and political identity were integral, Opus Dei flourished under Franco. "They became a part of the Franco regime because Franco needed competent people and Opus Dei were competent," says Feltzman.

In 1939 Opus Dei had only a handful of members, no money, no headquarters, and no legal status. Escrivá and his loyal followers devised a simple plan—recruit new members, find a stable location to build a new headquarters, gain papal approval, and spread the word of Opus Dei.

Furthermore, suggest some members of Opus Dei, it was around this time that the organization could have picked up its "secretive" tag, which, ultimately, has led to the suspicion that surrounds Opus Dei. "At the end of the war the Founder [Escrivá] regathered the members of Opus Dei," suggests Andrew Soane, Opus Dei communications officer, "but I don't think he had the mentality that Opus Dei was something to be hidden. Especially not, looking back on it, with the Catholic authorities in charge. There was no need to be secretive. But, during this time, most Catholics were being open about being Catholic and talking about the triumph of the civil war. The Founder didn't do that kind of thing. He didn't approve of banners. He didn't approve of religious writings on the church doors—the graffiti. So, in the context of that time, this was another possible reason why the label 'secretive' was given to Opus Dei."

As stressed, the tendency during this period to link Catholicism and support of Franco's regime also jarred with Opus Dei's stress on the political freedom of Catholics. As Escrivá said: "In temporal and debatable matters, Opus Dei does not wish to have and cannot have any opinion, since its goals are *exclusively* spiritual. In all matters of free discussion, each member of the Work has and freely expresses his own *personal* opinion, for which he is also *personally responsible*." Nevertheless, it has been a continual theme to link Opus Dei with Franco, and this has contributed to the ongoing misunderstandings between the organization and its critics.

In 1939, within months of the end of the civil war, Escrivá had opened a new residence hall in Madrid (the DYA residence), on 6 Jenner Street, near the Paseo de la Castellana, Madrid's main thoroughfare. He spent his time travelling to different cities in Spain each weekend, seeking out new young recruits. In 1941, when Escrivá was away on one of these "missions", preaching to priests at a retreat in Lerida, his mother died. Years later, Escrivá said: "I have always thought that our Lord wanted that sacrifice from me, as an external proof of my love for diocesan priests, and that my mother especially continues to intercede for that work."

The priest was now solely responsible for the two remaining members of his family—his brother Santiago and sister Carmen. However, Escrivá also had another family to care for—Opus Dei. As the father and mentor of the organization, he had pastoral duties towards the ever-growing number of his disciples. By 1945 about ten houses containing numeraries, or celibate members, had been opened in Spain—but, at this stage, the organization was still relatively small.

Until 1944, Escrivá was the only serving Opus Dei priest, but three veteran members of the movement were close to ordination—José Luis Múzquiz, who, ultimately, would help launch Opus Dei in the United States in 1949; José María Hernández de Garnica, who worked in many European countries, and Alvaro del Portillo, who later became President General of Opus Dei.

On June 25th, 1944, Múzquiz, Hernández de Garnica and del Portillo received Holy Orders at the hands of the Bishop of Madrid. According to reports, Escrivá did not want to be present at what could appear to be a success or a triumph. He stayed at home, praying. As he later wrote: "My role is to hide and disappear, so that only Jesus shines forth." Despite not being at the trio's ordination, Escrivá did, however, make one strange request...

"Escrivá used to smoke when he was a student," wrote Cardinal Luciani, later Pope John Paul I, in an Italian newspaper, "but when he went to the seminary he gave his pipes and tobacco to the porter. He never smoked again. However, on the day that the first three priests of Opus Dei were ordained, he said: 'I don't smoke; none of you three do either. Alvaro, you will have to take up smoking, because I don't want the others to feel that they are not free to smoke if they want to'."

Smoking aside, during the 1940s Escrivá's main concern was obtaining legal recognition from the Vatican to become part of the Roman Catholic Church, rather than simply gaining fellow priests. For the apostolic phenomenon to succeed it had to have a legal framework. Escrivá knew that Opus Dei would never succeed if it cut itself off from the ecclesiastical hierarchy.

However, in the following years, many within the Roman Curia came to regard Opus Dei with great suspicion as it was gaining in both influence and power. Opus Dei, despite its traditional beliefs, was the newcomer within the Roman Curia and, as a result, was upsetting the status quo of its contemporaries. Not only was Opus Dei different, but it was proving to be successful—gaining members, and influential ones at that. As a result of the politics and resentment towards Opus Dei within the Church, some members of the clergy instigated verbal attacks and spread sly rumors around this period in an attempt to discredit Escrivá and his work.

Critics of Opus Dei wrote that the movement was "Masonic" and a "heretical sect", while in Barcelona, Escrivá's book *The Way* was thrown onto a bonfire. At one stage, a young university student attending a public Mass organized by the Marian congregation (a church association) was identified as a member of Opus Dei by the preacher from the pulpit, and was expelled from the association. Meanwhile, in Madrid, there were rumors that Escrivá had been officially denounced to the Holy Office for his heretical beliefs (that is, for involving lay people in spiritual matters)—this never happened, although there were some informal efforts to try and have Escrivá condemned by the Vatican.

During this time, Escrivá described his hurt and disappointment caused by those who criticized him and his movement. However, Escrivá found some powerful supporters, including the Bishop of Madrid, who gave Opus Dei an approval in writing, which served to help Opus Dei's cause in gaining further recognition and validity. The abbot of Montserrat, a Benedictine monastery near Barcelona, had written to the Bishop of Madrid, Leopoldo Eijo y Garay, to ask him about the rumors concerning Opus Dei. "I know everything about the Opus," the bishop wrote, "Believe me, Most Reverend Father, the Opus [Work] is truly Dei [of God], from its first conception and in all of its steps and works...Nevertheless, it is good people who attack it. It would be a cause for amazement, if our Lord had not already made us accustomed to see this same thing happen in many other works of his."

In a later letter to the abbot, Eijo y Garay described Escrivá as "a model priest, chosen by God for the sanctification of many souls, humble, prudent, self-sacrificing, extremely obedient to his prelate, outstanding in intellect, of very solid doctrinal and spiritual formation, ardently zealous, an apostle of the Christian formation of young students."

In fact, on March 19th, 1941, Eijo y Garay granted the first diocesan, and therefore ecclesiastical, approval of Opus Dei. As an Opus Dei member said of the event: "Fully aware of the Opus' spirit, aims, means, and ends, the Bishop of Madrid had encouraged the Founder from the beginning, and had blessed his work."

The support from the bishop appeared to have the desired effect. Over the next three years, Opus Dei received various Holy See approvals. In 1943, the canonical problem of ordination was solved when it was agreed that Opus Dei members would be ordained priests—as a result, the Priestly Society of the Holy Cross was founded. One year later, 1944 saw the first priestly ordination of Opus Dei members—Múzquiz, Hernández de Garnica, and del Portillo—administered by the Bishop of Madrid. Soon after this, Escrivá was granted the title "Monsignor" by Pope Pius XII.

So Pope Pius gave Escrivá the Monsignor title, but just why had there been such virulent opposition—what had Opus Dei actually done to deserve the abuse and rumors? During this time, a number of priests had visited the houses of young people who had joined Opus Dei (or those who were considering it), and warned parents that their children were joining a heretical group and were in danger of losing their eternal souls. Is this where the cult accusations stemmed from? It is a possible origin for some of the later problems that Opus Dei has encountered.

Yet why was the movement attracting all this anger? One theory is that Opus Dei's opponents were critical of the Work's message about the universal call to holiness, as well as the possibility of sanctifying oneself through one's work in the world without being a priest or joining a religious order. In short, Opus Dei's innovations were a threat to the standing order of the Church. There was a fear that the movement would steal potential vocations from the priesthood and religious orders.

During this time, the papal nuncio to Spain demanded answers from Opus Dei—were they truly stealing away potential candidates for the priesthood? As it turns out, during the 1940s, the majority of people who joined Opus Dei at this time had never even thought about a future as a priest or of joining a religious order—but they were intrigued by, and drawn to, the prospect of sanctification. As Pope John Paul II later explained it, Opus Dei "has as its aim the sanctification of one's life, while remaining within the world at one's place of work and profession."

Opus Dei weathered the opposition, and outside of Madrid, the organization was spreading rapidly into new Spanish cities—Valencia, Barcelona, Zaragoza, Valladolid, and Seville. The expansion continued throughout Europe as members were being recruited in Portugal, England, Italy, France, Germany, and Ireland. As it began to grow internationally, Opus Dei needed, more than ever, the approval of the Pope.

In 1946 Escrivá moved to Rome to deal with Vatican officials and was welcomed by Monsignor Giovanni Battista Montini, the Vatican's Under-Secretary of State (later to become Pope Paul VI). Although Escrivá travelled throughout Europe to prepare the beginning of the "work of Opus Dei", by making Rome his base he emphasized Opus Dei's desire to "serve the Church as the Church wishes to be served". On several occasions it was reported that Pius XII and John XXIII sent Escrivá expressions of their affection and esteem.

"For me, in the hierarchy of love, the Pope comes right after the Most Holy Trinity and our Mother the Virgin," said Escrivá in a later interview. "I cannot forget that it was his Holiness Pius XII who approved Opus Dei at a time when some people considered our spirituality a *heresy*. Nor can I forget that the first words of kindness and affection I received in Rome in 1946 came from the then Msgr Montini. The affable and paternal charm of John XXIII, every time I had occasion to visit him, remains engraved in my memory. Once I told him: 'In our Work all men, Catholics or not, have always been lovingly received. It is not from your Holiness that I learned ecumenism.' And Pope John laughed with obvious emotion. What more can I tell you? The Roman pontiffs, all of them, have always had understanding and affection for Opus Dei."

On August 31st, 1946, Escrivá returned to Madrid with an "approval of aims" from Pope Pius XII, a document that the Papal State had not issued for over a century. Then, one year later, the Pope recognized Opus Dei as a "secular institute". Despite Escrivá's obvious affection for the Pope and his gratitude, Escrivá wasn't satisfied with the title "secular institute," as he believed that the secular institutes that came after were more like traditional religious orders and quite different from Opus Dei.

Such was Escrivá's belief in his movement that he wanted to give Opus Dei a new status to mark it as original and important. To do this, the movement had to make changes within its constitution: "oblates" became "associates", and "superiors" became "directors". Associates are similar to numeraries, in that they live in celibacy, but they typically do not live in Opus Dei facilities. (Their personal circumstances do not permit them to be as available to Opus Dei as a numerary, perhaps because they have an elderly parent they have to take care of, or they run a family business that would interfere with their ability to move to another city.) The whole aim was to avoid giving any impression that Opus Dei resembled a religious order or a secular institute. In fact, Escrivá claimed, as his followers still do today, that he had invented something new in Catholic spirituality.

Escrivá's work in Rome, and ultimate acceptance by many within the Curia, provided the basis for complete approval from the Vatican, which was granted on June 16th, 1950. Since then it has been possible to admit men and women as "Cooperators of Opus Dei", which allows followers who are not Catholic or even Christian, but who wish to help with Opus Dei's apostolic works, alms, and prayer. Opus Dei had won papal approval and acceptance.

While Escrivá strengthened his Italian links, life in Spain under Franco was developing nicely as members of Opus Dei began to rise up the ranks within the Spanish political parties. The firm relationship between Opus Dei and Franco's regime is shown in the friendship between Opus Dei member José María Albareda Herrera and José Ibañez Martin, Franco's Minister of Education (1939–51), who was not a member of the organization.

Ibañez Martin had become friends with Albareda during the civil war, when Ibañez Martin had taken refuge in the Chilean Embassy in Madrid. Following the war, Albareda became Ibañez Martin's vice-president at the Consejo Superior de Investigaciones Cientificas (CSIC), which had been established to improve educational standards in Spain. This was a prime position for anyone, especially for one of the integral members of Opus Dei. Thanks to Ibañez Martin's working relationship with Albareda, Opus Dei managed to establish its presence at various universities throughout Spain.

Using Opus Dei's newly set-up publishing house, called Ediciones Rialp, Florentino Pérez Embid and his colleagues set about translating European conservative thought into Spanish. Commentators at the time felt that Pérez Embid's work at the publishing house was a way of becoming part of the cultural arm of the Franco administration. Another link between Opus Dei and Franco's government was through Laureano López Rodó, who organized the CSIC administratively. López Rodó became friendly with Franco's long-time collaborator Admiral Carrero Blanco (who was not a member of Opus Dei), and these friendships helped Opus Dei gain momentum and recognition in the public eye.

Opus Dei was certainly in the ascendancy within the Spanish political field, and writer Penny Lernoux agrees that the organization's swift growth was down to Carrero Blanco, stating that many Opus Dei members made rapid advances in Franco's government when Carrero Blanco was running the country as premier. (Carrero Blanco was vice-admiral of Spain in 1963, admiral in 1966, controlled government affairs as vice-premier from 1967 to 1973, and became premier in June 1973.) Many Spanish political commentators also argue that until Carrero's assassination in December 1973 (see Chapter Thirteen), Opus Dei leaders were the strongest conservative political influence in Spain.

Following the civil war, there were several university chairs vacant throughout Spain. Many of the professors had either been executed or were in exile. The situation was so serious that many universities could barely function, and, naturally, the government was keen to fill these seats with ideologically compliant candidates. However, in order to ensure a fair hearing for potential professors, potential applicants sat an examination called an *oposición*, a tribunal consisting of other members of the university staff.

It was felt that, thanks to Albareda's role as vice-president of the CSIC, he was able to exert control over these *oposiciones*, and many members of Opus Dei were therefore available to fill the vacant professorships. According to later estimates, by the early 1950s one-third of all university departments in Spain were headed up by Opus Dei members.

It's a practise that continues today. Opus Dei continues to establish its main base and houses near elite universities. As a result, it often recruits new members from academic environments, which, of course, only enhances its reputation at the Vatican. While many Catholic movements are failing to make an impact, Opus Dei is successful in bringing in more Catholics to the fold, and, as a bonus, these are well-educated, articulate Catholics—a highly desirable force.

When Franco seized power, he managed to fuse the ideologically incompatible Falange ("phalanx", a far-right Spanish political party with close connections to Hitler and Mussolini) and Carlist parties under his rule. Despite the (then) strength of the Falangists and Carlist supporters, there were still key roles for Opus Dei members within Franco's political administration as the organization began to grow dominant within Franco's regime.

During this time, what exactly was Escrivá's relationship with Franco? According to Msgr Alvaro del Portillo, in an interview with Italian journalist Cesare Cavalleri, "In the case of Francoism, it is necessary to recall that the end of the Spanish Civil War signalled the rebirth of the life of the Church, of religious associations, of Catholic schools...in those circumstances, although the Father acknowledged Franco's achievements in bringing peace to the country, he had to counteract two dangers: on the one hand, a manipulation of the Catholic faith, an attempt on the part of certain groups to monopolize the representation of Catholics in public life; and, on the other hand, a tendency in some Catholic circles to use public power as a kind of secular arm."

Franco himself made this public statement on May 14th, 1946: "For us the perfect State is the Catholic State. It is not enough for us for the people to be Christian to ensure that the precepts of a morality of that order are fulfilled; laws are also needed to maintain principles and correct abuse. The chasm, the great difference between our system and the Nazi-Fascist system, is the Catholic character of the regime which today governs the destiny of Spain. Neither racism, nor religious persecutions, nor violence to consciences, nor imperialisms over our neighbors, nor the slightest shadow of cruelty, have a place under the spiritual and Catholic sentiment which presides over our life." With this attitude, Opus Dei members and, indeed practising Catholics, would have been welcomed by Franco with open arms. It is also important to remember that during this time, the Catholic faith in Spain during Franco's era was popular and widespread.

During the 1940s and 1950s, Opus Dei continued its work on "educational" organization—it had plenty of Opus Dei professors in positions of power—and by the late 1950s it was time to move on to the economy. Advisers judged the economy must be opened up to international market forces and investment, or Spain would face bankruptcy. A free market would also kill off the black market that was inevitable in a command economy. Franco could see dangers (economic liberalism as a breeding ground for political liberalism), but felt he had no choice. The reforms, led by the young university-educated members of Opus Dei, also known as the "Catholic technocrats", increased the prosperity of the people. Furthermore, from the late 1950s, European tourists and US investment began to flow into Spain.

Opus Dei combined conservative Catholic discipline with an ideology of capitalist success. Franco's 1957 government was seen as a "government of technocrats," with Opus Dei firmly in the driving seat. The Falangists were resistant to the idea of opening the regime to capitalistic influences, but their proposals were rejected, and members of Opus Dei assumed significant posts in Franco's 1957 cabinet. Among these were Alvaro (or Alberto) Ullastres Calvo, who was the Minister of Commerce and Mariano Navarro Rubio, who was a lawyer for the Council of State, Secretary of the Treasury, and, ultimately, head of the Bank of Spain. Finally, there was Laureano López Rodó, who was one of the main architects of the cabinet restructuring—the Falangists were on their way out.

Opus Dei was going from strength to strength. During the late 1950s and 1960s, Franco entrusted the faltering Spanish economy to a handful of Opus Dei members—the above three plus Gregorio López Bravo. It proved a shrewd move, as these technocrats managed to bring Spain back from the brink of financial disaster. They proposed measures to curb inflation, reduce government economic controls, and to bring Spanish economic policies and procedures in line with European standards. These were all incorporated in the "Stabilization Plan of 1959", which laid the way for Spain's remarkable economic transformation in the 1960s. During that decade, Spain's industrial production and standard of living increased dramatically.

The Stabilization Plan, which marked a turning point for the Spanish economy, resulted in the years 1959–67 becoming known as the *desarrollismo* (economic "developmentalism"). In their key roles in Franco's government, Opus Dei members imported models of "indicative planning" from France. In 1958, for example, a Collective Agreements Act allowed employers and employees to negotiate wages (which had previously been regulated by the Ministry of Labor) at factory level.

The problems with the Falangist movement continued to be an issue. On October 28th, 1966, Escrivá took action and wrote to José Solis, the minister who was head of the Falange movement:

> Most esteemed friend: Word has reached me about the campaign which the press of the Falange, which is in your Excellency's control, has been so unjustly waging against Opus Dei. I repeat to you once again that the members of Opus Dei—each and every one of them—are personally utterly free, as free as if they did not belong to Opus Dei, in all temporal matters and in those theological matters which are not of faith, which the Church leaves people to disagree about. It therefore makes no sense to publicize the fact that a particular person belongs to the Work, when it comes to political, professional, or social matters—just as it would make no sense, when speaking of the political activities of Your Excellency, to bring in your wife, your children, your family...I beg you to put an end to this campaign against Opus Dei, since Opus Dei has done nothing to deserve it...

Yet, while the Falange movement was attempting to cause problems for Opus Dei, the latter still had high-ranking members occupying important cabinet posts in education and finance. According to Arthur Jones, the *National Catholic Reporter*'s editor at large, "10 out of 19 new ministers in Spanish dictator Francisco Franco's 1969 cabinet" were members of Opus Dei.

But Luis Tellez, a regional director for Opus Dei in New York, denies this. He argues that although some Opus Dei members were cabinet ministers, there were other Opus Dei members who opposed Franco, at least one of them a prominent Spanish journalist who was exiled by the dictator.

Tellez is backed up by Vittorio Messori, author of *Opus Dei: Leadership and Vision in Today's Catholic Church*. Messori argues that, of the 116 ministers that were named by Franco for the 11 different cabinets between 1939 and 1975, only eight of these were members of Opus Dei. Of those eight, one died just three months after his appointment, while four were in office for only one term. Opus Dei members are keen to point out that, at no time, did members come close to representing a majority in any cabinet. Messori, in fact, claims that the idea of an Opus Dei-dominated cabinet is simply a "myth".

Del Portillo, in his interview with Cavalleri, also added: "It seems to me that those members of the Work, who freely collaborated with the government of Franco, on their own responsibility, worked for the good of their country; they achieved successes, unanimously recognized today, in improving the economy and in ending the isolation of Spain by turning her towards Europe."

Opus Dei has named these eight cabinet members. They were, according to the organization: Laureano López Rodó (1957–74: between 1957 and 1965 he was in the "Presidency" and not the "cabinet"), Alberto Ullastres Calvo (1957–65), Mariano Navarro Rubio (1957–65), Gregorio López Bravo (1962–74), Juan José García Espinosa (1965–9), Faustino García Moncó (1965–9), Vicente Mortes Alonso (1969–74), Fernando Herrero Tejedor (March–June 1975). So, if only these eight out of a total of 116 ministers were members of Opus Dei—hardly a dominant force—why do the rumors persist? What has Opus Dei done to earn its reputation as a Franco-loving movement? And as a dominant Spanish power?

"A good part of it, no doubt, is that you had people in these high positions," explains Andrew Soane, "and the fact that Opus Dei began in Spain, that's where they became famous. But, there were members of Opus Dei who were exiled by Franco."

Antonio Fontán, a member of Opus Dei, was the editor of the independent national daily newspaper, *Madrid*, from 1967 to 1971. The government suspended his liberal newspaper, which was in favor of democracy and against Franco's regime, for four months in 1968. Fontán himself was prosecuted on 19 occasions and fined some ten times, and by October 1971 the authorities demanded Fontán's resignation, closing down the paper for good a few weeks later. An Opus Dei member in opposition to Franco? Indeed. And he wasn't alone—a convenient fact that is often forgotten by those who choose to put all Opus Dei members in the Franco camp. This issue, in Opus Dei minds certainly, shows that Opus Dei followers are "free" to make their own political decisions and are not guided by an exterior "force" (i.e. their Opus Dei confessors).

Madrid's publisher and principal owner, Rafael Calvo Serer, was another Opus Dei member who spoke out about Franco. After his death in 1988, *The Times* in London wrote in his obituary: "[his] pioneering efforts during the latter years of the Franco regime helped lay the ground for today's flourishing press freedom in that country." After the newspaper's closure in 1971 and the offices had been sold off, the building was blown up in April 1973. Facing trial and a probable prison sentence, after a thinly disguised editorial that criticized Franco, Calvo Serer fled to Paris, where he continued his criticisms of Franco with his articles in *Le Monde, Le Figaro,* the *International Herald Tribune,* and other foreign publications.

One of the Opus Dei members who belonged to Franco's cabinet, López Rodó, argues that it would have been strange if none of the thousands of Opus Dei members in Spain had been in politics. His argument was that had none of them been in the government, then people would have thought that there was some kind of ban within Opus Dei against acting in public life or in a specific political orientation. Either way, Opus Dei can't win.

An Italian magazine, *Famiglia Cristiana,* which was published shortly before the beatification of Escrivá in 1992, contained a report on Opus Dei and explored Opus Dei's alleged involvement with the Franco regime in depth, quoting passages of a letter that Escrivá had written to Pope Paul VI in 1964:

> Permit me to say, Holy Father, that the numerary and supernumerary members of Opus Dei who work with Franco in government posts or in the administration do so of their own free will and under their own personal responsibility: and not as technical men, but as politicians, just like any other citizens—who are undoubtedly far more numerous—who work in similar posts and belong to Catholic Action, the Asociación Catolica Nacional de Propagandistas, etc. As far as I know, the only one to ask the hierarchy for permission to work in the Franco government was Martin Artajo [president of Spanish Catholic Action], for 13 years Minister of Foreign Affairs. When, instead, Professor Ullastres and Professor López Rodó were appointed respectively Minister of Commerce and Commissioner for the Economic and Social Development Plan, I got the news of those two appointments, which they had freely received, through the press."

The magazine also reported: "It seemed the ill feeling towards Opus Dei arose from the persistent refusal of the founder and members to act in politics according to an official criterion, like a 'single party'."

The claim that Escrivá himself showed support of Franco is brought up following this letter from the founder, written to the president on May 23rd, 1958.

To his Excellency Franciso Franco Bahamonde, Head of State of Spain

Your Excellency:

I wish to add my sincerest personal congratulations to the many you have received on the occasion of the promulgation of the Fundamental Principles.

My forced absence from our homeland in service of God and souls, far from weakening my love for Spain, has, if it were possible, increased it. From the perspective of the eternal city of Rome, I have been able to see better than ever the beauty of that especially beloved daughter of the Church, which is my homeland, which the Lord has so often used as an instrument for the defense and propagation of the holy, Catholic faith in the world.

Although alien to any political activity, I cannot help but rejoice as a priest and Spaniard that the Chief of State's authoritative voice should proclaim that, "The Spanish nation considers it a badge of honour to accept the law of God according to the one and true doctrine of the Holy Catholic Church, inseparable faith of the national conscience which will inspire its legislation." It is in fidelity to our people's Catholic tradition that the best guarantee of success in acts of government, the certainty of a just and lasting peace within the national community, as well as the divine blessing for those holding positions of authority, will always be found.

I ask God our Lord to bestow upon your Excellency with every sort of felicity and impart abundant grace to carry out the grave mission entrusted to you. Please accept, Excellency, the expression of my deepest personal esteem and be assured of my prayers for all your family.

Most devotedly yours in the Lord,
Josemaría Escrivá de Balaguer
Rome, May 23rd, 1958

Although at this stage of Escrivá's life he was actually living in Rome and not Spain, his letter and others of this ilk can be seen as political tools at the time and it needs to be judged in the context of the era. Most letters to Franco, at this time, were no doubt expressive, obsequious correspondences, and Escrivá is attempting to ensure that the general takes on board his points. The letter is, once again, affirming Escrivá's belief in "national Catholicism", as well as his ongoing support for Franco's regime.

This could have been, in this case, a purely "political" move by the priest to affirm his status and that of his followers with the Spanish leader but, by this stage, with Opus Dei firmly established in Franco's cabinet, this letter appears to be more a confirmation of his faith in Franco. Opus Dei not only had members who worked within Franco's government but also across the educational system.

As discussed before, Escrivá's support of Franco, when put in context, is justified. Having seen his fellow Catholics suffering during the civil war, he would naturally be in favor of Franco leading Spain—though followers and contemporaries of Escrivá's deny the priest was an out-and-out supporter.

During this period, Opus Dei came under suspicion for its organization and prominence within the country, but, looking back through history, the link between Church and State is not hard to find. Only centuries earlier, the Jesuits were using similar structures to gain support and new members—furthermore, there were plenty of other Catholic groups entrenched across Spain and within Spanish politics. Opus Dei, a new and different organization, however, attracted the most detractors, due to its status as new "kids on the block".

"Escrivá made Opus Dei's structure by copying Jesuits in their organization," according to members of the Maria Auxiliadora Prayer Group, "but adding the character of a secret lodge of masons and a totalitarian quality. As for its nature, it's Catholic fundamentalist; unfortunately they took the darkest of Catholicism and a fascist political character."

Naturally, Opus Dei feels affronted at the accusations of having a "fascist political character" (members of the organization constantly discuss their personal freedom) yet, throughout the 20th century, Opus Dei was constantly seen as a threat by other Catholics, as well as by some political commentators. From its humble beginnings in 1928, and in the space of only 30 years, the movement had risen up the ranks to "rescue" the country in the late 1950s. It was soon after this period that it became nicknamed "Octopus Dei" or "Holy Octopus" as, following its success in Spain, from the mid-1950s onwards it began to spread across Europe and into the ex-Spanish colonies of South America.

The Nazis, the Pope, the Occult, and Opus Dei

What the Church, especially certain towering personalities within the Church, undertook in those years [immediately after the war] to save the best of our nation, often from certain death, must never be forgotten. In Rome itself, the transit point of the escape routes, a vast amount was done.

Hans Ulrich Rudel, an international spokesman for the neo-Nazi movement, in 1970

On May 8th, 1945, Europe celebrated: the Nazis had been defeated. The war with Japan was still ongoing, but back in Europe Hitler had taken his cyanide phial and Germany had surrendered to the Allied forces. However, the continent's celebrations were short-lived. Once commanding nations were now financially ruined, and Europe was consequently also culturally barren: filmmakers, artists, architects, and visionaries had fled to safe havens during the war. World War II was the most extensive (and costly) armed conflict in the history of the world, with more civilian casualties than any war in history. It was during this period of confusion and chaos that the Vatican and Soviet "rat lines" came into being.

The so-called rat lines were the secret escape routes used by agents to smuggle fellow spies, fugitives, political prisoners, or undercover operatives out of (and into) countries across the globe, but it was, on the whole, mainly a European phenomenon. At the end of World War II there were hundreds of rat lines coming out of the Soviet-occupied countries in Eastern Europe. There were also the escape routes used by Nazi war criminals at the end of the Third Reich, as they fled to the likes of Argentina, Chile, and other countries across the globe with the help, among others, of the Vatican.

It should be noted, however, that it was only certain elements of the Vatican who were involved in the rat line allegations rather than the Vatican as a whole entity. For example, one well-known pro-Nazi prelate in Rome, Bishop Hudal, provided Red Cross passports, tickets, and visas to Latin America for Nazis on the run. Hudal was exposed in 1949, and his network was eventually closed down due to Vatican pressure. Yet, considering the elements within the Vatican who were involved and Opus Dei's broad and deep Vatican links, did the organization, too, play a part?

Ex-Opus Dei member Father Vladimir Feltzman says not: "Opus Dei wasn't influential in the Vatican until around 1948. I think they helped one Opus Dei member from Yugoslavia to escape, but they just weren't powerful enough at the time. Opus Dei didn't really hit the Vatican in any significant way until after the Second Vatican Council, until JP2 (John Paul II)." If that is the case, where did these conspiracy rumors start?

Throughout the latter half of the 20th century, it has been traditional for conspiracy theorists, when wanting to brand something as "evil", to bring links to the Nazi party and Nazi ideology into play. In the case of Opus Dei it is incorrect to ally the organization with the Nazi movement, but a scan across the internet shows that there are those who persist in linking the two. As Feltzman argues, Opus Dei was only in its infancy during World War II. Furthermore, during this period the movement was struggling for survival as Escrivá and his followers spent their time trying to dodge Communist bullets and *Paseos* (the midnight massacres doled out to men of the cloth).

Rumors persist, however. One of the reasons for these theories is because, for many, Escrivá's ideology is regarded as fascistic—people were expected to follow orders given to them by their leaders without doubting them. As ODAN (the Opus Dei Awareness Network, mostly made up of ex-Opus Dei members) writes: "Leaders have total control over the people subordinated to them through the weekly talk where they learn everything they need to manipulate followers."

"Opus Dei is often accused in the world press of being a political organization," says ex-Opus Dei member Dr John Roche. "In accordance with its constitution it is chiefly interested in the governing classes, and it does seek to acquire political influence. But such influence does *not* imply a particular political ideology, and in fairness to Opus Dei, *during my fourteen years of membership I did not detect any party political intention*. Its members do, however, loosely share a spread of political attitudes, which vary in emphasis with time and place. These result from its uncompromising anti-Communism, its fundamentalist religious outlook, its international business enterprises, and its long affiliation with the business and military classes of Spain. It is, therefore, very attractive to the far right." As a result, Opus Dei is often linked to fascist movements and, due to its present-day presence within the Vatican, it has often been linked to the rat lines.

Opus Dei's support of Francisco Franco was also seen as an indication of its compliance in helping right-wing movements at the end of World War II. Of course there is no proof that Opus Dei had any dealings with the many refugees who swamped Spain, as Franco tried to provide a haven for the Third Reich's dispossessed following the war. With treacherous, and many unmanned, borders, Spain proved an important early hide-out for Nazis, who had slipped past the Allies and needed a country to escape to before moving on to their new bases in either Latin America, or, in some cases, the Middle East.

Yet, as stated, during this period and especially in the years following the Spanish Civil War, Opus Dei was too busy trying to regroup and re-establish itself—in 1939 it had less than 20 members. There would have been no time for members to "man" rat lines or involve themselves in these activities, and they had little political presence in Spain during that time. Despite this, rumors remain.

Another reason why critics choose to link Opus Dei with the Nazi party is due to Escrivá's alleged attitude towards Hitler, who was seen by many Catholics during the war as a savior of Christianity against the attacking anti-religious Communist forces.

"After the war," says Feltzman, "Nazis were considered to be OK. One of my main criticisms [of Opus Dei] was that in the main church of the headquarters of Opus Dei in Rome, in a glass screen, there's a 'shrine', like the ones to medieval warriors. They put there swords belonging to members who had been in the army and become priests, and there were three daggers with swastikas on them. They're not there now of course. When I asked the rector of the Roman college he said: 'Ah, but they fought for what they believed.' There was that sort of attitude...as Escrivá said: 'You know, Hitler couldn't have killed six million, it couldn't have been more than three.' You can understand why he thought that. If somebody [Hitler] saves your life and then, only five years later, they're accused of being a mass murderer...and it's a person you've been dreaming about and thanking God for all those years? You get twisted up."

Opinions naturally change over time, but these were alleged to be Escrivá's initial thoughts at the end of the war. For many Christians during that period, Hitler was a hero. Such sentiments help to consolidate a theory that Opus Dei offered support to Nazis as they fled Europe. Of course, there is no proof that Opus Dei members and the organization itself did anything of the sort.

Father Vladimir Feltzman left the movement in the early 1980s. As a young man in Rome, from 1965 onwards, Feltzman had a close relationship with Escrivá since the founder, as he did to many others, served as a surrogate father to the junior priest. Thus, contends Feltzman, he was privy to a large amount of information as well as the private thoughts of the founder. Members of Opus Dei naturally dispute Feltzman's claims, as they have no written records or any further evidence of Escrivá's words in this case. They are adamant that Feltzman misheard or misinterpreted Escrivá. This issue continues to simmer between Opus Dei and Father Feltzman.

The debate began in January 1992 (the year of Escrivá's subsequent beatification) when *Newsweek* made the claim that Escrivá was pro-Hitler. Following the publication of the article, Domingo Diez-Ambrona, a Catholic, wrote to the then Prelate of Opus Dei in Rome to relate a conversation that he had with Escrivá after a chance encounter in 1941. He was not the only person to do so. *Newsweek* received letter after letter describing a "gentle man", who "loved Jews" and, that both Mary and Jesus, the two loves of his life, were Jewish.

"Here was a priest, who had accurate information about the position of the Church and of Catholics in Germany under Hitler's dictatorship," Diez-Ambrona told the *Catholic Herald* in February 1992. "Father Josemaría spoke very forcefully to me against that anti-Christian regime, and with an energy that clearly showed his great love of freedom. It is necessary to explain that it was not so easy in Spain at that time to find people who would condemn the Nazi system so categorically or who would denounce its anti-Christian roots with such clarity. And so, that conversation, taking place as it did at such an historically significant moment, before all the crimes of Nazism had been revealed, continues to impress me profoundly."

Bishop Alvaro del Portillo also made a statement following the *Newsweek* article, saying: "It is absolutely contrary to reality to affirm such a thing of a person who so deeply loved the Jewish people and who so vigorously condemned any kind of tyranny."

Escrivá himself, in 1975, while being interviewed in Venezuela, told his Jewish interviewer: "I love the Jews very much because I love Jesus Christ madly, and He is Jewish. I don't say He was but He is. *Iesus Christus heri et hodie, ipse et in saecula* [Jesus Christ the same yesterday, and today, and forever]. Jesus Christ continues to live and he is Jewish like you. And the second love of my life is also Jewish—the Blessed Virgin Mary, Mother of Jesus Christ. So I look on you with affection."

The information office of the Opus Dei Prelature in Britain points out: "St Josemaría published books, appeared on videos, and lived his life in the public gaze. From at least as early as 1959, when he was profiled in *The Times*, he was well known internationally. In his writings and actions (recorded or not) there is nothing that could support a charge of being anti-Semitic or a supporter of Hitler. Also, nobody alleged during his life that he harbored such tendencies."

Father José Orlandis, one of the oldest surviving members of Opus Dei (as of 2005), has said: "On September 15th, 1939, the day after he [Escrivá] asked me to join Opus Dei, during a retreat in Valencia, being with the Father in his room, without me asking him anything, he confided: 'This morning I have offered the Holy Mass for Poland, this Catholic country undergoing a terrible trial with the Nazi invasion'."

Despite Opus Dei and Escrivá's protestations and proof, commentators are still keen to link the organization with another Nazi affair—that of the earlier mentioned rat lines. The reason behind this theory is that one of the key players in the rat lines controversy was alleged to be Bishop Giovanni Montini, who later became Pope Paul VI during the 1960s. Montini has been named in several books and on several websites as a collaborator working on the rat lines, but has never been officially declared a traitor, nor has he ever been publicly denounced as a Nazi sympathizer. Still, with his name linked to the rat lines, Opus Dei has in turn been pulled into the drama as Montini had proved a useful ally to Opus Dei when Escrivá first arrived in Rome to petition the Vatican for support.

Montini worked closely with Cardinal Pacelli, and when Pacelli was elected Pope Pius XII, Montini held the title of Substitute Secretary of State. Much of Montini's work during this period remains a mystery—most importantly his involvement in the Vatican's diplomatic activities during World War II. The Vatican's repeated contacts with Count Galeazzo Ciano, fascist Minister of Foreign affairs and son-in-law of Mussolini, remains an issue of criticism. Are the links there to be made? Some would allege so: Montini, a leader with alleged fascist sympathies and Opus Dei, a branch of the Catholic Church, which needed Montini's patronage.

There are some conflicting thoughts on Montini being a supporter of Opus Dei. A few other contemporary reports describe hearing Escrivá "denouncing how Montini dared to join the European clamor against the death penalties signed by Franco", which had proved a problematic issue for Escrivá as he had been uneasy at the number of people executed by Franco after his victory. However, despite these reports of anger towards Montini, there is no denying Opus Dei's burgeoning relationship with the papal forces after the movement moved to Rome. Also, there are several passages within Escrivá's books that are filled with praise for the man whom Opus Dei history refers to as a friend of the movement.

While Opus Dei attempted to curry favor with Pope Pius XII during this time, the latter was allegedly involved in other, more sinister, activities. According to authors John Loftus and Mark Aarons in their book, *Unholy Trinity: The Vatican, the Nazis, & Soviet Intelligence*, the Nazi smuggling was personally authorized by Pope Pius XII and directed by his political advisor: Montini. The book explores the role of Vatican rat lines in Nazi smuggling and the involvement of Soviet intelligence in manipulating events. Elements of the Vatican had long been sympathetic to the Nazis' extreme anti-Communist stand, and organized large-scale programs to facilitate the escape of tens of thousands of Nazis and collaborators from Germany, Austria, Croatia, Slovakia, the Ukraine, and a number of other Eastern European states.

Further to the Pope being a Nazi sympathizer, there have been rumors that during the early career of the Pope, while a papal nuncio in Munich, he received Hitler at his residence late one evening and gave the Führer a large amount of money to invest in the rising Germany economy. The report came from an eyewitness account by his housekeeper, Sister Pascalina Lehnert, but there has been some dispute about the veracity of this account.

Critics of Sister Pascalina's account note the public stance that

Pacelli (Pope Pius XII) took against the Nazis in 1937, when he was the Vatican's Secretary of State. Pacelli drafted Pius XI's encyclical condemning Nazism as un-Christian—which led to the confiscation of presses and imprisonment of many Catholics in Germany. Then, in 1942, after Pacelli had become Pius XII, he made a public statement condemning persecutions—this again led to more persecutions and, as a result, Pius XII stopped making public protests, so the argument goes, because persecuted groups pleaded with him not to upset the Nazis.

Furthermore, in the monthly magazine *Inside The Vatican*, in February 2005, Sister Pascalina is quoted as saying in her testimony before the Congregation (Session CLXIII, March 17th, 1972): "The Pope not only opened the doors of the Vatican to protect the persecuted, but he encouraged convents and monasteries to offer hospitality. The Vatican provided provisions for these people. The accusation that Pius XII was indifferent to the needs of the victims is without foundation. He ordered me to spend his inheritance and personal funds to provide for those who wished to leave Italy and go to Canada, Brazil, or elsewhere. Note that $800 was needed for each person who emigrated. Many times the Pope would ask me to deliver to Jewish families a sealed envelope containing $1,000 or more."

Pius XII's actions during the Holocaust remain controversial. He refused pleas for help on the grounds of neutrality, while making statements condemning injustices in general. Privately, he sheltered a small number of Jews and spoke to a few select officials, encouraging them to help the Jews. It is estimated that the Pope saved an estimated 700,000 Jews from the concentration camps by the issuing of false Christian baptismal certificates and hiding many within the sanctuaries of monasteries and convents.

The Pope's success in saving 700,000 Jews only highlights the amount of influence he might have had, had he not chosen to remain silent on so many other occasions. It is said that not only was Pius XII worried there might be Nazi reprisals and that his words might not actually help, but there was also a fear of the growth of Communism were the Nazis to be defeated.

"One may otherwise view Catholicism as one wishes," said Hans Ulrich Rudel, international spokesman for the neo-Nazi movement, in 1970. "But what the Church, especially certain towering personalities within the Church, undertook in those years [immediately after the war] to save the best of our nation, often from certain death, must never be forgotten. In Rome itself, the transit point of the escape routes, a vast amount was done. With its own immense resources, the Church helped many of us to go overseas. In this manner, in quiet and secrecy, the demented victors' mad craving for revenge and retribution could be effectively counteracted."

As Nazi Germany collapsed, Church officials made it their duty to organize a massive campaign of refugee relief for the millions of Catholics fleeing from Eastern Europe and Communism. It was during this time that the moral fiber of the candidates being helped to escape became blurred. This is a point noted by Christopher Simpson in his book *Blowback*, where he explores US recruitment of the Nazis. Simpson argues that, after the war, there was little distinction made between Catholics who were "responsible for the crimes against humanity" committed in the Axis states and those being "persecuted simply for opposition to the Soviets". Europe was in a massive state of confusion after the war, refugees poured into Rome to escape the marauding German or Soviet armies who had stormed their villages, and Rome welcomed them with open arms. This was a huge issue for the Vatican—commentators noted that the Papal States' emphasis was on getting "good" people away from "evil" Communism.

As a result, reports estimate that around 30,000 Nazis were helped to escape to locations including the US, Britain, Canada, Australia, New Zealand, and the most famous haven of all, South America. Included among those "saved" were Klaus Barbie, the "Butcher of Lyons"; Franz Stangl, Commandant at Treblinka; Gustav Wagner, Commandant of Sorbibor extermination camp; Alois Brunner, an official in the Jewish deportation program; Adolf Eichmann; Dr Joseph Mengele; and Deputy Führer Martin Bormann.

John L. Allen Jr, who writes for the *National Catholic Reporter* newspaper, has tried to explain Pope Pius XII's actions by using "evil" Communism as an excuse: "There is no evidence that Pius XII was specifically aware of any of these goings-on. Nonetheless, the Pope had to be aware of the general picture: ex-Nazis were using Vatican offices to flee Europe. Why would he tolerate it? One word: anti-Communism. The Vatican all along regarded the atheistic Soviet Union, not Nazi Germany, as the ultimate global threat. In the years prior to World War II, that analysis had closely aligned the Vatican with a number of conservative Christian Democratic and clerical-fascist parties in Eastern Europe. Those governments that extended the quickest welcome to the Nazis were almost invariably Catholic—Slovakia under Msgr Jozef Tiso, for example, and Croatia under Ante Pavelic. Indeed, the basic Catholic calculus of most of the 20th century was to the effect that an anti-Communist is a friend of the Church."

In 1998 the Vatican issued a 14-page confession of the Vatican's sins of omission in the Nazi era. Deemed "a disappointing failure" by many leading Jews, one of the criticisms levelled at the document was its failure to recognize their [the Church's] role in the post-war period. According to Dr Efraim, director of the Israel office of the Simon Wiesenthal Center: "The document makes no mention of the Nazi escape routes—the rat lines—aided by some priests; it makes no mention of the shelter offered to fleeing Nazis by some churches, or of the continuing anti-Semitic statements of some post-war church leaders."

The relationship between former Nazis who fled using the rat lines and the Vatican was brought to the world's attention at Adolf Eichmann's trial in 1961. The Vatican had issued Eichmann a refugee passport in the name of Ricardo Klement after Eichmann had met an unnamed Franciscan friar and the Croatian priest Father Krunoslav Draganovic. Draganovic worked on one of the main rat runs, the Intermarium, which was run by US intelligence, with Draganovic's help in Genoa. Both the US and the British were deeply involved in the Intermarium as they needed the former Nazis to become intelligence agents in the West—they were important assets in the new cold war ahead. Another rat run, the ODESSA (Organisation der Ehemaligen SS Angehorigen), was made famous by novelist Frederick Forsyth and his source, Jewish Nazi hunter Simon Wiesenthal, is yet to be entirely proven.

During World War II the upper echelons of the Nazi Party weren't associated only with the Vatican. There were tales of "secret" societies and "occult" orders surrounding the higher-ranking members of the Third Reich. One such group was the "Thule" Society (Thulegesellschaft), founded in 1919, a racist, religious, ethnic-biased and anti-Semitic satanic cult.

Theories abound that all of Hitler's "inner circle", such as Heinrich Himmler (the son of a Catholic schoolmaster), Joseph Goebbels (born into a strict, Catholic working-class family from Rheydt in the Rhineland), and Julius Streicher (publisher, editor, and writer for the German propaganda paper, *Der Stürmer*) were not only good Catholics but members of both the Nazi Party and the "Thule" Society. The "Thule" was seen as the "mother" of the German Socialist Party, led by Streicher, and the right-wing radical Oberland Free Corps.

In his book *The Gods Of Eden*, William Bradley draws attention to the fact that Hitler, following his performance in Munich in 1919 when he identified pro-Communist soldiers who should be shot, was assigned to a secret political department—the Army District Command. This was a significant posting, especially as the District Command was being funded by German industrialists in their bid to help fight Communism. Furthermore, one of the prominent leaders of the District Command at the time was Ernst Röhm—a member of the "Thule" Society. Röhm was not alone; many members of the District Command at that time were also connected to "Thule", which believed in the "Aryan super race" and preached the coming of a German "Messiah" who would lead Germany to glory and a new Aryan civilization.

Hitler, of course, fitted the bill as a messianic leader and Bradley isn't alone in linking the Führer to the "Thule" organization. In *The Unknown Hitler*, written by Wulf Schwarzwaller, the author comments on Hitler's activities in 1919. Not only did the Nazi leader join the District Command but he also met a man called Dietrich Eckart, who had a significant influence on Hitler's life. A wealthy publisher and editor-in-chief of an anti-Semitic journal (*In Plain German*), Eckart was also a committed occultist and belonged to the inner circle of the "Thule" Society as well as other esoteric orders. Furthermore, Hitler dedicated his book *Mein Kampf* to Eckart.

Other writers of this period also discuss the creation of new religions devised by Himmler, based on the ancient neo-pagan cults, which formed the basis of several secret societies. In *Satan and the Swastika*, Francis King reports on various neo-pagan ceremonies that SS recruits were forced to attend—Himmler himself had invented an SS religion, which clearly originated in his love of the occult and his worship of the god Woden.

Such underground orders and secret societies, especially when leading Catholics such as Himmler are alleged to have been involved, mean that critics of Opus Dei, when looking for an easy target, tend to link the two since both had dynamic individuals within a small organization. As a result, people have been swift to judge, and the very nature of a secret organization (or, as Opus Dei likes to stress, "private" organization), like those invented by the members of the Nazi party, leads to suspicion, confusion, fear and, in Opus Dei's case, ignorance.

Since Opus Dei is viewed as a secretive society, the question remains—just what does it have to hide? During the period of post-war confusion and terror, some saw the foundation and spread of Opus Dei as a sinister force rather than a religious force for good. Obviously not in the same league as that of the "Thule" Society, Opus Dei is a group that appears selective, powerful, and not fully out in the open—resembling other menacing societies. Naturally, it looked like it had something to hide within its murky depths. As explained previously, following the Spanish Civil War, Opus Dei's lack of overt "Catholicness" often led to it being seen as secretive, especially while the rest of Spain was celebrating its faith.

As a result, confusion and ignorance led to paranoia, which is why many feel that Opus Dei must be part of a wider force. Some digging links Opus Dei with some other secret societies such as the Knights of Malta, which is the Sovereign Military Order of Malta and also known as the original Sovereign Military Order of St John of Jerusalem. A closed fraternity of the Roman Catholic Church, initiated members must be Catholic and have served in the military. They participate in secret ceremonies, wear feudal ritual dress, and embrace a strong class/caste mentality as part of their initiation into Rosicrucian dogma (which also includes Freemasons, the Knights Templar, and the Priory of Sion).

"The Knights of Malta is a club that aristocratic Catholics join," explains Feltzman. "This is a revival of the medieval Renaissance. It's a club you join, but you've got to be invited. You dress up in a big robe, and it's a club for rich aristocratic right-wing Catholics, whose aims are to look decorative, to be one of us. It's a club, a select club." And are there crossovers with Opus Dei? Apparently so. Opus Dei, used to targeting the wealthy and powerful, would find a rich seam of potential Opus Dei members among the affluent, aristocratic, right-wing, Catholic gatherings at the Knights of Malta meetings. "It's the sort of pond in which Opus Dei will fish," adds Feltzman, "because Opus Dei lives to make Opus Dei grow. They believe that Opus Dei is the salvation."

As for the other societies (like the Knights Templar), these Rosicrucians are devoted to the study of metaphysical and mystical lore—hardly Opus Dei territory. Yet, this hasn't stopped theorists heading off into unproven (and unchartered territory) with madcap theories alleging that Pope John XXIII was the Grand Master of the Priory of Sion during his papal reign, or that the creator of the Cistercian order (founded in 1098), St Bernard, was involved in the formation of the Knights Templar (founded 1118). All this is unproven but such theories are allowed to fester unchecked as allegations are strewn across the internet.

Comparisons between Opus Dei and these religious groups have been made but can they actually be linked together? Only, at present, in works of fiction—more recent scholarly investigations have disproved many allegations involving the Priory of Sion. The idea of a pope as a grand master is worthy of Dan Brown's fictional work, *The Da Vinci Code*, but the allegations remain.

As for the Freemasons, while they had links with the far right, it again seems unlikely, during the 1940s, that the group was associated with Hitler. "There is one dangerous element and that is the element I have copied from them," said Hitler when describing the Masons. "They form a sort of priestly nobility. They have developed an esoteric doctrine more than merely formulated, but imparted through the symbols and mysteries in degrees of initiation. The hierarchical organization and the initiation through symbolic rites, that is to say, without bothering the brain by working on the imagination through magic and the symbols of a cult, all this has a dangerous element, and the element I have taken over. Don't you see that our party must be of this character...? An Order, the hierarchical Order of a secular priesthood."

The Masons, a secular priesthood, however, had no links with Opus Dei. According to Feltzman: "Opus Dei was very much anti-Masons, because Masons on the continent were always traditionally anti-Christian, anti-Catholic, since the revolution in France. The

Masons were the enemy." Still, during this period and prior to his election to the papacy, Montini's hand was at work again: "Another generation will not pass before peace is established between these two religious societies [i.e. the Freemasons and the Church]", wrote the clergyman. Montini was trying to bring the two forces together. In fact, on Montini's death, a Freemasonic review stated in an obituary notice: "This is the first time that the leader of one of the greatest religious bodies in the West has passed away without considering the Masons as a hostile organization."

Despite Feltzman's protestations, as stated, the perceived secretive nature of Opus Dei continues to link them with other closed societies. And, as it turns out, later in Opus Dei's history some of their alleged members were linked to high-profile scandals and were also thought to be (or at least linked with) members of other organizations such as the Italian Masonic, right-wing group P2 (Propaganda Due). Nothing has been proved to link Opus Dei with the Nazis and it is highly unlikely that anyone will ever be able to do so. It is an impossible leap, yet due to the suspicion Opus Dei receives, the unfounded rumors continue to persist.

Taking Over the Vatican

Lord, could you have allowed me to deceive so many souls
in good faith, when I've done it all for your glory, knowing it
was your will? Is it possible that the Holy See will say that
we've arrived a century too soon? Behold we have left all things
and followed you! I never wanted to deceive anybody. I never
wanted to do anything other than serve you. Is there any
possibility that I could be a fraud?

Josemaría Escrivá, 1940s

The growing influence of Opus Dei within the Vatican has caused critics to worry. To outsiders, the organization is viewed as the power
behind the papal throne—a group that has the ability to elect a new
pope of its own choosing and the influence to make major changes
to the Catholic doctrine. How true are these allegations? How much
power does it wield in Rome?

Conspiracy theorists would argue that Opus Dei is "all powerful",
but while no one denies Opus Dei's presence in Rome, what many
commentators fail to remember is that not only has Opus Dei been
welcomed with open arms by the Vatican, but also, and especially at
the start, its members were few. This chapter strives to explore just
how, and why, Opus Dei has the reputation of having a strong public
presence within the Holy See.

To recap: during the 1940s, Escrivá had sent out experienced
members of Opus Dei to recruit new members in Portugal, England,
and Italy. Later, the movement spread to France, Germany, and
Ireland. The organization was expanding internationally, and it
became swiftly apparent that Escrivá had to prove that Opus Dei was
a serious religious organization. If it was going to expand and gain
support in the Catholic world it needed approval from the Holy See.

Escrivá believed that Opus Dei was different from other Catholic
organizations within the Church—the full apostolic vocation of Opus
Dei distinguished it from other confraternities and pious unions,

which were recognized by the Code of Canon Law. Furthermore, in the 1940s, a group of Opus Dei members were hoping to become ordained into the priesthood; it was vital to solve the points of law that their ordination would pose. Could they be Opus Dei priests? Legal recognition from the Vatican was vital.

As a result, Alvaro del Portillo, one of Escrivá's followers, visited the Holy See in February 1946 to present the Vatican with documents, but was told that Escrivá himself should come, if they were to make any kind of headway. Critics have often wondered why Escrivá didn't make the initial journey himself, but, according to his official website, the priest was ill and had been suffering from an acute form of diabetes since 1944.

"The doctors felt," said Escrivá, "that I could die at any moment. When I went to bed, I did not know if I would get up again. And when I got up in the morning I didn't know if I would last until the evening."

Escrivá recovered enough to travel to Barcelona and from there the plan was to move on to Genoa by ship. While in Barcelona, Escrivá preached to some of his followers: "Lord, could you have allowed me to deceive so many souls in good faith, when I've done it all for your glory, knowing it was your will? Is it possible that the Holy See will say that we've arrived a century too soon? Behold we have left all things and followed you! I never wanted to deceive anybody. I never wanted to do anything other than serve you. Is there any possibility that I could be a fraud?"

His fears for the movement were compounded as he continued his journey to Genoa. Together with José Orlandis, a young legal history student, the duo embarked on the steamship *JJ Sister*. By the time they reached the Gulf of Lyons, a storm rocked the boat to such an extent that everyone on board (including the captain) was suffering from seasickness. "It appears that the devil does not want us to get to Rome!" said Escrivá at the time.

Del Portillo, who was still acting as Escrivá's envoy in Rome, arrived in Genoa to drive Orlandis and Escrivá back to the Vatican, where Escrivá spent most of 1946 working with Vatican officials. While Escrivá and Opus Dei were welcomed by Msgr Giovanni Battista Montini, the Vatican's Under-Secretary of State, others were sceptical about finding an adequate place for Opus Dei within the structure of the Church.

As it turns out, Escrivá and the future Pope Paul VI were personal friends from 1946 and Montini was, apparently, the first curial official to take an interest in what Escrivá was trying to do. Escrivá called him the first friendly face he encountered in Rome. What is a little-known fact, however, is that in 1947, when Escrivá was made domestic prelate to the Pope (a position that brings with it the title "Monsignor"), the nomination was championed by Montini, who (Escrivá later learned) also paid the fee for the nomination out of his own pocket. In a letter of that year (April 22nd) to the new Monsignor, Montini wrote that Opus Dei was a sign of hope ("*una speranza*") for the Church.

Later, when Montini became Pope, he had several meetings with Escrivá, one of which stands out. On November 21st, 1965, the Holy Father opened the Centro ELIS—a technical school for worker-students entrusted to Opus Dei (by Pope John XXIII) as regards the spiritual dimension. Montini embraced Escrivá, visibly moved, and exclaimed that everything there was God's Work (a play on words: "*Tutto, tutto qui e Opus Dei*"). These are hardly the words of a man who did not trust or admire Opus Dei.

Montini is also reported to have used *The Way*, the meditation book written by Escrivá, and afterwards made it known that it had helped him spiritually. He had written even before they first met, in a letter dated February 2nd, 1945: "its pages are a deeply felt and vibrant appeal to the generous hearts of our youth; by revealing sublime ideals to them, they lead young people to think reflectively and seriously, as a preparation for living supernatural life to the full...[This book] has already produced plentiful fruits in the Spanish university environment. I am immensely joyful that *The Way* has already had such encouraging results, and I ask the Lord to continue to bless it and to let it become more widely known, for the good of many souls."

The criticism and gossip that revolved around Opus Dei and its work, including allegations that the organization had used underhand means to gain access and recognition, upset Escrivá, as he was later to write: "At first this murmuring hurt me, but it made a love for the Roman pontiff that was less 'Spanish,' i.e. less emotional, arise in my heart—born of more solid, more theological reflection, and therefore more profound. Since then I've always said that 'in Rome I lost my innocence', and this event has been most useful for my soul."

By the mid-1940s, the first three priests of Opus Dei were ordained. All three were engineers. Del Portillo continued in his role as Escrivá's closest collaborator and, as mentioned in Chapter Three, José María Hernández de Garnica worked in Europe while José Luis Múzquiz went to the United States. In 1946, six more members of Opus Dei were ordained, and from then on, ordinations became a regular event.

With Escrivá moving the center of his operations to Rome, it was time for the organization to find a home in the Eternal City. "This he did in 1947 through the efforts of an Italian duchess right out of the pages of Henry James—Virginia Sforza Cesarini," writes John Martin in *The Remnant* newspaper. "Largely through her efforts, Opus Dei was able to acquire a building in the Viale Bruno Buozzi that had once housed the Hungarian Embassy to the Holy See. Escrivá renamed it the Villa Tevere (Tiber), refurbished it, and, with his position secure at the center of things Catholic, pushed forward on other fronts."

One of Opus Dei's websites, which devotes itself to the writings and work of Escrivá, makes no mention of Cesarini on its pages. Instead, the site reports that the property was obtained with "almost no funds" and with the "encouragement of various Curia officials". In fact, the only detail that both sides appear to agree on is that the house did indeed stand on Bruno Buozzi Avenue. While the Opus Dei center was in the process of being built, members of Opus Dei lived in the small gatehouse at the entrance (known as the *pensionato*) until they were ready to move into the Villa Tevere.

Another critic of Escrivá's Roman vision describes a different home—harking back to John Martin's grandiose visions of the center in his article—with no mention of poverty. According to Martin, Miguel Fisac, a leading Spanish architect and one of Opus Dei's early numeraries (he remained one from 1936 to 1955), remembered Escrivá as someone who was not above insisting on a considerable degree of splendor in his surroundings, and especially in the mother house in Rome. As Fisac says: "Millions and millions of pesetas were invested in luxuries of low artistic quality, but in the Renaissance manner, because all of these frivolous details were of the greatest importance to him."

Construction work took around 12 years to complete and though no figures have ever been published, Robert Hutchison, in *Their*

Kingdom Come, estimates the final cost to be around $10 million. Where did Opus Dei get its money? The likelihood is through fundraising and donations (there was, apparently, a worldwide project to raise funds for the building), but Hutchison appears to imply a more sinister source, without going into any further detail.

Villa Tevere is still revered by Opus Dei members today. "I was shown last year round the Villa Tevere by Don Flavio Capucci," said Martin Ketterer at a conference in 2003. "You feel the Founder's presence everywhere. At every corner, on every landing, he erected little shrines, full of creative care for his children: Flavio showed me one in particular, a small hollow inside the prelatic Church of Our Lady of Peace. Saint Josemaría had collected a number of swords which belonged to members of the Work who served as soldiers for their different countries. Coming upon it suddenly as you sweep down the stairs, you're stopped in your tracks. He wanted you to pause and reflect on the vital importance of the interior life. It's the point he made in *The Way*: 'What is peace? Peace is something intimately associated with war. Peace is a result of victory. Peace demands of me a continual struggle'."

By 1948, Escrivá had established the Roman College of the Holy Cross, where from that time on, numerous male members of Opus Dei would study and receive a deep spiritual and pastoral formation, while taking courses at various pontifical teaching establishments in Rome. For the women, their new center (established later in 1953) was known as the Roman College of Saint Mary. After several years in Rome these men and women returned to their native lands, or somewhere new, to recruit for Opus Dei.

"They set up an institution called *Centro Romano de Incontri Sacerdotali* (CRIS)," explains Father Vladimir Feltzman. "It's a Roman center for meeting. Overtly, the aim of that was to have a place where students from all over the world, studying in Rome, feeling lonely, could come and get support, emotional and spiritual support. Covertly, the reason was that you wanted a platform to which you could invite present and future luminaries of the Church, to give them a chance to interface with Opus Dei."

The institution affords members of Opus Dei the chance to receive spiritual and pastoral formation in the spirit of Opus Dei directly from Escrivá, while pursuing degrees in philosophy, theology, canon law, and Sacred Scripture at pontifical universities in Rome. During the mid- to late 1940s, graduates of the Rome center were sent to Europe, with Escrivá often going out to visit them to check on their progress. In 1945, Sister Lucia, the visionary of Fatima, asked Escrivá to come to Portugal, and in 1949 Cardinal Faulhaber of Munich invited him to Germany to present his vision. Opus Dei was gaining European recognition. Italy, meanwhile, was growing rapidly for Opus Dei. In August 1949, 30 Italian students began their training at a villa near the Pope's summer residence at Castelgandolfo. This was later replaced with a more opulent building, the Villa delle Rose, a women's residence attached to the Roman College of Saint Mary.

1950 is viewed as a golden year in Opus Dei's history. By this stage, the men's branch had some 2,400 members and the women's branch numbered another 550. Furthermore, Escrivá got his wish: Pius XII granted the definitive approval to Opus Dei. This enabled married people to join Opus Dei, and secular clergy to be admitted to the Priestly Society of the Holy Cross.

Only two years later, Opus Dei founded its first university—the University of Navarre in Pamplona. Escrivá saw it as a place to infuse science and culture with faith: "Every now and then, monotonously sounding like a broken record, some people try to resurrect a supposed incompatibility between faith and science, between human knowledge and divine revelation. But such incompatibility could only arise—and then only apparently—from a misunderstanding of the elements of the problem. If the world has come from God, if He has created man in His image and likeness and given him a spark of divine light, the task of our intellect should be to uncover the divine meaning embedded in all things by their nature, even if this can be attained only by dint of hard work." While Escrivá no doubt saw Navarre as an educational masterpiece, there's no doubting it could also be used as the perfect recruiting ground for the organization. By admitting the brightest and the best, what better place to find or groom new members to its cause?

In Rome, Escrivá was still making inroads. The center was expanding and, thanks to the support of the Vatican, slowly but surely becoming more influential. Escrivá often heaped praise on the various Popes he worked with over the years. This "understanding" and "affection" hit a rough spot, however, during one of the most turbulent years of Vatican history—the Vatican Council of 1962, known more widely as Vatican II.

Opus Dei's presence and politics in Rome contrasted starkly with Italian daily life during that era. The late 1950s and 1960s in Italy was characterized by Federico Fellini's 1960 film *La Dolce Vita*. In the epic film Marcello Mastronianni played Marcello Rubini, a playboy journalist who spends his days with celebrities and wealthy acquaintances seeking fleeting joy in parties and, of course, sex. Splashing about in the Trevi fountain and having carefree sex with blonde models was hardly the world of Opus Dei. It was during this time that Opus Dei invited a young Polish bishop to come to its center in Rome. His name was Karol Wojtyla, and he would eventually become Pope John Paul II.

"Wojtyla came from Poland, which was all squeaky clean morally because it was controlled by Communism," says Feltzman, "and he arrives in Rome and it's sex, drugs, and rock and roll: the *dolce vita*. He's invited to *Christ Centro* and everybody is immaculate, respectable, traditional...So, when he becomes Cardinal and later Pope, who does he remember?" The answer, according to Feltzman, is naturally Opus Dei.

At this point in time, Wojtyla was still a young bishop, and the most pressing issue during the early 1960s was Vatican II (the 21st ecumenical council of the Roman Catholic Church). The council's purpose was to look at the spiritual renewal of the Church and reconsider its position in the modern world—issues that Opus Dei, naturally, was interested in.

The Council, summoned by Pope John XXIII, brought together more than 2,000 of the world's Roman Catholic bishops to discuss the Pope's visions of *aggiornamento* ("bringing up to date") of the Church. One issue in particular caught Escrivá's eye: the Council's emphasis on the important role to be played by lay Christians in the Church.

"When John XXIII announced his decision to call an Ecumenical Council," says the Vatican, "Blessed Josemaría began to pray and get others to 'pray for the happy outcome of this great initiative of the Second Vatican Ecumenical Council', as the Vatican wrote in a letter in 1962. As a result of the deliberations of the Council, the Church's solemn *magisterium* was to confirm fundamental aspects of the spirit of Opus Dei, such as the universal call to holiness; professional work as a means to holiness and apostolate; the value and lawful limits of Christian freedom in temporal affairs; and the Holy Mass as the center and root of the interior life. Blessed Josemaría met numerous Council Fathers and experts, who saw him as a forerunner of many of the master lines of the Second Vatican Council. Profoundly identified with the Council's teaching, he diligently fostered its implementation through the formative activities of Opus Dei all over the world."

Despite this pomp from the Vatican, at the time, according to ex-Opus Dei priest Vladimir Feltzman, Vatican II was in fact a blow to both Opus Dei and Escrivá. "Escrivá had been pro-laity and pro-early Church," explains Feltzman, "because the whole Church was pro-clerical and medieval and Renaissance and fervor. Latin Mass and so on. In the 1960s, Opus Dei started having Mass in English, readings in English, and we had altars facing people. Along comes Vatican II and that says that it's OK to have altars facing people and Mass in the vernacular. So what does Opus Dei do? It turns the altars back to front just to be different. It's almost like tacking into the wind if you're sailing: 'Wherever they're going we're going the other way'."

It was said, by critics of Opus Dei, that elements of the third session of Vatican II in November 1964, which brought in women, religious men, and lay people, as auditors, enraged Escrivá—as, allegedly, did a new Constitution on Liturgy. This constitution promoted more active communal participation in the Mass as the central act of Roman Catholic public worship and was the initial step in changes, which, by 1971, included the replacement of Latin, the ancient language of the service, by vernacular languages.

While initial reaction to the council within the Catholic faith was generally in favor, there was, of course, some opposition. Conservative Roman Catholic groups began to fear that the reforms had become too radical. Later, organized dissent became apparent, and some critics challenged the authority both of the council and of the popes who carried out its decrees.

Opposition to changes in the Church's liturgy became a rallying point for those angry with the changes. It should be noted, however, that Opus Dei was not part of this group. In fact, many priests of Opus Dei used the new rite, unlike other organizations within the Church. The most prominent leader of the "Catholic Traditionalists", those who rejected the doctrinal and disciplinary reforms instituted by

Vatican II, was a retired French archbishop, Marcel Lefebvre. In 1970, Lefebvre founded an international group known as the Priestly Fraternity of St Pius X, and declared that the Vatican Council's reforms "spring from heresy and end in heresy". Efforts at reconciliation between Rome and Archbishop Lefebvre proved unsuccessful—Pope Paul VI suspended him from the exercise of his functions as priest and bishop in 1976, but he continued his activities, including ordination of priests to serve traditionalist churches. Lefebvre was excommunicated in 1988. Compare this with Opus Dei, which was given "Personal Prelature" status in 1982—hardly something that would be given as a reward for "dissent".

Opus Dei continues to deny that Escrivá was livid concerning Vatican II, but the rumors live on. It has also been suggested that Pope John had asked Escrivá to participate in Vatican II, but when he turned down a role in the proceedings, Alvaro del Portillo was made secretary of the Commission on Discipline of the Faith. During this period, Pope John died and Cardinal Giovanni Montini became the next Pope, a man who had been supportive towards Opus Dei from the time of Escrivá's arrival in Rome.

There have even been some stories stating that Escrivá was so frustrated and incensed with Vatican II that he considered moving to Greece and becoming a Greek Orthodox minister. As it turned out, in 1966, Escrivá did visit Greece, but it was an apostolic journey made with del Portillo and Echevarría on February 26th.

On March 10th, Escrivá wrote from Athens to the General Council: "This journey is already coming to an end, and it is without doubt the history of the Work in these lands. Let us pray—at times one would want to pray less, but it is inevitable—remind yourselves and think about the future of the work—the Work of God—that we will have to do in this corner of the Mediterranean: it will not be easy, but not difficult either."

These are not the words of a man keen to leave the Catholic Church and settle in Greece. Furthermore, according to Andrew Soane, "The general impression that the Founder took from this journey was it would be difficult to start the Work in Greece. The social and religious climate at that moment was not favorable for developing an apostolic activity to any great extent. As in all places, it would go ahead through the strength of prayer, mortification, and work.

However, while the circumstances did not improve, it was prudent to be calm. It was not the opportune moment to begin Opus Dei in Greece."

Reports continue to state that Escrivá initially turned his back on Vatican II—again, an accusation that Opus Dei categorically denies. "The Founder's attitude to the Second Vatican Council," continues Soane, "was a mixture of being very happy and positive about the message (which was wonderful for Opus Dei) and being concerned at the delicate situation of the Church when the Council was used to further some more personal agendas—something [Pope John Paul II] put a stop to."

"As I see it," said Escrivá in 1967 in an interview with the Madrid newspaper *Palabra*: "The present doctrinal position of the Church could be expressed as 'positive' and at the same time 'delicate', as in all crises of growth. Positive, undoubtedly, because the doctrinal wealth of the Second Vatican Council has set the entire Church, the entire priestly People of God, on a new supremely hopeful track of renewed fidelity to the divine plan of salvation which has been entrusted to it. But, delicate as well, because the theological conclusions which have been reached are not, let us say, of an abstract or theoretical nature. They are part of a supremely *living* theology..."

"It was not the Council that the Founder disagreed with," continues Soane, "but some of the unofficial interpretations of it, the aftermath which (apparently) caused confusion among lay people about the teachings of the Church. To take very concrete examples, which Escrivá spoke about, some people were saying that confession was no longer necessary, that devotion to the saints was now discouraged, that it was no longer necessary to insist on doctrine but rather good intentions. These are not ideas that the Council promoted, but the founder of Opus Dei got a reputation nonetheless because he spoke out against them (he can be seen doing so, in get-togethers which were captured on video in the 1970s)."

For Opus Dei, the central theme of Vatican II—that everyone was called to holiness—gave the organization the confirmation of all the principles that Escrivá had been preaching; and an issue over which Escrivá had initially been labelled "heterodox". "Perhaps the best locus of these ideas is the homily 'Passionately loving the world'," says Soane, "with the concepts of Christian materialism (which 'flatly rejects' the presentation of the Christian life as something purely spiritual) and also, perhaps especially, the freedom of lay people."

"Freedom is a key idea to grasp in Opus Dei," adds Soane. "Members of Opus Dei, and indeed Catholics in public life, do not represent the Opus Dei or the Catholic Church when they propose solutions to the problems faced by society. They represent nobody but themselves. Failure to understand freedom and its implications is historically perhaps the single area that has led to the most misunderstandings about Opus Dei."

Opus Dei's reports on Vatican II contradict Feltzman's account, which describes a man who was upset by the reforms of Vatican II as he felt that all the discipline and hard work he promoted was going to fall apart. Though some of the reforms followed many of Opus Dei's beliefs, Escrivá's sense that control was slipping from his grasp disturbed him. "He was scared that everything was going to fall apart," says Feltzman. "All the discipline, all the orthodoxy. He got so terrified; he started codifying everything, writing everything down from how many pairs of underpants you should have to how many cups. His fear was breeding that kind of control."

Despite these contradictions, nearly everyone (even critics of Opus Dei) agree that Vatican II did give Opus Dei and Escrivá some opportunities and validation. The Church accepted, for the first time, that work was part of the divine plan and Opus Dei publicly declared that *Lumen Gentium*, the Decree on the Apostolate of the Laity, and *Gaudium et Spes* all drew their inspiration from Escrivá's teachings. Before Vatican II, the laity were seen as passive units of a Church run exclusively by the clergy, rather than as responsible members of the faithful playing their part—as they do within Opus Dei. *Lumen Gentium* stated that "all Christians, in any state or walk of life, are called to the fullness of Christian life and to the perfection of love."

"Contrary to many distorted interpretations, the Council was not principally about the role of the lay person in the Church," wrote C. John McCloskey, an Opus Dei priest, "but rather about the role of the lay Catholic in the world, an essential distinction and one with many profound consequences for both society and culture. All of this might serve as an introduction to the phenomenon of the growth of Opus Dei throughout the world, and how it may be an aspect of the worldwide strategy of the pontificate of John Paul II as the oft-heralded millennium rapidly approaches. It is no secret that while all the Roman pontiffs whose reigns have coincided with the growth and development of Opus Dei since 1928 have highly approved of its message and mission, John Paul II—perhaps as a result of his varied work and educational background—has grasped its importance in a deeper fashion and has played an essential role in encouraging its development through the granting of its definitive juridical status, the establishment of the Pontifical University of the Holy Cross, and finally the beatification of its founder, Blessed (now Saint) Josemaría Escrivá."

Vatican II was also important in another way: it created the canonical form known as the "Personal Prelature", and thus opened the way for Opus Dei to become a Church with a Personal Prelature two decades later, in 1982.

In 1968, a few years after Vatican II, Pope Paul VI also issued *Humanae Vitae*, which discussed birth control, and condemned artificial methods of contraception. The document stated that there are two purposes of human sexual intercourse: the "unitive" purpose and the procreative purpose. As a result, condoms, even when used during the infertile period or in order to avoid infection, still destroy the "unitive" purpose of sexual intercourse; their use is therefore opposed to the Church's teaching, as was made clear in *Humanae Vitae*. When *Humanae Vitae* was released it was said that Escrivá had rejected it, declaring that the statement wasn't strong enough in its opposition to contraception. Rumors abound that Karol Wojtyla (later Pope John Paul II) resolved the issue, as it has been said that it was he who had convinced the then Pope to reject changing the Church doctrine in favor of artificial birth control.

Incidentally, although Opus Dei has been criticized for being too stringent in its attitude towards sex and contraception, it should be noted that years later, in July 2004, an Opus Dei priest, Father Martin Rhonheimer, wrote in *The Tablet*: "Campaigns to promote abstinence and fidelity are certainly and ultimately the only effective long-term remedy to combat AIDS. So there is no reason for the Church to consider the campaigns promoting condoms as helpful for the future of human society. But nor can the Church possibly teach that people engaged in immoral lifestyles should avoid them [condoms]."

With all this change occurring at the heart of the Catholic Church,

Escrivá saw Opus Dei as the core, or pure center, of the Church. "God has chosen Opus Dei to save His Church," was a familiar mantra of Escrivá's, and now it was more apt than ever. And, as long as Wojtyla remained a friend, the organization knew its time would come. It is perhaps Opus Dei's strong relationship with Wojtyla and the Work's more stringent views, especially in a constantly changing modern society, that causes it to be the subject of frequent attacks. Is this justified? Not entirely, though of course there are some doubts as regards attitudes towards Vatican II; but in terms of doctrinal practises, at this stage at least—post-Vatican II in the early 1970s—there is little reason to suspect that Opus Dei was "taking over the Vatican" and little evidence to show that it, especially at this stage, had any major influence on the papacy.

The New Conquistadors of South America

**Latin America is a fertile field ripe for the proselytizing by
Opus Dei...**
**Opus Dei...especially in Latin America, is associated with
dictatorships, death squads, and oppressive policies.**
Lee Cormie, a professor of theology at the University of Toronto

Like the Spanish conquistadors who invaded and overwhelmed
the New World in the 16th century, Opus Dei set itself the task of
capturing South America. The mission began in 1949 in Mexico, and
within a few short years had spread to Chile, Argentina, and beyond.
Mexico quickly became an Opus Dei stronghold and the organization's largest outpost in the New World. Its numbers grew at tremendous speed, and it was soon ranked behind only Spain and Italy in
terms of membership.

But that success came at a price. The mid-20th century was a time
of enormous social and political change for the continent. It was also
a time of tyranny, rapid industrialization, and brutal repression. Opus
Dei moved freely between countries, encountering despots and dictators, opposing Catholic liberals, and all the while advancing its own
cause.

Opus Dei's envoy to Mexico was Pedro Casciaro, architect, theologian, and close confidant of Josemaría Escrivá. The two had a close
bond, having escaped together during the Spanish Civil War (see
Chapter Two). In the winter of 1937 they had made a long and arduous journey across the Pyrenees and through Andorra, celebrating
Mass along the way, finally re-entering Spain in the free zone in
the north. Their friendship and devotion was sealed: there were
few others whom Escrivá would have trusted with such an important
mission.

Casciaro left Madrid and set sail from Bilbao, Spain, with a mission to convert a continent lying before him. Arriving in the Mexican
port of Veracruz on January 18th, 1949, he carried a modest amount

of cash and a portrait of Nuestra Señora del Rocio, the "Madonna of the Dew". Most importantly in his bag was a list of wealthy contacts. He set to work immediately, and one month later had established the first Opus Dei center outside Europe, at 33 London Street (Calle Londres), in the federal district of Mexico City, in Mexico's capital.

An impressive central location, Opus Dei's first home on Calle Londres was in an area filled with people, as the Federal District in Mexico City is one of the world's most populated areas with an estimated 22 million inhabitants living inside an area of 750km² (290m²). It was from here that Casciaro began building the Opus Dei network. His list of contacts opened the doors of Mexico's great and good.

Casciaro may have had useful contacts, but he must also have been aware that relations between the Mexican State and the Catholic Church had been highly problematic in the 1920s and 1930s. During the 1920s, the president, Plutarco Elías Calles, had battled the Catholic Church throughout his rule. The major crisis started in 1926 when José Mora y del Río, the Archbishop of Mexico City, declared that Catholics could not follow the religious provisions of the 1917 Constitution. Ignoring del Río's declaration, Calles decided to implement several of the constitutional provisions: religious processions were prohibited; the Church's educational establishments, convents, and monasteries were closed; foreign priests and nuns were deported; and priests were required to register with the government before receiving permission to perform their religious duties.

As a result, the Church and her servants decided to go on strike on July 31st, 1926. In the three years that followed no sacraments were administered, and all around the country bands of militant Roman Catholics (the *Cristeros*) attacked government officials and facilities, as well as burning public schools. The government, in turn, reacted with overwhelming force, using the army and partisan bands of Red Shirts to fight the *Cristeros*.

By 1929 the revolt had been largely contained, and the *Cristeros* were compelled to lay down their arms and accept most of the government's terms. The Church and Catholic worshippers viewed it as a battle for survival—their religious traditions pitted against the force of modernization. According to Edwin Williamson, in *The Penguin History of Latin America*, rural Mexico was "overwhelmingly" Catholic. As a result, the anti-Church *caudillos*' attempts to bring in a secular style to the schools, rather than the Church education that the peasants were more used to, proved incredibly unpopular.

Mexico was suffering—internal struggles, religious discord, and, like many other nations during the 1930s, an economic depression—and the country's output suffered. Although no longer the elected President, Calles still worked behind the scenes from 1928 to 1934, encouraging the tightening of state controls and brutal repression across the country. In these difficult times, anti-clericalism flourished, and fascist-style Goldshirts terrorized Catholics and other opponents of the regime. The governor of the state of Tabasco passed extreme anti-Catholic laws, enforced by church-burning *pistoleros*—many Catholics lived in fear during this era.

By 1934, the oppressive government was in decline. With the presidential elections approaching, Calles pacified the left-wing elements of his party by nominating Lázaro Cárdenas, a popular state governor, to succeed Abelardo Rodríguez, president of Mexico since 1932. Cárdenas had participated in the revolutionary conflict and had risen through the ranks from a military officer to brigadier-general. Initially suspicious of Cárdenas, Calles hoped that he would fall into line like the three previous incumbents before him (Emilio Portes Gil, 1928–30; Pascual Ortiz Rubio, 1930–2; and Rodríguez, 1932–4). This was not to be the case.

Cárdenas proved to be an honest and radical president, and sensed that Calles wanted to regroup, regain his power, and remove Cárdenas from power. As a result, Cárdenas struck first. On April 9th, 1936, he had Calles arrested and dumped over the border. When a detachment of soldiers and police burst into Calles' bedroom, they found him reading a Spanish edition of *Mein Kampf*.

President Cárdenas set about giving the restless peasants what they wanted: land. This act earned his revolution a fund of popular goodwill. At the same time, he began to work on a proposal of reconciliation with the Church. This was continued by his successor Ávila Camacho, a practicing Catholic.

It was Camacho who pushed forward with a rapid industrialization of the country. The economy finally began to pick up during World War II. The United States built factories, and offered technical and financial aid in exchange for exploring Mexico's mineral wealth, with the result that Mexico became an important part of the US war effort.

When the United States went to war with the Axis powers, Mexico followed.

With the friendship between the two countries came wealth. Mexico City was transformed, with new roads, schools, and factories being constructed. A middle class appeared and expanded, servicing the ever-increasing financial and professional demands of a booming economy. The time was ripe for Opus Dei to arrive in Mexico.

Just as Mexico's economy was being transformed so, too, was its politics. Opus Dei's arrival in the late 1940s also coincided with the new direction of the political fight of the Synarchism (Sinarquista) movement and other groups affiliated to the right. The National Synarchist Union (Unión Nacional Sinarquista; UNS) had been founded in May 1937 by a group of Catholic political activists led by José Antonio Urquiza (who was murdered in April 1938). The group published the radical *Sinarquista Manifesto*, opposing the policies of the government of the then PRI (Institutional Revolutionary Party) led by President Lázaro Cárdenas. (PRI was formerly known as the PRM, Party of the Mexican Revolution.)

"It is absolutely necessary that an organization composed of true patriots exists," the UNS manifesto declared, "an organization which works for the restoration of the fundamental rights of each citizen and the salvation of the Motherland. As opposed to the Utopians who dream of a society without governors and laws, Synarchism supports a society governed by a legitimate authority, emanating from the free democratic activity of the people, that truly guarantees the social order within which all find true happiness." The manifesto certainly could be said to have shades of Opus Dei within it.

UNS's ideology is derived from the conservative Catholic social thinking of the 1920s and 1930s. It is based on the papal encyclical *Rerum Novarum* of Pope Leo XIII, which had already left its mark on the regimes of Engelbert Dollfuss in Austria, Antonio Salazar in Portugal, and Francisco Franco in Spain. The Mexican ideology stressed social cooperation as opposed to class conflict and socialism, as well as hierarchy and respect for authority as opposed to liberalism. In the context of Mexican politics, this meant opposition to the centralist, semi-socialist, and anti-clerical policies of the PRI regime. As a result, UNS members were denounced as fascists and persecuted by the Cárdenas government. The UNS movement, however, with its links to Franco, was immediately seen by outsiders as a perfect springboard for a group such as Opus Dei. Yet, once again, Opus Dei strenuously denies any political links within the organization.

On a pastoral level, Opus Dei was making rapid progress from its new base. The Montefalco complex (in the Morelos state) now consisted of a countryside promotion center, an old people's home, two schools, an agrarian college, and a women's "domestic science" institute/school. It was a source of much pride to members of Opus Dei, especially considering the struggle behind its creation.

"Montefalco was where dreams became reality for the first Opus Dei members in Mexico," remembers one of Opus Dei's devotees. "At the turn of the century, there was an old colonial property in the valley of Amilpas, in the state of Morelos, which had been sacked, set fire to, and completely devastated. It remained empty and abandoned for years until its owner donated it in 1949 towards good works. When Don Pedro Casciaro first saw the building it had little of its old splendor. Instead, it was just an enormous mass of buildings, covered with weeds and in ruins. It seemed like madness, but they began to reconstruct the complex. The Opus Dei members remembered the surprise of the architect as he arrived at the estate: 'ruined walls, damaged stones...Pedro, this is impossible. These are ruins.' But they explained that they had dreams and hopes...We will finish it, with your sacrifice, and the help, as ever, of so many people who are willing to collaborate in a task that will be for the greater good of all Mexico... It is a madness, but a madness for the love of God."

Their "madness" complete, Opus Dei now has around 7,000 members in Mexico and, like Spain and Italy before, the membership is mostly made up of professionals from the banking, commercial, teaching and university sectors. Apparently, it was during the 1970s that Opus Dei mounted a strong promotion campaign, allegedly thanks to the backing of Miguel Azcárraga, who was manager of the Chrysler Corporation in Mexico at the time. However, no one at Opus Dei can confirm this as fact.

What is factually proven, however, is that Opus Dei has emerged as one of the few successful Catholic movements in Mexico. It opened doors for its members, delivering connections between Mexico's wealthiest, and playing to the widely held belief that it is not what you know that matters, but who you know, and using those contacts to get things done—especially in the field of education.

The Catholic movement had influential supporters around the country, and its economic might in Mexico is huge. This could stem from a particular Opus Dei trait—unlike many other religious groups, Opus Dei members are encouraged to involve themselves in secular jobs and enterprises. Furthermore, building on the original Spanish model, which founded the University of Navarre, the Opus Dei movement in Mexico has a number of educational centers.

The third article of the Mexican Constitution states that education has to be secular and independent of any religious affiliation. Technically then, is the Opus Dei educational system contrary to the law? It seems unlikely, considering Opus Dei's penchant for organization, that it would operate outside the law, but this is yet another unproven accusation that has brought Opus Dei into question abroad.

Despite this, Opus Dei has left an impressive imprint on Mexican education. The new institutions founded by Opus Dei include the technological institute in Yalbi, located in the old house of the Mimiahupan in Tlaxcala, which is part of a hospitality and catering education center; the school of Capacitación Hotelera (CECAHO), which borders on the Laguna de Chapala in Jalisco and is attached to the Jaltepec conference center; the Pan-American Institute of High Management of Companies (Instituto Panamericano de Alta Dirección de Empresas), known as IPADE, which was founded in 1967 in Mexico City; the Pan-American University, which sits in the Federal District of Guadalajara and Monterrey; the Pan-American University Residence (la Residencia Universitaria Panamericana), founded in 1949; the Latin-American University Residence (la Residencia Universitaria Latinoamericana), founded in 1950; and the Center of Technology and Sport Jarales (Centro Tecnológico y Deportivo Jarales) in Zapopan, which is in Jalisco.

One such school, the IPADE, is roundly praised by the *Wall Street Journal* and the *Financial Times*. Founded in 1967, it is similar to the IESE (Instituto de Estudios Superiores de la Emresa) in Barcelona, and the *FT* ranks IPADE as the number one business school in Latin America. The school has left the doctrinal and spiritual aspects of its teaching firmly in the hands of Opus Dei.

Another flourishing venture is the Montefalco Women's School in Jonacatepec in Mexico. Founded in 1958, it is not just a girls' school but, according to Opus Dei: "inspired by St Josemaría's desire to meet the needs of Mexicans with fewer material resources. Over the years it has developed not only a girls' school, but numerous programs for other women as well."

Having made inroads in Mexico, the mission spread to Chile and Argentina in 1950. It was Opus Dei's involvement in the southern countries of South America that really brought it to the world's attention.

When Opus Dei first arrived in Argentina, the country was in turmoil. In 1943 a military junta had ousted Argentina's constitutional government. It allowed Juan Perón, one of the *coup*'s leaders and an army colonel, into a key position of power within the government as Minister of Labor. Protests in 1945 lead to Perón winning the presidential elections in 1946 and, initially, he gave an economic and political voice to the working classes and began rapidly expanding nationalized industries.

Today, Perón is better known worldwide for his dynamic wife Eva Perón, also called Evita, a former actress from a working-class background, who helped her husband develop strength with labor and women's groups; women obtained the right to vote in 1947.

Evita also played another role. On June 6th, 1947, she left Argentina for a tour of Europe. She began by visiting Franco in Spain, before meeting Pope Pius XII, bowing before him to kiss his ring at the Vatican. The Pope gave her a gold rosary which years later was placed in her hands at her death. The glamorous ambassador met Italian and French foreign ministers. Her mission, she said, was to strengthen diplomatic, business, and cultural ties between Argentina and the leaders of Europe.

Few others were better placed to advance the Argentinian cause. "Although Señora Perón insisted repeatedly that she was only interested in social work," reported the *New York Times* in 1952, "political observers began to credit her with influence in Government affairs that was second only to her husband's—if indeed that."

It was alleged, years later, that Evita's European trip had a more sinister motive: coordinating a network to support the hundreds of Nazis relocated in Argentina, who had arrived via the rat lines generated out of the Vatican after World War II (see Chapter Four).

Evita made a dramatic impression on the Pope during her half-hour audience. Glamorous, exotic, and rich, she lit up the ascetic and male world of the Vatican. But the Holy See didn't appreciate the potential of sending Catholic missions to Perón's Argentina and across South America. Opus Dei didn't make the same mistake.

Returning from her European sojourn, Evita's position of power, and that of her husband, grew stronger. In 1949, Perón pushed through a constitutional amendment to allow him to run for a second term (which he won in 1952). However, the Argentinian economy was heading for disaster. Exports dropped by almost a third, and the country's reserves of foreign cash were quickly wiped out. The factories were paralyzed and unemployment grew out of control. Inflation was rampant, and shot up by 33 percent.

Like Mexico before it, Argentina turned to foreign investors, and in 1954 Perón made a notorious deal with Standard Oil, giving the US corporation the right to develop the oil fields of Patagonia. For a while, Argentina's economic situation improved, but the underlying problems never disappeared. In time, state-protected industries stagnated and energy supplies faltered. Inflation began to pick up once again.

As a result, Perón took steps to tighten his grip on the country—individual rights, political freedoms, and the free institutions of civil society were steadily eroded by the Peronist state. It is at this time, while the country was in the grip of what many deem a fascist dictatorship, that Opus Dei first made its mark on Argentina. The parallels between Spain, Italy, and Mexico appear clear.

Perón's grip on the country was not to last. The growing economic crisis, high levels of corruption, and conflict with the Roman Catholic Church resulted in an army–navy coup sweeping Perón from power in September 1955. He went into exile in Paraguay, before eventually moving to Madrid.

But Perón's exile would not be permanent. Nearly 20 years later, after the Argentine government had failed to suppress the growing terrorist threats (mainly from pro-Perón groups like the Montoneros) and deal with the failing economy, a return to power for the former president was on the cards. In March 1973, Argentina held its general elections, and Héctor Cámpora, Perón's stand-in, was elected as president. He resigned in July of that year, new elections were called, and

Argentina was in turmoil. Perón was asked to return, and by October 1973 he was elected president of Argentina for a third time.

Following Perón's triumph, Licio Gelli, the grand master of Italy's right-wing Masonic P2 (Propaganda Due) lodge, was appointed the honorary Argentine Consul in Florence, and became one of the government's economic advisers. Gelli is said to have chartered the DC-8 jet that returned Perón to Argentine soil for a brief visit in late 1971; is alleged to have dealt arms in Latin America; and reputedly became the linkman between the CIA (Central Intelligence Agency) and Perón. During the "Calvi affair" (see Chapter Eight), Gelli's name and P2 were constantly linked with Opus Dei in a number of conspiracy theories, although the organization denies all links with Gelli.

Did Opus Dei assist in returning Perón to power in the early 1970s? This is a rumor that has persisted throughout the years. Critics have constantly tried to link Opus Dei with the financial dealings between Perón and Gelli that occurred during this period. One of the reasons for this was Opus Dei's alleged (and unproven) links with P2, said to have taken place in Italy during the Calvi scandals. Opus Dei strenuously denies any involvement with Gelli and Perón, stating: "Opus Dei cannot be in league with any secular authority."

Yet it is natural that Opus Dei, and other organizations at the time, would have tried to maintain good relations with the head of state, just as they did with Franco. As Perón became more powerful, however, Opus Dei and other Catholic organizations became unwelcome friends of the Argentine president, as he turned against the Catholic Church as a whole.

The mere fact that Perón was not a supporter of the Catholic Church in his native country should serve to further distance any involvement with Opus Dei, but the rumors of Opus Dei's collaboration with Perón persist.

When Perón turned on the Church with his anti-clerical reforms of the early 1950s, the army also lost patience with its leader. The Church, too, became hostile after Peronism began to encroach on its traditional domains of education, welfare, and public morals. By June 1955, Perón's anti-clerical campaign led to his excommunication. The unusual coalition of labor, reactionaries, nationalists, churchmen, and military leaders that had supported Perón came apart.

The Catholic Church became the focus of resistance to Perón. During 1955, the Church's supporters in the military attempted to launch a *coup d'etat* and bombed the presidential palace during a mass rally of Peronists, which resulted in the death of several hundred people. Naturally, there was outrage, which resulted in Peronists taking their revenge by burning several churches in Buenos Aires. Ultimately, Perón was ousted by September 1955 and made his escape to Paraguay.

At the time, Argentina was an important base for Opus Dei, and the movements of the Catholic group were directed, initially, from Europe. During this period, European powers, especially those in Spain and Italy, were worried about the growth of Communist forces—anything that promoted an anti-Marxist philosophy in Latin America was actively supported by European and US powers. Opus Dei, with its right-wing philosophies and stringent reputation, was viewed as a perfect foil against the Communist threat. Again, Opus Dei denies that the organization was ever involved in active anti-Communist activities as this goes against its credo. While individual members might have stood up to Communism, there was no group policy that demanded them to do so.

On the religious front, the first emissaries worked hard in Argentina, and by the mid-1960s the institute had recruited 1,000 members throughout the country—it was alleged that, among them, Opus Dei had won over General Juan Carlos Ongania. Ongania was commander-in-chief of the army and, in 1962, lead a revolt within the army that purged the extreme right-wing faction. He became president in 1966 following a military junta, and proved a useful ally for Opus Dei—it is thought that Ongania's triumphant takeover of the country occurred after he had visited a religious retreat sponsored by Opus Dei. Again, Opus Dei denies that Ongania was ever a member, yet critics of Opus Dei are keen to claim him—he fulfils Escrivá's supposed policy of *Cuius regio, eius religio.* This mantra is also one that the organization has distanced itself from, insisting that its mission is for all and does not just involve targeting the elite alone.

A further reason why Ongania has been linked to Opus Dei is because he is said to have filled his cabinet with generals and industrialists who shared his belief that the "Christian and military virtues of Spanish knighthood"—authoritarian clericalism blended with enlightened dictatorship—would restore Argentina to health. Robert Hutchison also claims that Ongania's belief in an elite corps of lay people—professional and military—called by God to serve the nation was pure "Opus Dei dogma".

Opus Dei's growth during the late 1960s and early 1970s saw Escrivá himself visiting South America. According to Opus Dei: "The founder of Opus Dei decided to undertake catechetical trips to various countries. With doubt and uncertainty spreading among the faithful, it was time to put his shoulder to the wheel, to proclaim the authentic teachings of the Church to large numbers of people and thus strengthen their faith. The method that he liked to use was one of personal contact, and personal it was for each of those present, despite the numbers that came to listen to him. Questions and answers, jokes and prayer, stories and truths, proclaimed loudly and firmly."

Escrivá started off in Mexico in 1970, in conjunction with his pilgrimage to Guadalupe, and then between May and August of 1974, he travelled through South America, visiting Brazil, Argentina, Chile, Peru, Ecuador, and Venezuela.

"The founder of Opus Dei arrived in Buenos Aires on June 7th, 1974," recalls one Opus Dei member, "and remained until June 28th. Besides many from the capital, people from all over Argentina, Paraguay, and Uruguay came to be with Blessed Josemaría. The gatherings were held in theaters and auditoriums. In one of the theaters, close to five thousand persons took part on two occasions. There were also frequent small family gatherings with the faithful of Opus Dei and their families in La Chacra, the center where he stayed."

Escrivá's tour of Latin America proved popular, and he helped consolidate Opus Dei's position across the continent. Like a papal visit, Escrivá met Opus Dei followers, held meetings and prayer groups, and preached the Opus Dei message to anyone who would listen. The testimonies from his followers and supporters at this time are numerous—even Angel Vera, a retired police sergeant who was one of those providing security for Escrivá in Argentina, made a statement regarding the Opus Dei leader: "Meeting Blessed Josemaría was the most important thing that has happened to me in my life."

"I often remember Josemaría's great love for the poorest and those most in need. His example has helped me to love them more each day," said Alfonso Delgado, now Archbishop of San Juan, as he reminisced about a meeting that Escrivá had held with priests.

However, another former Argentine numerary, Mariano Curat, presents a different view of Opus Dei: "I was a numerary for many years and as we all know very well, they repeated to us so many things in 'The Work' that we came to believe were true: 'Numeraries are the aristocracy of the intelligentsia' and 'One of our dominant passions is to give doctrine', and we went through the streets with our heads up high thinking that we were the only ones who had clear ideas and that the rest were ignorant and didn't know what they were talking about. Now when I look back, I realize how arrogant I was."

It is believed that Opus Dei became so established in Argentina that, by the end of the 20th century, like Spain, it had key members in established roles around the country. For example, alleged members included Rodolfo Barra, who became Carlos Menem's Public Works Secretary when Menem (President of Argentina until December 1999) first came to power in 1989. Barra was also a Supreme Court judge from 1993 to 1994, as well as a Minister of Justice for the following two years. Hardly the most noteworthy of Opus Dei's supposed recruits, the Justice Minister was forced to resign his post after revelations about his past membership in a violent anti-Semitic group. Barra belonged to the right-wing group UNES, a youth group affiliated with Tacuara, an organization responsible for hundreds of anti-Semitic actions including attacks against synagogues, violent riots in the Jewish neighborhood, and the murder of Jewish lawyer Alberto Alterman. Barra said in his defense: "I was a nationalist and an anti-Zionist, because I was told all Jews were Communists and I was adamantly anti-Communist." No one within Opus Dei can confirm whether he is indeed a member—it looks like another myth that continues to link Opus Dei to yet more unsavory characters without proof.

Others have linked Admiral Emilio Eduardo Massera to both Opus Dei and P2, but there is no proof that the military man was a member of the Catholic group. Added to this, Opus Dei stresses that were Massera a member of P2 it would be "impossible" for him to be an Opus Dei member—Catholics are not allowed to be members of Masonic lodges.

Massera was a navy commander-in-chief who, on March 24th, 1976, was involved in the military *coup* and a member of the military

junta that took power. The junta was responsible for the disappearance, execution, and jailing of tens of thousands of Argentinian political activists, and drove millions into exile. After being jailed for some
of the crimes he committed during this time, he was pardoned by
President Carlos Menem in 1990. Again, there appears to be a pattern
across South America. Political figures involved in scandal are often
linked to Opus Dei, even without any proof. It serves the purpose,
however, of implying that Opus Dei is filled with shadowy untrust-
worthy servants, further blackening the organization's name.

Like other countries associated with Opus Dei, educational matters feature just as highly as politics within Opus Dei. A fact often
overlooked is that Opus Dei's Argentine academic base is the
Universidad Austral in Buenos Aires and a business school (also in
Buenos Aires): IAE. An important jewel in Opus Dei's crown, the school
is ranked ninth among quality brands for Argentine executives.

The Opus Dei school was also praised by the *Financial Times* in
2003: "For the fourth year in a row, IAE ranks among the top 30 business schools in the world. Columbia, Duke, Harvard, IESE, and
Stanford lead, in that order, Executive Education worldwide. IAE
ranked 27th, climbing two positions since last year. As regards open
programs—for top and middle management, IAE came out 22nd,
having ranked 29th in 2002 and 33rd in 2001. The Argentine business
school is number one in Latin America."

Visit IAE's official website and it is clear on the university's affiliation to Opus Dei: "Throughout its Programs, it [IAE] provides a service to society in general and to the business world in particular. Its
rigorous and qualified teaching is based on solid research of the problems affecting business. As every school of the Universidad Austral,
IAE entrusts the prelature of the Opus Dei with the religious, ethical,
and anthropological aspects of its academic activity."

Opus Dei's reputation is that it frequently seeks out and works
with the best. Opus Dei's "plan" is to recruit the best, so if it creates
the best universities, naturally, it will always continue to produce
people who are part of the elite. If you attend an Opus Dei university,
this does not make you an automatic member, but by participating
in an efficient, well-run, prestigious university environment it is likely
that you would at least become more sympathetic towards the organization that runs through it.

Opus Dei's success also gives the organization a respectable moral profile on the world stage. How can anyone criticize an organization or movement that does well and gets positive results? While the Argentine economy has been suffering, IAE provides pride and success within the country, and Argentina isn't Opus Dei's only success story.

In the same year that Opus Dei entered Argentina (1950), another Escrivá envoy, Adolfo Rodríguez Vidal (1920–2003), headed for Chile. Having recently been ordained as a priest, he was fresh and eager to start Opus Dei's cause in the country. A success in Chile, he went on to become Bishop of Los Angeles—also in Chile, not the United States.

A conversation in Rome that took place in 1950 shows just how Opus Dei had full Vatican approval for its work across South America. A priest in Rome who wanted to do something to improve the spirituality of university students in Chile spoke of his concern to the then Msgr Montini, who was later to become Pope Paul VI. Montini encouraged the priest to contact Escrivá, telling him that he had plenty of experience of university students. Only months later, in 1950, the apostolic work in Chile started in earnest.

In 1950, Chile, like the rest of South America, was a country in decline. With some considerable financial backing, Opus Dei's work in Chile was said to have claimed 2,000 members and 15,000 cooperators by the end of the century—a triumph.

Chile, during the 1950s, was a country in turmoil. Strikes and rioting were rampant and the rift between the Communists and the Radicals was deepening. In 1948, Congress passed a "Law for the Defense of Democracy", which effectively outlawed the Communist Party. Communist militants went underground or fled into exile. Having fallen out with the left, the Radicals and other center parties had nowhere else to turn except towards the right. As a result, the next two presidents emerged from the center and right, respectively, but both failed to alleviate Chile's economic problems, particularly when it came to inflation.

In 1964, Chile elected Eduardo Frei Montalva as its president, on a huge majority vote. A Christian Democrat, he initiated a period of major reform under the slogan "Revolution in Liberty", with far-reaching social and economic programs in education, housing, and agrarian reform, including the rural unionization of agricultural workers.

The Vatican initially supported Frei but, rumor has it, due to reports from José Miguel Ibañez Langlois, an Opus Dei priest in Chile, the Vatican became worried that Frei was working too closely with the radical trade union movement. During this period, there were reports that the Jesuits wanted Frei to remain in charge, as they felt he was one of the few people capable of halting the march of Marxism in Chile. In opposition to this, Ibañez Langlois is alleged to have formed a Conservative think-tank, the "Institute for General Studies", which attracted a following of free-market economists, lawyers, publicists, and technocrats. Stories like this also play on the rivalry between the Jesuits and Opus Dei. These two religious factions within Roman Catholicism have a long-standing history between them, as Opus Dei began its successful worldwide apostolic work in areas already served by the Jesuits.

If this think-tank truly existed, then it was an impressive innovation attracting "the best" political thinkers—exactly the type of people Opus Dei would want to become members. While Opus Dei claims it wants to recruit from all sectors of society, there is no denying that, as with any religious group, gaining members from the elite (bright, wealthy, and university educated) was also an attractive prospect.

Pablo Baraona, who was alleged to be involved in Langlois' think-thank, went on to become Chile's Minister of Economy (1976–9). Opus Dei categorically states that he was not a member, while non-Opus Dei commentators insist that he was. Two of Opus Dei's earliest alleged recruits in Chile were right-wing activists Jaime Guzmán and Alvaro Puga. By the 1960s both recruits had become editors of El Mercurio, Chile's oldest newspaper. Ibañez Langlois is also said to have joined them on the paper, becoming a literary critic. Puga was not only said to be a member of Opus Dei, but also a CIA agent. Again, Opus Dei stress that neither Guzmán nor Puga were members of the organization.

The El Mercurio network was an important base in Chile as it dominated the Chilean media with its newspapers, radio station, ad agencies, and wire service—it also included the three largest newspapers in Santiago, as well as seven provincial papers. The CIA's involvement with the paper saw at least $1.5 million invested during the early 1970s alone, and many felt that El Mercurio was used by the CIA as a propaganda tool. Later, named agents at the organization were listed as Puga, Enno Hobbing, and Juraj Domic.

This wasn't the CIA's only involvement with Chile during this period. Investigations into Chilean politics have revealed that Frei's social program infuriated US President Richard Nixon. With a cold war battle raging, Nixon had to do everything within his power to prevent the spread or even the encouragement of Communism. Allegations at the time claimed that the CIA had helped fund Baraona and Ibañez Langlois' think-tank in the hope that it would become a rival to the Christian Democrat Party, and a rival to Communism. Opus Dei's information office in Chile has no record of this think-tank in the country—but instead refers to a cultural and literary review that ran for a while during the 1960s. Despite this, the legend of "Langlois's think-tank" continues.

In 1970 Allende's Marxist government, which had been elected on the basis of its left-wing program, finally came to power after two failed election attempts in 1958 and 1964. Allende attempted to change radically the structure and direction of the country, which brought about a second political crisis. In 1973 a right-wing *coup* led by General Augusto Pinochet Ugarte seized power, with help from the CIA. Allende was killed in the takeover, and Pinochet's government kept an iron grip on power for the next decade and a half, frequently resorting to terror in order to stifle discontent.

According to Penny Lernoux's book *People of God*, and a 1984 article in *Time* magazine, Opus Dei members were among those who supported the CIA-backed *coup* that overthrew Allende. Members named during this period were said to be Hernan Cubillos, who later became General Pinochet's Foreign Minister. Cubillos had also founded *Que Pasa*, a magazine later identified by the *Los Angeles Times* as an "important" outlet for CIA views. Following Allende's death, Puga wrote a book *Dario De Vida de Ud* about his campaign to bring down Allende. Furthermore, according to Fred Landis, in *Covert Action*, it was published with a CIA grant and reprinted many of Puga's damning columns written during Allende's rule. Opus Dei denies that Cubillos was a member of Opus Dei.

In a rebuttal to Lernoux's book, William Schmitt, an Opus Dei communications director in the United States, wrote of the allegations concerning the Chilean government: "The facts contradict the author's allegation that members or sympathizers supported an illegal criminal *coup* that was widely condemned by international public opinion. No member of Opus Dei has ever worked as a minister or adviser in the Pinochet government, nor occupied any high-level directive function during the Pinochet regime."

Despite Schmitt's rebuttal, the rumors continue. While Opus Dei continues to deny that Puga and Guzmán were members, it was easier for others to claim they were, in order to substantiate conspiracy theory claims. These stories have continued through the years with tales that there were Opus Dei men in positions of power and authority throughout Chile and the rest of South America. One named man was Chile's General Secretary, Javier Cuadra, although Opus Dei says he was "not a member". Furthermore, it was believed that during the Pinochet regime, the previously mentioned CIA-funded think-tank (the "Institute for General Studies") was filled with bright, able businessmen and politicians, who were more than ready to step up to the "challenge" of assisting Pinochet.

The dictator's spokesman was none other than Puga; another director at the "Institute". With rumors spreading that these were Opus Dei men (including Cubillos and Baraona), it was felt that Opus Dei's influence was right across the country. At least two members of the military junta, Admiral José Merino and General Jaime Estrada Leigh, are said to be "sons" of Escrivá. There is no proof that either man was a member of Opus Dei, and Opus Dei certainly denies it. Finally, there is Estrada, who previously headed the Nuclear Energy Commission, before becoming Housing Minister. However, these named members have not been confirmed by the present-day office of Opus Dei and could, in fact, be further red herrings, as theorists try and assert their hypothesis that Opus Dei is an all-powerful organization, ready to influence governments to put its own agendas into play.

It is at this time that one of the most impressive conspiracy theories comes into play. It has been claimed that basic Opus Dei principles are contained in Chile's Constitution. The reason in this case was due to Guzmán. The alleged Opus Dei man wrote Pinochet's "Declaration of Principles", which was released in 1974 and was later distilled in the document, "National Objective of the Government of Chile". One of Guzmán's statements promised to "cleanse our

democratic system of the vices that had facilitated its destruction".
This was seen as Opus Dei dogma.

Chile then followed the path of other countries that had been
visited by Opus Dei on its evangelizing mission—from the beginning,
Escrivá had emphasized the power of education. Recruiting directly
from universities or placing Opus Dei members in influential positions is viewed as the key to building and continuing the movement's
work. Chile's educational system was said to have been taken in hand
by three successive Opus Dei ministers, an Opus Dei superintendent
of education, and an Opus Dei dean of the Catholic university.

Although Opus Dei is alleged to be a part of Chilean politics and
history, it is an issue that Chileans, by and large, continue to ignore.
"Opus Dei is an issue that no one in Chile really addresses, about
which there is a lot of talk, but no real in-depth discussion," explained
film director Marcela Said at a showing of her documentary on
Pinochet. "I want to take a good look at it. I like challenges." Said
sees her project as a direct challenge to Opus Dei and its reliance
on wealthy, influential members to make its mark in a country.

Another alleged Chilean recruit was Manuel Cruzat—an entre-
preneur whom Opus Dei denies was a member of the organization.
During the 1970s, Cruzat controlled pension-fund companies, forestry
and fishing concerns, copper mines, vineyards, banks, and brewers,
an empire that earned him the nickname of "Chile's Howard Hughes",
according to the *Wall Street Journal*. In the 1980s, Cruzat continued to
build his wealth, and set up a company called Provida with his
brother-in-law Fernando Larrain, also said to be a member. As the
Wall Street Journal reported: "Provida came into being in 1981, when
the pension-fund system was first set up. It was formed by the
Cruzat-Larrain group, whose curious mixture of Opus Dei religious
fundamentalism and wild commercial audacity twice brought it to
the brink of insolvency..."

As with many religious organizations across the globe, financial
contributions are passed on by generous benefactors and Opus Dei
is no different. Yet, when companies donate sums to Opus Dei, or are
alleged to have given the organization some capital, rumors of decep-
tion and intrigue invariably abound. Such is the case with Cruzat-
Larrain. Both Michael Walsh, author of *Opus Dei: An Investigation into
the Powerful, Secretive Society Within the Catholic Church*, and a German-

based website allege that the South American company donated around $3 million per year. According to the *Wall Street Journal*, during this period "for the first time, a number of Chileans appeared in the Forbes list of the world's billionaires, with the most uneven distribution of wealth—coming in sixth."

While Opus Dei continued to grow within Chile, times changed after the 1988 plebiscite when Pinochet was defeated. The constitution was amended, creating more seats in the senate, diminishing the role of the National Security Council, and equalizing the number of civilian and military members (four each). In December 1989, Christian Democrat Patricio Aylwin, running as the candidate of the Concertacion (a coalition of parties), was elected president.

More theories concerning Opus Dei came into being when, in 1991, Jaime Guzmán, the right-wing senator and collaborator of General Pinochet, was assassinated in a revenge attack for the atrocities committed by Pinochet's secret police. In August 1993 police investigators captured Mauricio Hernández Norambuena, number two in the FPMR/D (a paramilitary dissident wing of the Chilean Communist Party). He was accused of participating in Guzmán's murder and in three attacks on US government representatives in Chile.

One year later, Eduardo Frei Ruíz-Tagle of the Christian Democratic Party was elected president for a six-year term leading the Concertacion coalition, and took office in March 1994. A presidential election was held on December 12th, 1999, but none of the six candidates obtained a majority, which led to an unprecedented runoff election on January 16th, 2000. Ricardo Lagos Escobar of the Socialist Party and the Party for Democracy (PPD) led the Concertacion coalition to a narrow victory, with 51.32 percent of the votes. He was sworn in on March 11th, 2000, for his six-year term.

Lagos's win was a defeat for one of the more prominent and open Opus Dei members, the right-wing Joaquín Lavin, a confirmed member of Opus Dei and a supporter of Pinochet's regime in its early years, before he fell out with the dictator. Lavin has plenty of high-profile support around the country. At one stage, Cardinal Jorge Medina Estévez (who is not a member of Opus Dei), the Bishop of Valparaiso, Chile's second largest city, stated: "Catholics know who they ought to vote for" and "a Catholic wouldn't vote for people whose program includes principles and postures contrary to the faith and morals of Christians", which was interpreted as an endorsement of Lavin.

By 1998, Pinochet had left Chile and moved to Britain. Spain sought his extradition from Britain to face charges connected with the "disappearance" of Spanish nationals, but Britain ruled that he was not fit to stand trial and continued to keep him under "house arrest"—albeit in a mansion on the outskirts of London. After more than a year in custody, the general was allowed to return to Chile in March 2000.

During this period, many were surprised when the Vatican spoke out in support of Augusto Pinochet. Naturally, there were those who believed that the hand of Opus Dei was at work. Opus Dei continues to maintain that the Vatican is not made up of Opus Dei puppets, yet the rumors of their involvement proved especially damaging when it was revealed that high-ranking Vatican officials supported Pinochet's release. Opus Dei was seen as the instigator behind the support for Pinochet. The Chilean general was allegedly responsible for thousands of deaths and disappearances during his 17 years in power, and in the light of John Paul II's strong stance on human rights, this expression of solidarity with one of Latin America's most infamous dictators appeared out of place.

There has been much legal wrangling since Pinochet's return to Chile, and as of 2005, Pinochet has still not stood trial. However, in December 2004, the Santiago Appeals Court stripped Pinochet of immunity from prosecution over the 1974 assassination of his predecessor, General Carlos Prats, who was killed by a car bomb during exile in Argentina; and on December 13th, 2004, Judge Juan Guzmán placed him under house arrest and indicted him over the disappearance of nine opposition activists and the killing of one of them during his regime.

Medina Estévez, who is also the head of the Vatican's liturgy office, told a newspaper in January 1999: "There have been discussions at every level on this affair, and we're hoping that they will have a positive outcome. I've prayed and prayed for Senator Pinochet, as I pray for all people who have suffered."

The Cardinal's stance is unsurprising. "Like the other three Latin Americans who occupy top-run positions in the Roman Curia," writes

John L. Allen Jr in the *National Catholic Reporter*, "as well as Italians with extensive experience of Latin America in the papal diplomatic corps, Medina rose through the ranks as a friend of right-wing governments and a staunch opponent of liberation theology, which seeks to align the Catholic Church with movements for social justice. Sympathy for Pinochet was of a piece with the values and policy decisions, on both secular and ecclesiastical matters, that have propelled these men to the peak of the Vatican's power structure."

In contrast to this, many Catholics find the Vatican's weak stance towards Pinochet disturbing. Furthermore, many feel that Opus Dei clerical and lay members could have done more during the military dictatorships in Latin America—religious leaders could have held protests, preached from their pulpits, and used their power and influence within the Church to highlight the issues and injustices within Pinochet's regime. But then, Opus Dei was not alone in this failing. The Vatican itself and other religious organizations could also have "done more", yet few made any constructive stands against the political leader.

By the end of the 20th century, Opus Dei's work in Latin America appeared to be going smoothly. However, despite strong representations in Mexico, Argentina, and Chile, it still faced opposition from a major source—other Catholics, namely, the followers of "liberation theology".

Liberation theology dates to the Second Vatican Council (1962–5), which instituted reforms intended to make the Roman Catholic Church more dynamic in its service to "the people of God". In its evolution over the years, liberation theology has blended Catholic teachings with Marxist economic analysis to provide the theoretical basis for what is called "a preferential option for the poor".

In the late 1960s, radical priest organizations emerged in Colombia, Argentina, and Peru. In public statements they used Marxist analysis in condemning dependent capitalist development. Movements of Christians for Socialism also appeared in the 1970s in western Europe, as well as North and South America, criticizing the identification of religious symbols with bourgeois ideology, and urging closer structural ties between local Church communities and political movements working for socialism. In their perspective, socialism is the only economic system compatible with Christianity, and they claim churches must become predominantly rooted in the culture of the working classes to achieve their mission authentically.

Liberation theology, the creation of Peruvian priest Gustavo Gutiérrez, was established after Gutiérrez became disillusioned by the corruption of the Christian Democrats in Latin America. It stands in direct opposition to authoritarian clericalism and, in turn, to Opus Dei. Due to the reality of mass poverty and political powerlessness, common in Latin America, liberation theology became a popular credo.

To Opus Dei, liberation theology proved a threat, as its philosophy teaches that the poor must work to improve their life on earth within the existing social structures, while preparing through devotion and obedience for eternal salvation. Furthermore, liberation theology believes that the Christian gospel demands "a preferential option for the poor" and that the Church should be involved in the struggle for economic and political justice in the contemporary world—particularly in the Third World. By contrast, while Opus Dei also does good works to help the poor, its more fundamentalist brand of theology is seen as one that leaves little freedom for an individual's conscience and is associated with secular power structures.

Opus Dei's more conservative brand of theology differs so widely from liberation theology that the latter has been excluded from the syllabus of the University of Los Andes in Santiago. As a belief system, liberation theology was in direct opposition to authoritarian clericalism—Escrivá rejected it, and some interpreted this move of Escrivá's as another major theological battleground between the Jesuits and Opus Dei.

In later years, Pope John Paul II made it clear that he, like Escrivá, was unhappy with elements within the liberal developments within the Church. On his first visit to Central America, in March 1983, the Pope warned the supporters of liberation theology that they were going too far. In Managua, he publicly chastized the Rev Ernesto Cardenal, a prominent liberation theology advocate, who has since been suspended from the priesthood.

Publicly naming and shaming liberation supporters wasn't the Pope's only act during his visit. Pope John Paul II battled Church progressives in Latin America over the theology of liberation. Travelling in Peru in 1984, the Pope knew that Gutiérrez lived in an urban slum in Lima, but refused to meet him. The Pope, it is alleged, regarded Gutiérrez's theology as being tainted by Marxism.

The battle between the two raged on. A year after Pope John Paul's visit, Colombian Cardinal Dario Castrillón Hoyos, a leader of the conservative wing of the Roman Catholic Church in Latin America (and not a member of Opus Dei), denounced liberation theologians, saying: "When I see a church with a machine gun, I cannot see the crucified Christ in that church. We can never use hate as a system of change. The core of being a church is love."

Following in Hoyos' footsteps was the Bishop of Esteli, Nicaragua, Juan Abelardo Mata Guevara (not a member of Opus Dei). On arriving at his diocese in 1988, he spoke of purging it of what he deemed "red clergy" as well as "imposing order": "Certain priests pushed the idea of a people's church, and thought the bridge for this people's church was in place in Esteli," said the bishop. "They took Esteli as a laboratory for their pastoral experiments, which were nothing more than putting in practise the directives of the Sandanista Front."

Liberation theology also has to contend with Opus Dei's strength across Latin and South America. Mexico, Argentina, and Chile were not the only countries that welcomed Opus Dei. A year after Opus Dei missionaries had arrived in Argentina and Chile, they set off for Colombia and Venezuela. By the late 1950s, there was an Opus Dei presence in Guatemala, Peru, Ecuador, Uruguay, and Brazil. The Vatican noted Opus Dei's rapid spread across the region and, in 1957, the Pope entrusted the prelature of Yauyos, a mountainous region of Peru, to Opus Dei.

By the new millennium, Opus Dei had members in various Mexican, Argentinian, and Chilean governments and positions of power, and this was a pattern that took place across the rest of South America. Again, Opus Dei is keen to stress the distinction between an Opus Dei individual's actions and responsibilities, as opposed to the group ethic. Opus Dei continues to argue that its members are free and it, as an organization, cannot take any responsibility for a good, or bad, politician who is a member. Despite this, conspiracy theories continue, as each individual member is seen as being guided by an invisible hand...that of Opus Dei as they work towards a collective aim—to rule the world.

Venezuela was another country where Opus Dei saw a level of

success. In the early 1900s, Venezuela was a conflict-ridden nation, but after the discovery of oil by the 1920s it was beginning to develop economically. However, as is often the case, most of the wealth remained with the ruling classes and dictators controlled the country until 1945 when Rómulo Betancourt led a popular revolt and rewrote the constitution.

The first president-elect in Venezuela's history took office in 1947—the novelist Rómulo Gallegos. But Gallegos was ousted by another dictator, and the country had presidential elections marred by violence right up until 1963. An oil boom during the 1970s saw more wealth pour into the country, although the vast lower class didn't benefit from this. Oil prices dropped in the late 1980s and the country was thrown into crisis once again. Riots swept through Caracas and were violently repressed, and two *coup* attempts took place in 1992.

In 1994 President Caldera made several unconstitutional crackdowns on economic speculation and civic freedoms, which incensed civil libertarians, but it wasn't until early 1996 that popular opinion started going against him. In December 1998 Venezuelans elected an army colonel, Hugo Chávez, to the presidency with the largest vote margin in 40 years. Just six years earlier, Chávez had attempted a *coup* against the government and had spent two years in jail. Chávez was also re-elected by a comfortable margin again in 2000.

On April 11th, 2002, a *coup* to overthrow Chávez saw divisions within the ruling class reach a stand-off. The two groups were known as the "hawks" and the "doves". According to *Socialism Today*, the anti-Chávez group, the hawks, "included far right-wing generals" and, allegedly, "members of Opus Dei". This group supported the retired general, Ruben Rojas (not a member of Opus Dei), the son-in-law of former President Rafael Caldera, founder of the Christian Democrats, in their bid to oust Chávez. According to recent reports, the CIA was aware of and in contact with this grouping, which had been planning a *coup* on February 27th.

On April 14th, STRATFOR (an online strategic research news organization, which claims to have contacts in the US security forces) reported that the February *coup* plan was aborted because Bush and the State Department were more intent on developing widespread opposition to Chávez and pushing him out "constitutionally", thereby supporting the "doves". *Socialism Today* reports that "representatives of the Bush administration met with the doves".

After the April 11th *coup* in 2002, Pedro Carmona Estanga, a leading businessman and another alleged member of Opus Dei, was briefly named interim president. The government was made up of far-right representatives of big business, members of the old corrupt capitalist parties. The Defense Minister of the new regime was Rear-Admiral Hector Ramirez Pérez; the Foreign Minister, José Rodríguez Iturbe, was also said to have been a member of Opus Dei. Key members of the military and others were outraged. The new government was to be a coalition government of major elements of Venezuelan society.

Carmona's rule did not last. On Saturday April 13th, less than 36 hours after Carmona and his men had assumed control, the new goverment collapsed in a welter of confusion. Shortly after 10pm, Interim President Pedro Carmona resigned and was reportedly under arrest. National Assembly president, William Lara, swore in Vice-President Diosdado Cabello as president after Carmona was forced to reinstate the assembly's elected members and other public officials he had fired on April 12th. Finally, amid scenes of wild rejoicing, Hugo Chávez, having been flown by military helicopter to the Miraflores Presidential Palace, was reinstated as President of Venezuela. Again, with a few Opus Dei members in prominent positions across Venezuela, this has led to theories about Opus Dei attempting to be a world power by "taking over" countries.

Meanwhile, in Peru, the Roman Catholic bishop, Luis Cipriani, a member of Opus Dei, is a strong supporter of disgraced president, Alberto Fujimori. Cipriani is popular in Peru and a poll in 1994 found his approval rating to be at 52 percent, against a miserable eight percent for the then president, Alejandro Toledo. Again, this is taken by Opus Dei critics to mean that the organization is allying itself with high-ranking politicians as it continues its worldwide crusade...

"Opus Dei forged a coalition of business and banking leaders with high-ranking bureaucrats that gave its backing to President Alberto Fujimori," wrote Robert Hutchison in the *Guardian* in 1997. "When Tupac Amaru rebels seized the Japanese embassy last December, creating the 126-day hostage crisis, Fujimori called upon Archbishop Juan Luis Cipriani, from the mountain diocese of Ayacucho, to mediate—

over the head of the Archbishop of Lima, Cardinal Augusto Vargas Zamora, a Jesuit. Cipriani, one of seven Opus Dei bishops in Peru, is now favored to succeed Cardinal Vargas, who is past the retirement age, as Archbishop of Lima, which traditionally means promotion to the cardinalate." As Hutchison, a noted critic of Opus Dei, feared, Cipriani became Opus Dei's first cardinal in 2001. Incidentally, since Cipriani's appointment to cardinal, he has complained of an alleged smear campaign against him.

One of two Opus Dei members in the College of Cardinals, Cipriani spoke to the *National Catholic Reporter* in an interview at his residence in Lima. "The story, which resembles a potboiler novel, begins in October 2001, when the then-Minister of Justice in the Peruvian government, Fernando Olivera, secretly carried three letters to the Vatican," reported John L. Allen Jr, in the feature.

The letters, which were later proved to be forgeries, suggested that there were links between Ciprani and Vladimiro Montesinos, the head of the Peruvian security forces under Fujimori. Olivera met Archbishop Leonardo Sandri, the number two official in the Secretariat of State, and showed Sandri the letters, but stated that he did not have the authority to turn them over.

One of the letters was allegedly written by Cipriani, while the other two were from the papal nuncio in Peru, Archbishop Rino Passigato. According to sources, the letter that had Cipriani's signature allegedly had him asking for the "elimination and incineration" of various videotapes that showed him meeting and talking to Montesinos. Apparently, the other letters had Cipriani thanking Montesinos for a contribution of $120,000 before he went on to ask for more money.

"Cipriani is widely seen in Peru as critical of the current president, Alejandro Toledo," explains Allen, "and hence the motive for transmitting the letters to the Vatican, in the eyes of most observers, was to discredit Cipriani. Since the nuncio is seen as subservient to Cipriani, he too, or so this theory runs, was targeted."

The fake letters were later acknowledged by Toledo's government to be forgeries, but the question remains—who was behind the effort? And why? Cipriani thinks he has the answer: "bishops are involved," he said bluntly, describing himself as "completely convinced". Still, if Cipriani has any further troubles, there are other bishops in Peru who belong to Opus Dei, on whom he could call. These include the Archbishop of Cuzco, Juan Antonio Ugarte Pérez; the Archbishop of Chiclayo, Jesus Moline Labarte; the Bishop of Abancay, Isidro Sala Rivera (both Labarte and Rivera are members of the Priestly Society of the Holy Cross); the Bishop of Chuquibamba, Mario Busquets Jorda; and the auxiliary of Ayacucho, Gabino Miranda Melgarejo. If these religious allies cannot provide Cipriani with the support he needs, there are also plenty of high-ranking officials who could rally to Cipriani's side.

Peruvian Foreign Minister, Francisco Tudela, has been named as an alleged Opus Dei sympathizer, and it was his law that helped acquit Fujimori's Grupo Colina death squad. However, it is more than likely that Tudela has nothing to do with Opus Dei—by using his name and his links with the death squad, Opus Dei's name can be blackened yet further. Added to this, Opus Dei denies that Tudela is, in fact, a member.

In some regions of the jungle—in Ayacucho, for example—there are rumors of priests who train and lead the army's paramilitary *rondas*. Among these supposed paramilitary priests, the most notorious is alleged to be the Archbishop of Huamanga known as "Cristiani", who is said to be a member of Opus Dei. Again this adds fuel to the paranoia theories—if these theories and allegations are to be believed, Opus Dei is a real force to be reckoned with here. After all, the movement now has priests training soldiers in death squads.

This is one important example of how twisted rumors about Opus Dei eventually become upheld as fact. Even if Opus Dei's mission, as stated, is to contribute to the evangelizing mission of the Church, would it really carry out such a mission with guns? Such allegations seem unfounded but are allowed to fester thanks to the sinister fears that appear to surround this organization.

This myth of a paramilitary priest can be proved to be just that— a myth. As an example of just how rumors start, note that the Huamanga "Cristiani" priest mentioned on the internet is a fiction. Firstly, the Catholic Church forbids priests to be paramilitaries, and there certainly would not be any paramilitary priests in Opus Dei. Secondly, Huamanga is the old name for Ayacucho (the name was changed by General Bolivar in the 19th century) and Ayacucho was the region where Archbishop Cipriani preached before he moved to

Lima. So what this turns out to be is a complete untruth combined with a spelling mistake and a non-existent diocese. Cipriani is of course well known, so this libel crumbles quite significantly and is yet another example of one of the stories allowed to fester and grow when discussing or researching Opus Dei.

It has also been noted that gradually, but systematically, all over Latin America, the late John Paul II replaced left-wing senior clerics with right-wingers, some of them connected with Opus Dei, leaving liberation theology out in the cold. As yet, the new Pope's views on liberation theology remain to be seen. While this is a statement of fact, many choose to interpret this as further Opus Dei infiltration— yet, it came directly from the Pope, not members of Opus Dei, whose numbers in the Curia are, in fact, surprisingly small.

These thoughts increased after 1980, when a right-wing death squad gunned down Archbishop Oscar Arnulfo Romero in San Salvador as he was celebrating Mass. Since then, he has been revered as "a saint, prophet, and martyr of Latin America" by the progressive wing of the Roman Catholic Church, both in San Salvador and throughout the region. His successor, chosen by the Pope, was Arturo Rivera y Damas, who carried on Romero's traditions. Following his death in the mid-1990s, Pope John Paul II had to elect a new archbishop. A debate raged—would he pick another liberal progressive bishop or would he change direction?

John Paul II selected Bishop Fernando Saenz Lacalle, a Spanish-born prelate, a former Vatican liaison with the Salvadoran Armed Forces, and a clerical member of Opus Dei. Rome's decision came as a shock. According to Larry Rohter, writing in the *New York Times*: "Perhaps more than any other recent development, the elevation of Bishop Saenz signals that the theology of liberation, the doctrine that has largely defined the character of the Roman Catholic Church in Latin America for more than a quarter of a century, has been forced into retreat..."

Across Latin America, dozens of activist bishops are being replaced by clerics who "toe the line very carefully on issues of doctrine, who you might say are yes-men" doing Rome's bidding, said the Rev Joseph E. Mulligan, an American Jesuit, who lives in Nicaragua and who has written extensively on the Church in Central America. As a result, he added, the Church is experiencing "a pulling back from the strong commitment to social justice and liberation that we saw in the 1970s and 1980s".

Twenty years after Romero's assassination, in 2000 the tension between Romero's progressive theology and Opus Dei's more conservative values was still visible. During a Mass for the murdered former archbishop, which was presided over by Saenz Lacalle, the bishop praised Romero's holiness saying: "It was never his intention to stir up the people to hate and violence, but his messages were frequently fiery." However, according to an account in the *National Catholic Reporter*: "His listeners understood, giving the archbishop a polite round of applause, whereas every appearance of the 'Romero' bishops, Pedro Casaldaliga of Brazil and Samuel Ruiz García of Mexico, was met with thunderous applause."

Theories about Opus Dei's work abound because, across Latin America, the organization has forged alliances with other movements related to the Roman Catholic Church in a bid to increase supporters to their more conservative issues versus the more liberalizing tendencies in the Church and society. While some commentators, in particular Paul Rich and Guillermo De Los Reyes, in their academic paper on Opus Dei, feel that Opus Dei's work presents a threat, others contend that the movement is only continuing its evangelizing mission—and one that has received the support of the Vatican. Its members make no secret of the fact that they are more conservative than other liberals—yet in today's society, that makes the organization different and thus threatening.

In El Salvador, Bishop Lacalle, who is, as mentioned, an Opus Dei member, accepted an *honorary* commission as a brigadier-general in an army that has one of the most brutal track records in recent history. While this job is similar to a "military bishop" in Europe, where religious men are there for the army, in this case it was a foolish decision by Lacalle. The army he chose to link himself to was the same army responsible for the murder of Archbishop Oscar Romero—an asinine mistake by Lacalle, and one that would not have endeared him to his parish. But while some chose to take Lacalle's military title as one that includes some form of active service, it should be remembered that it was, as stated, merely honorary.

Over in Brazil, Moreira Neves, who is not a member of Opus Dei, was the lynchpin in the Vatican effort to bring the Brazilian Church under control during the 1980s and 1990s. Neves served as a secretary for the powerful Congregation of Bishops in the 1980s, where he was able to influence Brazilian appointments. In 1988, the Pope sent Neves back to Brazil as Archbishop of Sao Salvador de Bahia; in 1995, he was elected president of the bishops' conference, this marking the end of the progressive majority. In 1998, he returned to Rome as a prefect of the Congregation of Bishops.

As secretary to the bishops' congregation, Neves helps steer papal appointments in Brazil to the right and is often named as another Opus Dei member, who is part of a conspiracy, yet this is, again, another myth. According to John L. Allen Jr in the *National Catholic Reporter*: "Neves is widely believed to be close to Opus Dei. His signature appears on one of the most important documents in that organization's history, a 1982 decision from the Congregation of Bishops granting Opus Dei the status of 'personal prelature'...The letter signed by Neves said the decision was made with a view to the 'proven guarantees of apostolic vigor, discipline, and faithfulness to the teaching of the Church' shown by Opus Dei."

Opus Dei is not the only unifying element shared between various South American and Latin countries. There was another, powerful, force that was, albeit underground, sweeping the nation—the CIA. US efforts to bring down Communism meant allying itself with the far right governments and organizations that were making inroads in South America. One operation in the continent known to the CIA was "Operation Condor" (Operación Cóndor), a campaign of assassination and intelligence-gathering, conducted jointly by the security services of Argentina, Bolivia, Brazil, Chile, Paraguay, and Uruguay in the mid-1970s.

The right-wing military governments of these countries, led by dictators such as Videla, Pinochet, and Stroessner, agreed to cooperate in sending teams into other countries, including France, Portugal, and the United States to locate, observe, and assassinate political opponents. They also exchanged torture techniques, such as near drowning and playing the sound recordings of victims who were being tortured to their family. Many people disappeared and were killed without trial throughout this period. Their targets were "leftist guerrilla terrorists" but many are thought to have been political opponents and innocent people.

Operation Condor was unofficially supported by the United States, since it feared that left-wing powers in the region would create a second Communist Cuba. It appears that Henry Kissinger, Secretary of State in the Nixon administration, played an important role in giving US sanction to the operation. CIA documents show that the CIA was closely linked with Manuel Contreras (head of Pinochet's secret police) up to, and even after, the assassination of Orlando Letelier, former member of Salvador Allende's government. Killed by a car bomb in Washington DC in 1976, Letelier's death was seen as the first in the wave of Operation Condor assassinations—its targets were left-wing politicians, activists, and enemies of Pinochet and his allies.

There are no links between Opus Dei and Operation Condor, but what was allegedly apparent was that, throughout South America, it was believed there were consistent links between Opus Dei and the CIA. The US, in its fight against the rise of Communism as it fought the cold war, needed strong and predominantly right-wing forces, and the Opus Dei members heading up various cabinets and in positions of influence and power proved useful contacts and sources to maintain. While it might be true that members of Opus Dei helped the CIA, the organization, as an entity, insists that it does not get involved in politics or back particular political parties. Nevertheless, the stories remain.

The CIA was used to build up these regimes, but author Penny Lernoux also claims that the German Catholic aid-agency Adveniat "gradually replaced the CIA in the 1970s as the helpmate of military regimes". From this, a link was drawn to Opus Dei, as it was felt that Adveniat was run by the German bishops, who were allegedly "sympathetic" to Opus Dei. Note the word "sympathetic". As yet, none of the German bishops have come out as Opus Dei members, but the rumors continue to linger.

Opus Dei continues to deny that the organization has a political agenda. However, its rapid worldwide rise, with members in considerable positions of power, has led to commentators fearing something they do not understand. The organization, from the start, has been open about its evangelizing mission across the globe. This, of course, has been interpreted as wanting political domination rather than religious acceptance, and a bid to garner new members for Opus

Dei. For critics, again, the mere fact that Opus Dei members appear to dominate political institutions often overshadows the actual work Opus Dei carries out.

One example is the Montefalco site in Mexico. Opus Dei has four schools for the rural population in the area: a school of home economics, an agricultural school, a women's institute, and a teachers' training college. This initiative has given rise to many others and, following Montefalco's success, there are other medical centers and dispensaries and vocational schools in underdeveloped areas throughout Latin America. While some people naturally find the work and nature of Opus Dei's beliefs and culture oppressive and conservative, nevertheless the organization still receives Vatican backing and has achieved a remarkable amount of success across Latin and South America in providing education and hope. The rumors persist but, as yet, the conspiracies surrounding the organization as a political force are yet to be, ultimately, proven.

Achieving the American Dream

A missionary—you dream of being a missionary. Another Francis Xavier... And you long to conquer an empire for Christ. Japan, China, India, Russia...the peoples of the North of Europe, or America, or Africa, or Australia? Stir up that fire in your heart, that hunger for souls. But don't forget that you are more of a missionary "obeying". Geographically distant from those apostolic fields, you work both "here" and "there": don't you— like Xavier—feel your arm tired after administering baptism to so many?

Josemaría Escrivá

In 2001, Opus Dei achieved a milestone in the United States. The Rev José Gomez became an auxiliary bishop in Denver, making him the first Opus Dei priest to be ordained a bishop in the United States. This sign of Opus Dei's prominent place in the Church came weeks after the Archbishop of Lima, Peru (Juan Luis Thorne), became Opus Dei's first cardinal. In 2005 he was made archbishop of San Antonio, Texas.

Opus Dei's growth in the United States has been impressive, and research into Opus Dei-affiliated organizations suggests assets of $0.5 billion in the US alone. An impressive financial figure for this Catholic organization, but with all this wealth, does it have power, political influence, and a firm foothold across the nation? Many would argue that this is indeed the case for Opus Dei. Yet, a swift investigation into its actual membership shows only a small percentage of the population are actually members.

"There are over 3,000 Opus Dei members in the United States," writes Jesuit priest James Martin in *America* magazine, "with 64 centers, or residences for members, in 17 cities: Boston; Providence, R.I.; New York; South Orange, N.J.; Princeton, N.J.; Pittsburgh; Washington; Delray Beach, Fla.; South Bend, Ind.; Chicago; Milwaukee; Urbana, Ill.; St Louis; Houston; Dallas; Los Angeles and San Francisco."

As Brian Finnerty, the US communications director, points out:

"That is correct [of the 3,000 members of Opus Dei in the US]. Of course, there are many more people who have been in contact with our activities. Also, there were 4,000 people who travelled from the United States to Rome for the canonization of Opus Dei's founder, Saint Josemaría Escrivá." With a limited number of devotees, this makes Opus Dei's work across the US even more impressive—it carries out a number of activities including working at schools, colleges, universities, and outreach programs as just some examples. How? Some would say it is down to the amounts of money raised by the movement, as well as the organization carried out by its members.

"Opus Dei has not acquired its considerable wealth and influence by attracting the down and out," wrote Kenneth Woodward in *Newsweek*. "Its student centers are placed near pricey campuses like Princeton, Harvard, Columbia, and Notre Dame, where gifted—but often lonely—students are targeted according to the axioms of Escrivá."

"Each center typically houses 10 to 15 members, with separate centers for women and men," adds Martin in *America* magazine. "Opus Dei also sponsors other programs, such as retreat houses, programs for married Catholics, and outreach programs to the poor, like its education program for children in the South Bronx. Other activities are run in Syracuse, Philadelphia, Miami, San Antonio, Minneapolis/St Paul, Denver, and Phoenix."

However, while Opus Dei's charitable foundations have been allowed to function without interference, when the Catholic group has ventured on to university campuses it has led to conflict with other groups.

Donald R. McCrabb is executive director of the Catholic Campus Ministry Association (CCMA), an organization of 1,000 of the 1,800 Catholic chaplains in the United States. Speaking to James Martin, McCrabb reports: "We are aware that Opus Dei is present at a number of campuses across the country. I'm also aware that some campus ministers find their activities on campus to be counterproductive."

One of McCrabb's concerns was Opus Dei's emphasis on recruiting, supported by an apparently large base of funding. "They are not taking on the broader responsibility that a campus minister has." He had other concerns as well (note that McCrabb is reporting "hearsay" evidence). "*I have heard* through campus ministers that there is a spiritual director that's assigned to the candidate who basically has to approve every action taken by that person, including reading mail, what classes they take or don't take, what they read or don't read." Naturally, Opus Dei would contend McCrabb's hearsay claims, as Opus Dei continually refers to its members' "freedom," but these issues still stand between Opus Dei and other campus ministers.

Thanks to the large sums of money raised by its charitable work and its continual drive in the United States, Opus Dei now operates five high schools in the US: The Heights (for boys) and Oak Crest (girls) in Washington DC, the Montrose School (girls) in Boston, and Northridge Prep (boys) and The Willows (girls) in Chicago. "We're not out to change the world," says Barbara Faulk, the headmistress of Oak Crest. "We're not shrouded in something weird."

As Martin describes, since first arriving in the United States back in 1949, the organization has certainly grown. Yet, the figure Martin gives—3,000 members—seems small when compared with the actual population of the United States as of 2004: 293 million. However, such is the structure of Opus Dei that one doesn't necessarily need to become a "member" or "numerary" in order to be affiliated to the organization. As Finnerty pointed out, 4,000 US citizens travelled to Rome for Escrivá's beatification.

To clarify, numeraries are single members who pledge a "commitment" of celibacy and normally live in "centers". These members, who account for around 20 percent of the membership, choose to give their income and receive a stipend for personal expenses. Stricter members of the order, they follow the "plan of life", which includes Mass, devotional reading, private prayer, and, depending on the person, physical mortification. Every year an oral commitment to Opus Dei is made, and after five years the "fidelity" is made, which is a lifetime commitment.

Most members are supernumeraries, married people who contribute financially and sometimes serve in corporate works like schools. Associates are single individuals, who are "less available", and who remain at home because of other commitments. Finally, there are cooperators, who, strictly speaking, are not members because "they do not yet have the divine vocation". The cooperators make up the vast majority of Opus Dei, and they "cooperate" through work, financial aid, and prayers.

Figures from early 2000 showed that 70 percent of members were married or single supernumerary members. The rest were celibate numerary members. In addition to the members of Opus Dei, there are also cooperators. In the New York area alone there are some 200 members and 500 cooperators, who are said to make monthly contributions or lump-sum grants to Opus Dei. However, it is important to stress that Opus Dei is not a tithe religion. No member is forced to give a certain percentage of his or her salary to the cause.

Opus Dei's fundraising work in the US is impressive, having raised millions of dollars to support its charitable work, and is said to have one of the largest fundraising centers—in New Rochelle, at the Woodlawn Foundation, which has raised more than $50 million over the last decade. The money has apparently gone to an Opus Dei university in Rome, as well as Opus Dei programs in other cities. Another fundraising success is the National Center Foundation, which helped to raise funds to pay for the million-dollar construction of the Opus Dei headquarters on New York's Lexington Avenue.

"The Woodlawn Foundation, which is based in New Rochelle, is the most significant fundraising entity to support the work of Opus Dei in the United States," explains Finnerty. "Woodlawn grants have gone to various projects in the United States, as well as the Pontifical University of the Holy Cross in Rome, which is run by Opus Dei. Woodlawn has also allocated funds to the National Center Foundation, which raised money to support the construction of Murray Hill Place. This building, located on Lexington Avenue, is a retreat and conference center, as well as the US headquarters for Opus Dei. The financial statements (the 1990s) of Woodlawn and the National Center Foundation are public information and are available on the Web [www.guidestar.org, the national database of non-profit organizations, which has a complete list on the internet of the financial reports from Lexington College in Chicago and Arnold Hall, which is in Massachusetts]."

"If you can bring the message of Christ in the workplace here, in the crossroads of Manhattan, you can do it any place," said Rev Arne Panula, the main official in the United States for Opus Dei. "Three thousand members is not many. The goal of the Founder was that if someone wanted to be affiliated with Opus Dei, in any town, they would be able to. It's a big challenge, and we have a long way to go."

Along with Opus Dei's growing financial strength, the organiza-tion also received a boost in 1991 when Chicago's Cardinal Joseph Bernardin appointed two Opus Dei priests, Rev John Twist and Rev John Paul Debicki, as pastor and associate pastor of St Mary of the Angels Church, which serves a gentrifying Puerto Rican and Polish community on the Near North Side. When Rev William Stetson arrived in Chicago in 1983 to head up Opus Dei's Midwest region, he recalled: "I spoke to Cardinal Bernardin about the possibility of pro-viding a couple of priests to run an inner-city parish when the time was right."

"Given the shortage of priests in the archdiocese," said Sister Joy Clough, Archdiocesan Director of Public Information, "the current needs of this parish and the willingness and ability of Opus Dei to take on the challenge involved, the cardinal decided this was an appropriate action. It was difficult to find anyone else for this parish." Both Twist and Debicki speak Spanish, while Debicki also speaks Polish—a useful advantage. As of 2005, Twist is now based in Barcelona, while Fathers Stetson and Debicki are both based in Washington DC—Stetson followed Father C. John McCloskey as direc-tor of the Catholic Information Center.

Naturally, many opponents of Opus Dei were not happy and there was a consensus among critics that the organization was seeking to gain as many parishes as possible, a charge Opus Dei has naturally denied. "We're not eager to pick up parishes," said Tom Bohlin, direc-tor of communications for the movement's Midwest office to the *Chicago Tribune*. "We're open to serving in this capacity if the circum-stances are right, but we basically see this as a one-time thing." He noted that there are only 50 Opus Dei priests in the US.

Furthermore, as Andrew Soane from Opus Dei's London branch, points out: "I do think it is very important, i.e. a member of Opus Dei in public life, or indeed any secular profession, represents only him-or herself, not Opus Dei. Opus Dei's function is only spiritual. The same is also true of bishops who run dioceses; they are responsible to the Pope and the Vatican to whom they report, not to Opus Dei."

James Martin reports in *America* magazine that when he contacted each of the seven US cardinals and one archbishop for comments on Opus Dei to gauge the opinions of the North American Catholic lead-ership no one would comment—either positively or negatively: "The majority said they had either no substantial knowledge or no contact with them, though Opus Dei is active in nearly every large archdiocese in the country."

Throughout Europe, Opus Dei has often been accused in the media of trying to infiltrate governments, especially during the final years of Franco's regime in Spain when Opus Dei had developed a reputation as being part of his cabinets—but as has been shown, there was never an occasion when more than half of his cabinet ministers were members of Opus Dei. Furthermore, during the cold war, Opus Dei was viewed as a strident foe of Communism. So, what can the United States expect?

Michael Walsh, in his book *Opus Dei: An Investigation into the Powerful, Secretive Society Within the Catholic Church*, thinks this theme of "political power" is old news. He argues that after the negative comments the organization received following its involvement in the Franco era, it would be "unwilling" to "risk" political involvement again. Yet, this theory depends on the notion that Opus Dei is a political organization. As has been stated before, Opus Dei continually denies these accusations. Escrivá himself pointed out the "freedom" he feels his followers should adhere to.

Opus Dei first began its apostolic activities in the United States in Chicago in 1949, when Salvador Martinez (Sal) Ferigle, a young physics graduate student, and Father Joseph Múzquiz, one of the first priests to be ordained for Opus Dei (see Chapter Three), arrived in Chicago. Ferigle, a Spanish native who was born in Valencia, was a typical Opus Dei recruit. A high-flying scholar, he was also a committed Catholic and an ideal candidate to lead Opus Dei's US charge when Opus Dei's first US center was established near the University of Chicago, a prime spot to recruit new members. The two Opus Dei men were joined in their activities by Joseph Barredo, one of the first members of Opus Dei having met Escrivá while at university and joined in 1932.

Barredo had in fact arrived in the United States in April 1948, slightly earlier than his two companions, as he had been on an initial exploratory tour of North America with Father Pedro Casciaro (who initiated Opus Dei in Mexico) to study the country and make some contacts. The pair had started their tour in New York, but after a visit to Chicago's archbishop, Cardinal Samuel Stritch, the latter suggested that the city's central location and excellent universities would make Chicago the logical place to begin their work.

Once Barredo and his companions had settled in the Windy City, they started introducing themselves to people and laid the foundations of their work. An important issue to note here is that throughout its history Opus Dei has frequently been accused of practically "invading" a country to push its doctrines. Yet often, and certainly in the case here in the United States, it was after meeting with various bishops across the country that Opus Dei was in fact invited to carry out its work, rather than being the unwelcome invaders the organization is often accused of.

Cardinal Stritch, the fourth archbishop and ninth ordinary (governing bishop) of Chicago, had a ten-year relationship with Opus Dei that ended only with his death, in Rome, in 1958. To begin with, Opus Dei was something of an anomaly within the Church. It was a different type of Catholicism, due to its emphasis on involvement by its lay members and, furthermore, it had only recently been granted the status of a "Secular Institute" but Stritch understood that and was concerned that Opus Dei should be understood and accepted. Opus Dei members met with Cardinal Stritch on 13 recorded occasions between April 1948 and April 1958—there were also exchanges of letters and reports on a number of occasions. Furthermore, the Cardinal wanted people to realize that the distinction between religious and secular entities in the Church was clear, and approved every petition for centers of men and women as well as faculties for priests—a sign that Opus Dei was welcome, in Chicago at least.

The pioneers worked hard in the United States, and the early months saw the men making every effort to familiarize themselves with the English language, which they practiced by introducing themselves to as many people as they could at the University of Chicago, at IIT, (a private, PhD-granting institution with programs in engineering, science, psychology, architecture, business, design, and law) and around the city, mainly through Barredo's daily round of appointments while Ferigle and Múzquiz were at their tasks.

By 1959, residences had opened in Milwaukee and Madison, Wisconsin; Boston and Cambridge, Massachusetts; St Louis, Missouri; and Silver Spring, Maryland (suburban Washington DC). The appointment of an Opus Dei priest, Father William Porras, as Catholic chaplain

at Harvard University was followed by the first major influx of vocations (those with a spiritual/religious calling for Opus Dei), many of
whom were subsequently ordained. Ferigle, following his time spent
in the United States, moved on in 1956 to help launch new Opus Dei
centers across Japan, the Philippines, and Australia. Ferigle then
returned to the US to serve Opus Dei in Milwaukee, Washington, and
St Louis, before settling in Boston in 1971, working as the chaplain
for a student residence just off Harvard Square.

By 1969, 20 years after Opus Dei had begun its apostolic activities
in the United States, there were new centers in South Bend, Indiana;
Washington DC; Manhattan and Scarsdale, New York; and San
Francisco, California. Some young American members were helping
to begin the apostolate in Kenya, Australia, and Nigeria. By 1979,
Opus Dei had started its work in the US suburbs and was working
with high school students. Centers were opened in Oak Park and
Northfield, Illinois; Mill Valley, California; Park Ridge and South
Orange, New Jersey; Brookfield, Wisconsin; Chestnut Hill and Dedham,
Massachusetts; and Kirkwood, Missouri; while high schools con-
ducted by members of Opus Dei and their friends were established
in metropolitan Washington, Chicago, and Boston.

By the turn of the new millennium, Opus Dei had more milestones
to record—the organization had achieved the entrustment of St Mary
of the Angels to priests of the Prelature, the planning and construction of a major national center in Manhattan, the participation in the
Beatification of Escrivá in Rome, along with the first pastoral visit of
the current Prelate.

The establishment of Opus Dei in the United States was, in fact,
part of the initial expansion that became possible when the Pope
granted Opus Dei canonical approval as an institution of pontifical
right on February 24th, 1947 (the *Decretum Laudis*). This action set in
motion preparations to send the first members of Opus Dei to Ireland
and France (that same year), Mexico and the United States (1949),
Argentina and Chile (1950), Venezuela and Colombia (1951).

In Robert Hutchison's book, *Their Kingdom Come*, the writer
describes the American missionaries' proselytizing in the US as initially "hard-going", and names an influential recruit to Opus Dei: Yale
graduate R. Sargent Shriver Jr, who married Eunice Mary Kennedy (the
sister of JFK). Eunice went on to become the first director of the US

Peace Corps, as well as taking a leading role in her brother's presidential campaign, and both were named as active Opus Dei cooperators. Father C. John McCloskey, an Opus Dei priest in the United States, when asked whether Kennedy or Shriver were in fact members, stated: "Neither to my knowledge." Furthermore, in Scott Stossel's biography of Sargent Shriver, he states that Shriver liked Opus Dei but was not, in fact, a full member, though the biographer notes that Shriver was a cooperator.

It is from this point that the conspiracy theories surrounding Opus Dei really began to take off. The first major Opus Dei rumors in the US took place following the presidential campaign of 1972 when George Stanley McGovern, a US senator from South Dakota (1963–81) who opposed the Vietnam War, was defeated as the 1972 Democratic candidate for president. McGovern's running mate in the election was none other than Sargent Shriver Jr, a friend of Opus Dei. From this, people have made the leap that Arnold Schwarzenegger, the former actor who became the Republican governor of California, has also been "influenced" by Opus Dei—the reason being that he is Shriver's son-in-law following his marriage to Eunice and Sargent's daughter, Maria Shriver. Opus Dei has categorically denied Schwarzenegger's involvement in the movement, yet the rumors persist, and the more fantastical and entertaining they are (Arnie as an Opus Dei protector), the quicker they appear to spread.

A link with Hollywood supplies the Opus Dei rumors with glamor and, during this period, Michael Butler, a theater producer and former special advisor to Senator John F. Kennedy on the Middle East, describing his conversion to Catholicism (thanks to the guidance of Sargent Shriver) recalls his "enlightenment": "In my early 20s, I was living with Linda Christian and Tyrone ['Rawhide'] Power. I was very much in love with them. As Ty had before me, I came under Linda's strong influence to become a Catholic. I asked Sargent Shriver to help me with instruction and he arranged this with his Monsignor. Like most converts I became very involved with the Church. I eventually was part of Opus Dei, which at that time was a powerful lay organization which had tremendous political and economic influence."

If the Shrivers (and indeed the Kennedys) were members of Opus Dei they would have been important, vital even, contacts for the organization. They had wealth, power, and more importantly, influence.

Considered by many to be America's version of the British royal family, the Kennedys of Boston, led by the family patriarch Joseph Patrick Kennedy, were all devout Catholics. While there is no evidence to suggest that Joseph Kennedy and his sons were ever members of Opus Dei, it is plausible that through Joe's daughter Eunice they would have been aware of the organization and, as Catholics, would have appreciated the movement's work.

Once again, this theory fits in neatly for any conspiracist since throughout American history, following the Kennedy assassination in 1963, every "good" conspiracy usually links to the Kennedy family. In this case, on the one hand, there's Opus Dei as a supposedly sinister organization and, on the other, there's the Kennedys, one of America's leading Catholic families—it's conspiracy gold! Delve deeper, however, and there is no proof whatsoever that the two were linked, but it appears that nothing usually comes between a good conspiracy and fact.

During the 1950s, when Opus Dei first arrived in the United States, McCarthyism was still in full swing. To its critics, it was felt that Opus Dei, with its "far-right" philosophy, would have been sympathetic to the strident right, which swept across the US seeking out potential Communists—no matter how insignificant the links. Joseph Raymond McCarthy drove a vicious anti-Communist campaign, which fed on the paranoias of post-war Americans. Anyone with a hint of sympathy towards the USSR was swiftly dealt with, by being either blacklisted (which led to your name being on a list of persons who were under suspicion, disfavor, or censure, or listed as not to be hired or otherwise accepted, especially in the entertainment industry) or imprisoned. With Opus Dei's initial anti-Communist reputation, which is linked back to the movement's experiences during the Civil War and which the organization subsequently distanced itself from, as well as Opus Dei's subsequent supposed alliances with the CIA in South America, the organization gained US support to pick up new affiliates. Opus Dei denies contact with the CIA and, furthermore, due to its stated non-political ideology, also denies any part in the McCarthy era or contact with McCarthy himself.

Despite this supposed and unproven link (conspiracy theories litter the internet) with McCarthy and his organization, Opus Dei's growth in the US was slow, especially when compared with the rapid spread of the faith throughout Central and Latin America. However, the organization received a boost during the 1960s when John F. Kennedy, a Catholic, became president, albeit a tragically short-lived one. Catholics were back in the limelight, they had a glamorous figurehead with an attractive family and were in positions of power. Being Catholic was nothing to be ashamed of—it was, in fact, something to be proud of.

Since Opus Dei's arrival in the United States, rumors have circulated about Opus Dei's relationship, not only with the CIA but also with the US Senate and White House itself. There is no proof that there is a working relationship between Opus Dei and any of these organizations, yet the conspiracies continue to run.

Throughout Ronald Reagan's presidential rule, rumors abounded that dozens of Opus Dei members were in prominent jobs in the White House, on Capitol Hill, and throughout the government. One of the reasons for the linking by conspiracy theorists of Reagan with Opus Dei was due to the fact that, during his presidency, Reagan convinced the Senate to establish full diplomatic relations with the Holy See in 1984. According to the *National Catholic Reporter*: "Part of his [Reagan's] logic was to use Rome as leverage against the US bishops, since Reagan felt the bishops were drifting too far to the left on nuclear deterrence and the economy, and he worried that they might undercut American Catholic support for his agenda."

Reagan's move to improve US/Vatican relations is hardly surprising. The Pope is the supreme authority of a Church with 65 million adherents in the United States. Though American Catholics rarely vote as a "bloc", presidents dare not ignore them. As a result, Opus Dei's growing influence in the United States is a factor that all presidents and prospective presidents need to consider. And so, through the years, there have been plenty of allegations about presidents working too closely with Opus Dei.

One website, the M+G+R Foundation, is filled with such allegations against Opus Dei and is a useful example of the kind of intense, unbalanced allegations that Opus Dei attracts. One case on the website looks at the developing relationship of Opus Dei with past US presidents (including George Bush and Nixon) in conjunction with Opus Dei's subsequent relationship with the CIA—the website names former CIA director William Colby as a member of Opus Dei.

Appointed by Nixon, Colby was director of the CIA between 1973 and 1976. He is referred to on the website as a "rigid Catholic", and although he is not named as a member of Opus Dei, the allegations claim that his "personality profile" was one that fits into the typical Opus Dei world. Furthermore, due to the fact that he was a CIA operative in Rome during the 1950s, the online writers claim that this would have been an ideal opportunity for him to be recruited by Opus Dei. In addition, Colby died in allegedly suspicious circumstances—in a canoeing accident after his retirement in 1996 and after he had allegedly abandoned the Catholic faith.

"Search crews on Monday combed the muddy waters of the Wicomico River, and helicopters scoured the area in a search for former CIA Director William Colby, presumed drowned in a weekend boating accident," reported CNN at the time. "Colby, 76, the CIA's chief spy in Saigon during the Vietnam War and the agency's director in the mid-1970s, was reported missing by neighbors after his canoe was found filled with water about a quarter mile from his vacation home. No foul play was suspected, but an investigation is ongoing, Charles County Sheriff Fred Davis said."

The "suspicious circumstances" mentioned on M+G+R were not borne out, as it was later discovered that his cause of death was reported as an aneurysm, which caused him to drown, resulting in hypothermia. Still, the rumors about Colby continue.

The website also alleges that, because Colby abandoned Catholicism—and thus, had he been a member of Opus Dei, he would have abandoned that too—he would have become a liability and was therefore in all probability, killed. However, there is no proof to substantiate these claims and most websites and obituaries following Colby's death make no mention of Colby's abandonment of his faith, although he did divorce his wife in 1984 to remarry... It is this kind of paranoid, wild conjecture that has led to Opus Dei unfairly gaining the reputation that it has. Such fanciful notions are perfect fodder for schlock novels but totally divorced from reality.

The accusations also bring former president George Bush (senior) into the equation, claiming that following his defeat to Bill Clinton his travels across the globe took him to Spain and thus to Opus Dei, with whom, it's alleged, he enjoys a "close relationship". While Bush certainly visited Spain, a country with a strong Opus Dei presence, there is little evidence to back up claims that the close relationship between Bush Senior and Opus Dei actually exists.

As for the relationship between Opus Dei and George W. Bush, US political commentator Gore Vidal certainly feels it is worth investigation—he maintains that President Bush was appointed by an Opus Dei "bloc". How likely is this to be true given that, as stated before, there are only around 3,000 known members of Opus Dei in the United States and hundreds of millions of potential voters?

Furthermore, although 45 percent of the nearly 65 million Catholics in the United States are registered voters, Opus Dei still represents a minor percentage, even within the country's Catholic "bloc". US political commentators have noted that while Republicans gained the support of fundamental Protestants, in the past the Catholic vote has been evenly divided. Yet, for George W. Bush's election campaign, using the tag-line of "compassionate conservatism", the Republicans attempted to court Catholic conservatives to their cause.

Catholics, as well as other religious groups, are often actively targeted and courted by the major US political parties. This could be possibly useful for Opus Dei. If the organization could become the major Catholic force in the United States, then by getting its candidates and spokesmen in place, the scene could be set for Opus Dei to influence major constitutional decisions across the US. However, it would need to gain an enormously large power base in order to do so, something that the organization doesn't appear overeager to do.

After George W. Bush was elected, the plans to target Catholic conservatives by the Republicans and the White House continued. In the lead up to Bush's re-election, the Republican Party announced the formulation of a National Catholic Leadership Forum to plan strategies in the 2002 congressional elections (as well as Bush's re-election campaign). Once again, some have chosen to put Opus Dei *and* this Catholic conservative push in the same bracket—if Bush was targeting Catholics, then, "obviously", the theory goes, Opus Dei was playing a major part. Again, this doesn't stand up under scrutiny, yet theories about Catholics in positions of power continue to be discussed and held up as some kind of proof that there is a Catholic conspiracy (also known as Opus Dei) taking place in the White House.

One example of this alleged Catholic takeover was cited when Bush appointed John Klink, a former Vatican diplomat, to a position in the State Department over one of Secretary of State Colin Powell's candidates. Then, in the summer of 2001, Catholic thinkers were central to the discussions on embryonic stem-cell research. It was felt that Bush and his team were on the rampage to secure the votes of conservative Catholics with the religious right. As Robert George, a leading Catholic thinker, told the *Washington Post*: "In 1960, John Kennedy went from Washington down to Texas to assure Protestant preachers that he would not obey the Pope. In 2001, George Bush came from Texas up to Washington to assure…Catholic bishops that he would." One year later, in 2002, a guest at the January 7–11 Congress in Rome was the Republican senator from Pennsylvania, Rick Santorum, who regards George W. Bush "as the first Catholic president of the United States". "From economic issues focusing on the poor and social justice, to issues of human life, George Bush is there," says Santorum. "He has every right to say, 'I'm where you are if you're a believing Catholic'." Incidentally, Santorum, is often described as an Opus Dei member. Apparently he is not, according to Opus Dei, though he did once give a talk in Rome praising Escrivá. Santorum himself has made it clear that he is not a member of Opus Dei.

So, with a "Catholic" in the White House, where, at this point, was Opus Dei? During this period of Opus Dei's history, it was still regarded as an elite, intensely secret society and, as in Europe, once again the organization has been frequently linked with other clandestine groups such as the Freemasons or Knights of Malta by the paranoid and suspicious.

"Their ranks are small, but a handful of key societies count as members some of the most influential Americans," write James Mann with Kathleen Phillips in *US News & World Report*. "While the Rev Jerry Falwell's Moral Majority draws most of the public attention, other religious groups are quietly trying to influence the nation's elite. Their names are unfamiliar to most Americans—the Knights of Malta, Opus Dei, Moral Re-Armament, the Christian Reconstructionists. Yet their principles, which include strict adherence to Christian values, are the guiding force in the lives of some of the most powerful people in the US. Despite coming from different faiths, members share a common belief that a small number of dedicated people can indeed change the world."

The article in *US News & World Report* once again draws parallels between the Knights of Malta, a Roman Catholic organization, and Opus Dei. Like Opus Dei, membership to the Knights of Malta is small, with only about 1,000 members (70 percent men). Again, similarly to Opus Dei, the US members are often all-impressive figures in business, government, or professional life. The report lists a number of impressive leaders within the community (Casey, a former, now deceased, CIA director, is named in this organization, too) as well as some Republican US senators and former high-ranking politicians. The list goes on, but already a swift glance at the type of members the Knights of Malta has attracted in the US looks like a supposed wish list for Opus Dei—definitely members an organization like Opus Dei would want to have on its books, with their influence, caliber, and power—as a result, many believe there are crossovers between the two organizations. However, this theory works only if you buy into the allegations that Opus Dei targets only the rich and the powerful in its bid to "rule the world".

"The main purpose of the Knights is to honor distinguished Catholics and raise money for charity, especially hospitals," writes *US News & World Report*. "But the close personal ties among members contribute to what some observers call a potent old-boy network of influential decision makers dedicated to thwarting Communism. The annual induction ceremony for new members at St Patrick's Cathedral in New York City is the only function of the US chapter open to non-members. Because many Knights and recipients of the Order's honors have worked in or around the CIA, critics sometimes suggest a link between the two. But members deny any connection, noting that the pattern of conservative members with overseas ties emerges naturally from the order's role as an international defender of the Church."

Articles like the above refer to the likes of Opus Dei as "secret" or "low key"—the organization continued to grind away across the country, gaining influence and members, but was still largely secretive. That was all to change, not only with the 2003 publication of *The Da Vinci Code* but, in 2001, with the arrest of Robert Hanssen, a CIA double agent who claimed to be a member of Opus Dei. Suddenly, the long-standing international debate about Opus Dei was cracked open, with Catholic liberals and progressives describing the conservative organization as a Catholic mafia—cunning, cult-like and secretive.

On February 20th, 2001, the FBI released this statement:

"Attorney-General John Ashcroft, FBI Director Louis J. Freeh, and United States Attorney Helen Fahey announced today that a veteran FBI counterintelligence agent was arrested Sunday by the FBI and charged with committing espionage by providing highly classified national security information to Russia and the former Soviet Union. At the time of the arrest at a park in Vienna, Virginia [USA], Robert Philip Hanssen, age 56, was clandestinely placing a package containing highly classified information at a pre-arranged, or 'dead drop', site for pick-up by his Russian handlers. Hanssen had previously received substantial sums of money from the Russians for the information he disclosed to them. FBI Director Louis J. Freeh expressed both outrage and sadness. He said the charges, if proven, represent 'the most serious violations of law—and threat to national security'."

Hanssen's arrest, and the subsequent revelation that he was both a spy and a Catholic, led to an "open season" on Opus Dei. Here was proof, for some, that Opus Dei members had a secret mission, they were against the US government, they had their own agendas... Yet, considering Hanssen was caught spying for the Russian government, this has led some more balanced commentators to note that if Opus Dei is a supposedly right-wing body of the Church, why would Hanssen be helping a Communist state? Could it, in fact, be that he was using Opus Dei as a cover? According to one source, Hanssen's motive for his treachery was a desire to afford the Opus Dei lifestyle and send his children to Opus Dei schools. The source goes on to say: "He justified his actions by the maxim of the old Jesuit moral theology of the greater or lesser good. Other psychological explanations are probably just Opus Dei disinformation." Whether or not that truly was Hanssen's motive is unclear, as his reasons have never been fully explained.

The debate still rages on—with critics of Opus Dei using the Hanssen case as an example of Opus Dei behaving badly, with the implication that all members must somehow also have disreputable aims. "We are here to keep Catholics from leading double lives," states Father C. John McCloskey, a leading Opus Dei priest in the United States. Despite McCloskey's claims, many refuse to believe him.

However, many Opus Dei members felt that the Hanssen arrest would, ultimately, result in positive exposure. "Even though it is a tremendous tragedy, God has the ability to bring good out of tragedy," said Brian Finnerty, Opus Dei's US spokesman. "The media attention could help us spread the message about finding Jesus Christ in daily life."

Hanssen was due to retire from his job as an FBI agent. When he suspected that his cover had been blown he wrote to his handlers in Russia, informing them that he was handing in his notice:

Dear Friends:

I thank you for your assistance these many years. It seems, however, that my greatest utility to you has come to an end, and it is time to seclude myself from active service.

I have been promoted to a higher do-nothing Senior Executive job outside of regular access to informaiton (sic) within the counterintelligence program. I am being isolated. Further, I believe I have detected repeated bursting radio signal emanations from my vehicle. The knowledge of their existence is sufficient. Amusing the games children play.

Something has aroused the sleeping tiger. Perhaps you know better than I.

Life is full of its ups and downs.

I will be in contact next year, same time, same place. Perhaps the correlation of forces and circumstance then will have improved.

Your friend,
Ramon García

According to the Associated Press: "Ramon García was one of his code names. He thought he had been cautious, never giving Moscow his real name and never meeting with the KGB. But he had not been careful enough. His biggest mistake had been leaving his fingerprints on the plastic garbage bags in which he delivered state secrets. When his file was sold by a former KGB higher-up in September 2000, the FBI lab had asked for everything. Surprisingly, the Russians had kept the Hefty bags, and once the prints had been dusted and traced, his fate was sealed."

When Hanssen's double life as a spy had been exposed, inves-tigative journalists soon "discovered" that Hanssen's brother-in-law was an Opus Dei priest in Rome, while one of his daughters is a numerary. According to the Associated Press: "Hanssen befriended best-selling espionage author James Bamford, and after pumping him for information about interviews he had had with Soviet leaders, would invite him to join him at Opus Dei meetings. 'He was a little obsessed about it. Bob would rant about the evil in organizations like Planned Parenthood and how abortion was immoral,' Bamford recalled."

Bamford, a Catholic, went on to write about Hanssen's preoccu-pation with Opus Dei in the *New York Times*: "Hanssen squeezed reli-gion into most conversations and hung a silver crucifix above his desk. Occasionally he would leave work to take part in anti-abortion rallies. He was forever trying to get me to go with him to meetings of Opus Dei. After weeks of urging, I finally agreed. At the meeting, Hanssen was in his element. He reveled in that closed society of true believers like a fraternity brother exchanging a secret handshake. His faith seemed too sincere to be a ruse."

One of Hanssen's chiefs at the FBI headquarters agreed with Bamford's assessment: "He [Hanssen] was a religious person who put the Soviets into a religious context. He would say that the Soviet Union is bound to fail because it is run by Communists and Communists don't have God in their life. He said to me, 'Without reli-gion, man is lost'."

Hanssen's arrest set off a short-lived, but intense, frenzy of spec-ulation about whom else in the nation's capital might be associated with the group, which, in other countries, has been politically linked with the far right. The speculation surmised that Opus Dei and its members have risen to the highest levels of the US government, including the Supreme Court and FBI. Again, none of this has ever been proven.

Critics noted that the order is the only one in the Catholic Church that reports directly to the Pope, thus diverting American citizens from their true allegiance—to the United States.

C. John McCloskey, a priest of the Prelature of Opus Dei, also nat-urally dismisses these theories. "Opus Dei is the most open order in the Catholic Church," he said in an interview with *Newsweek*. Of

Hanssen's connection, he says: "Only a very twisted mind would join Opus Dei, seeing it as a cover or mysterious secret organization, because it isn't." Naturally, there are plenty of people who disagree with McCloskey's argument. There is one theory that supposes that the secret service would rather spread rumors and attempt to alienate an organization (in this case Opus Dei) rather than take responsibility for a turncoat within its own organization.

"It is time to stop being polite to Opus Dei," says critic Eugene Kennedy. "Secret societies cannot be Catholic. Opus Dei does not constitute a community of love and support, like Jesus did, but seeks to divide, subvert and, as I believe we found with Mr Hanssen, appeal to the paranoid strain in life." Again, this mistakes the religious order's work and aims with that of state-controlled Secret Service. Kennedy is not alone in his distrust of the organization as allegations continue, especially when high-profile Opus Dei members are caught in a scandal.

Following Hanssen's arrest, there are those who have tried to build a conspiracy theory around Hanssen and the former FBI director, Louis Freeh—both are Catholic but was Freeh really a member of Opus Dei?

Before Freeh ran the FBI, he was a trusted agent in the mid-1970s, working out of the New York City field office. From there, he joined the US Attorney's Office, and in 1991 he was appointed as a US District Court Judge for the Southern District in NY. It was President Clinton himself who nominated Freeh to be the new FBI director on July 20th, 1993. A trusted position, yet Freeh has been dogged by conspiracy theories due to the fact that he has been linked to Opus Dei. His two eldest children are said to have attended The Heights, the Opus Dei school in Washington. However, according to Opus Dei: "Louis Freeh and his wife are not and have never been members of Opus Dei. The Freeh children have never attended The Heights School."

The journalist Robert Hutchison has made further Opus Dei links between Freeh and the papal nuncio in Baghdad, Opus Dei's Bishop Marian Oles, who was transferred to Almaty in Kazakhastan, becoming a papal nuncio in Kazakhastan, Kyrgystan, and Uzbekistan. Hutchison is keen to stress that when he contacted the inspector in charge of the FBI's Office of Public and Congressional Affairs, John E. Collingwood, to ask about Freeh's Opus Dei links, Collingwood stated:

"While I cannot answer your specific questions, I do note that you have been 'informed' incorrectly by whomever your sources might be."

Following the publication of Hutchison's book on Opus Dei, which contains the allegations against Freeh, Hutchison followed up this story with an article in the *Guardian* stating: "It seems that Special Agent Collingwood was himself 'misinformed', as Opus Dei subsequently admitted that Freeh's brother, John, was indeed a celibate director of the Work's large center in Pittsburgh." However, John Freeh resigned as a numerary in 1994 to marry, and it is uncertain whether or not he remains an Opus Dei member. Hutchison's logic here, however, seems unfair—merely because Louis' brother was a member does not automatically mean that Freeh was a member. As stated above, Freeh himself has not denied that he is a Catholic but continues to deny any affiliations with Opus Dei and, in return, Opus Dei has also denied he is a member of the organization. However, the rumors still linger on, no doubt in part due to Freeh's important standing within the US government.

During Freeh's time as FBI director, the agency cracked both the Unabomer and Oklahoma City bombing cases. "Most important," reports the *New York Post*, "Freeh refused to be cowed by the efforts of President Clinton and Attorney-General Janet Reno to blatantly politicize the Justice Department. He confronted Reno over her stifling of criminal probes into Clinton—Gore fundraising scandals—including what he rightly called 'compelling' evidence of Vice-President Al Gore's 'active, sophisticated' involvement in those schemes." However, inside the agency, Freeh faced criticism for his drastic streamlining within the Bureau, after he eliminated nearly 50 top-level posts and reassigned 600 supervisory agents to the field. Could the Opus Dei stories then be part of an elaborate smear campaign from disgruntled former agents? Possibly.

Due to the fact that people have refused to accept Freeh's statement that he is not a member of Opus Dei, a statement was released by the organization itself: "We can confirm that the Pope's spokesman, Joaquín Navarro-Valls, is a member, but we would like to *dispel* once and for all the rumors that Louis Freeh, Antonin Scalia, Clarence Thomas, and Mel Gibson are members."

Opus Dei continues its denial. Speaking to *Newsweek* magazine, McCloskey dismissed rumors of Freeh being a secret Opus Dei member, calling them "completely false". Indeed, added McCloskey, "I can't think of any Opus Dei members in government."

US journalists continue to disagree with Opus Dei: "FBI Director Louis Freeh and also Supreme Court Justices Scalia and Thomas are members of Opus Dei," writes Catharine A. Henningsen, editor of *SALT*, a liberal Catholic journal. Adrian Havill, author of *The Spy Who Stayed Out In the Cold*, offers further evidence that they could be. Freeh, according to Havill, attended the same church as Hanssen, St Catherine of Siena in Great Falls, Virginia, an orthodox Catholic church that still offers a Latin Mass. Another alleged parishioner is Justice Antonin Scalia, whose son, Father Paul Scalia, is alleged to have converted Judge Clarence Thomas to Catholicism. Here's where more Opus Dei conspiracy theories abound—Freeh is linked to Hanssen, while also being linked to Thomas and Scalia—more high-profile US citizens. The facts might prove otherwise, yet some are convinced that there is something sinister afoot—a conspiracy, obviously.

Antonin Scalia, a Justice on the Supreme Court, despite Opus Dei's official statement that he is not "a member", is often linked to the group and is regarded as the embodiment of the Catholic conservatives; while he is careful not to be seen mixing politics and religion, his faith clearly influences his work in the high court. According to *Newsweek*: "While he is not a member of Opus Dei, his wife Maureen has attended Opus Dei's 'spiritual functions', says an Opus Dei member."

"Thomas praised Pope John Paul II for taking unpopular stands," wrote *Newsweek*. "The conservative Catholics in the audience agreed with every word Thomas said. It's just that this elite Washington club wasn't entirely comfortable about the very public airing of a normally private agenda." Again, Thomas and Scalia's relationship with Opus Dei has never been proved. Furthermore, McCloskey points out: "All I know they [Antonin Scalia and Thomas] have in common is they both attended Holy Cross. Justice Thomas returned to the Catholic faith but was not a convert." Furthermore, Brian Finnerty, the US communications director of Opus Dei, adds: "Father Paul Scalia [Antonin's son] is not a priest of the Prelature of Opus Dei." Yet, despite Opus Dei's adamant stance that Scalia, Thomas, and Freeh are not members, unfounded rumors remain—nothing, it seems, not even truth, can dislodge decent conspiracy theory, even if it is founded on untruths.

Gore Vidal, the US author, has investigated the relationship between the Scalias and Thomas and has brought his only theory to the fore, alleging that Scalia (Antonin) and Thomas were vital components in George W. Bush's election battle against his cousin Al Gore in 2000. Both Supreme Justices, Vidal argues, should have withdrawn from the Gore vs Bush battle as Scalia's son was working for the Bush team of lawyers before the Supreme Court. Had Scalia and Thomas withdrawn from the case, the vote would have gone four to three in favor of Gore, who would now be president.

Naturally, Vidal is protective of his own cousin, Al Gore, but he also picks up on many US conspiracy themes when discussing the Bush "victory" in 2000. Was it a fix by those who wanted to see a Republican in the White House, and one who could guide the country into a more conservative lifestyle again, following Clinton's Democratic administration?

"We're all conspiratorial minded in America," adds Vidal in a later interview, "because there are so many conspiracies. We saw the Supreme Court conspiring to deny the presidency to the popular winner, it pulled every trick in the book and in full view of the world. We have big tobacco lying about the effects of nicotine, that's also a conspiracy. What is a political party but a conspiracy?"

Political conspiracies aside, figures such as Thomas and Scalia, with their supposed allegiances to Opus Dei, means the organization naturally suffers when an Opus Dei member is embroiled in a major scandal. Hanssen's involvement with both the US government and Opus Dei was an embarrassment but there were further public trials to come for Opus Dei.

The indictment of Mark Belnick, a lawyer at Tyco International Ltd, for fraud, brought the Catholic group more unwanted publicity.

"In July 2000, Mark Belnick, then the top in-house lawyer at Tyco International Ltd., received a $2 million payment toward a $12 million bonus," writes Laurie P. Cohen in the *Wall Street Journal*. "For Mr Belnick, it was the latest reward in a meteoric legal career that ran from some of the highest-profile business cases of the 1980s and 1990s to Tyco, a hugely successful conglomerate and Wall Street darling."

In 2002, Belnick faced an initial round of criminal charges by New York prosecutors and a civil-fraud lawsuit filed by the SEC (Securities and Exchange Commission). Prosecutors accused him of stealing the $12 million bonus from Tyco, which hadn't been approved by the company's board, as required by Tyco's by-laws. He was also charged with falsifying records by failing to disclose his relocation loans and compensation in federal securities filings. Prosecutors have taken testimony from Lewis Liman, the son of his late mentor. His lawyer called the charges "absurd".

Others might have spent the $2 million bonus he received two years earlier on a house, a car or three, trips abroad, or invested the cash—Belnick donated the money to charity. The majority of the cash went to a small Catholic college in California and to the Culture of Life Foundation, a Catholic pro-life group in Washington.

Three months earlier, Belnick, formerly a member of the Jewish faith, had quietly converted to Catholicism and become an active supporter of Opus Dei. In addition to his donations to the Catholic college and foundation, he gave money to a Catholic television network, two parishes, an Opus Dei bookstore, and an information center.

Just before Belnick's conversion and baptism, in April 2000, he e-mailed Father C. John McCloskey: "I've never felt so exhilarated—not since my bar mitzvah." A little more than a year later, the convert attended Mass with the Pope in his private chapel in Rome.

According to Cohen: "Belnick joined an elite fraternity of Father McCloskey's converts. Others include Lawrence Kudlow, the economist and television commentator; Sen. Sam Brownback of Kansas, and conservative political columnist Robert Novak. Bernard Nathanson, a one-time abortion doctor and pro-choice advocate who became a Catholic with the priest's guidance, helped counsel Mr Belnick on his conversion. At Father McCloskey's behest, Mr Belnick himself tried to persuade other prominent people—including former Nebraska Sen. Bob Kerrey—to join the Catholic faith."

McCloskey, who has an economics degree from Columbia, worked as a stockbroker for Merrill Lynch & Co. in the late 1970s, before joining the priesthood in 1981. He admits to playing squash at the University Club with *Washington Post* reporters and regularly appears on MSNBC television. His official job (until January 2005) was running the Catholic Information Center of the Archdiocese of Washington, but he is best known for shepherding prominent people into the Church. "The Holy Spirit uses me as a conduit," says the priest.

"C. John [McCloskey] is the most effective converter of high-profile people in the country," says Dr Nathanson, who, decades before his 1996 conversion from Judaism, helped start the organization now known as the National Abortion Rights Action League. "He wants to bring well-educated, affluent people to the Pope."

Some of the others the priest has helped through the conversion process are conservative publishing executive Alfred Regnery and financier Lewis Lehrman. Father McCloskey says that his Wall Street experience, as well as church postings in Manhattan, Princeton, N.J., and now Washington "put me in a circle I wouldn't otherwise be in".

In January 1998, Mr Belnick declared himself a "cooperator" of Opus Dei. On September 30th, 1999, he received the first of several huge Tyco payouts: $3.4 million from the sale of restricted company shares. According to Cohen: "Six days later, he e-mailed Father McCloskey to say, 'I'm sending you my check for $2M towards my pledge to the new Sanctuary/Altar' in the Catholic Information Center in Washington. Asked to clarify the amount of this pledge, Father McCloskey says Mr Belnick's donation was 'a minimal amount' and declines to be specific."

While McCloskey and Opus Dei stand by Belnick, who continues to maintain his innocence, there have been other scandals—more sinister, due to both their absurdity and their malice—that have plagued Opus Dei.

Some theorists have chosen to link Opus Dei with two major US events—the massacre at Waco (1993) and the bombings by Timothy McVeigh in Oklahoma City (1995). In the case of Waco, there are those who have claimed that it was a conspiracy to kill white Protestants, especially as there was an alleged Catholic sharpshooter among those at Waco. There is no basis for this theory whatsoever, yet, especially on the internet, the fables appear to fester.

During the siege of Waco, approximately 80 men, women, and children died on April 19th, 1993—William Sessions was the FBI director in charge. Initially, the US government and the Feds were seen as the guilty party, but a jury in 2000 decided that federal agents were not to blame for the deaths. The FBI version of events stresses that they wanted to rescue the children from David Koresh. As a result, armored vehicles were dispatched to spray tear gas on the parents and children who were the object of the rescue. But some perverse (and unnamed) Davidians set the place on fire. Some Davidians escaped, but many others, including those the FBI wanted to save, died in the fire. The FBI was suspected of foul play in the Davidian deaths. Sessions left the FBI in July and Louis Freeh became a candidate for his job.

Since Waco, many critics have asked for a thorough investigation (as well as complete reports) into the incident and feel that Freeh is covering up for alleged FBI mistakes, instead blaming the Davidians for killing their own. "No one in the FBI wanted anyone harmed," said Freeh to the *Dallas Morning News* in 2000. "Everyone did their best under extraordinarily difficult circumstances..."

Freeh is seen as the villain by many in this instance, and, due to the misguided belief that Freeh is a member of Opus Dei, the organization has been linked to the Waco deaths—an unproven conspiracy theory, and it is highly unlikely that Waco and Opus Dei are linked. To add fuel to the conspiracy claims, one report describes how Father Franklyn McAfee, the pastor of the church attended by both Robert Hanssen and Louis Freeh, threatened to have several supporters of the Waco Holocaust Electronic Museum arrested for handing out pamphlets that defamed Freeh.

"The incident occurred on Sunday, March 11th outside the property lines of St Catherine of Siena Catholic Church on Springvale Road, Great Falls, Virginia," reports Carol Valentine, the museum curator. "At 11.50am, two representatives of the Museum walked to the outlet of the driveway of St Catherine's, and began handing out pamphlets to parishioners as they left the parking lot after High Mass. The pamphlet, 'Should Christ's Words Set Standards For Public Morality?', documented Louis Freeh's seven-and-one-half year effort to cover up the Waco Holocaust. The pamphlet questioned the propriety of the Catholic Church in delivering the sacrament of confession to him; it also raised questions concerning the FBI allegations against Robert Hanssen... After 25 minutes (approximately 12.15pm), the stream of cars leaving the church parking ended and the parking lot was almost empty. It was then that Father McAfee ran down the church drive toward the pamphleteers. As he drew closer, he apparently saw the cameras and realized the incident was being recorded. Father McAfee stopped short and shouted: 'This is private property. Leave or I will call the police'."

Theories also abound when discussing the case of Timothy McVeigh, who was executed for the bombing in Oklahoma City that killed 168 people and injured more than 500 people on April 19th, 1995. Thanks to Opus Dei's supposed links with Freeh and, in turn, Freeh's links with the FBI, the Catholic organization's name has also been linked to McVeigh in terms of a cover-up. Again, the name of Gore Vidal pops up as one of the main theorists in this affair. He discussed McVeigh in a radio interview with Romana Koval in November 2001:

> The villain of the piece is pretty much the FBI out of control. For eight years the director of the FBI has been a man called Louis Freeh, and it has been revealed in the last year or so that he's a member of Opus Dei. Now we are essentially a Protestant Jewish country. So when I found out about Freeh being Opus Dei I thought 'now there's something that's odd here, how did he get into our secret police, who are the most powerful thing in the country?'
>
> I wrote Louis Freeh, who was then the head of the FBI, a letter which I include in the little book, a letter which I read aloud on the *Today Show*, just to make sure that he saw it. No answer, but I said there's certain very interesting leads here, and this is all from evidence at the pre-trials, which anybody can get at, and I said these should have been investigated, but they weren't. They decided it was McVeigh and that was it. Now a couple of days ago we find out that the FBI was faking it, some anti-McVeigh stuff in their labs, trying to prove that he built the bomb, that he had ammonia on his trousers or something. Well he may well have been in on it, I don't know, I'm not a prophet, but my impression is that he could not have done it alone. So there were others to follow up, and on television I said you've got to start doing your job, at the FBI, at the Justice Department, your job is to protect persons and property.

This was obviously something that Vidal felt the FBI weren't doing—could this be because Freeh was covering something up? Could it be because Freeh was an alleged member of Opus Dei? No matter what the facts of the matter, other political commentators were starting to notice that these supposed Opus Dei members were in positions of power and the commentators weren't getting straight answers. A common thought started floating around—Opus Dei had to be behind this. A poor allegation, especially as it is, again, completely unproven—but it once again shows how Opus Dei appears to attract a multitude of extreme stories. Any disaster, any major US incident, and there is often someone out there linking Opus Dei with the main players.

With all these negative stories flying around Opus Dei, whether discussing recruitment tactics, the secret nature of the organization, or Opus Dei's alleged political power, it's difficult to see quite where and how it can progress in the United States.

According to James Martin in *America* magazine: "Whether Opus Dei will continue to grow in the United States is difficult to predict. Its critics, including ODAN, are gaining a voice. But Opus Dei's widely acknowledged Vatican influence seems to provide a degree of protection, and its attraction for some, especially among college students, is a reminder of the desire for spirituality among Americans."

Martin isn't alone in his doubts surrounding Opus Dei's progress. David J. O'Brien, Loyola Professor of Roman Catholic Studies at Holy Cross in the United States, is of two minds. While admiring the organization's approach—drawing idealistic people together in a concerted manner—he thinks Opus Dei's appeal might be self-limiting: "They are so negative toward American culture that they can't understand how deeply our notions of freedom and individualism can go."

"Opus Dei has been approved and repeatedly encouraged to expand its apostolic outreach," argues Opus Dei's communications director, Bill Schmitt, "precisely because it has practises that have proven to be sound."

Robert Royal, president of the Washington-based Faith and Reason Institute, in an interview with *Newsday* in November 2003, said Opus Dei has "a kind of energizing spirit" that has attracted many well-educated young people. "It's kind of remarkable," said Royal. "I think the attack on it is because it's been successful and it's been powerful in its kind of way."

Furthermore, Opus Dei has supporters from cardinals and bishops across the United States. Cardinal Edward Egan (New York) stated: "It is with great pleasure that I express my appreciation for the work of Opus Dei here in the Archdiocese of New York for over 40 years.

Whether through programs for the needy in our inner city or through spiritual counselling in retreats and individual spiritual direction, Opus Dei has encouraged, and continues to encourage, the faithful to live the Gospel where they find themselves in the world, in their families, and in their place of work."

The rumors concerning the CIA and Opus Dei continue. Those that contend that Opus Dei is an "all-powerful political force" would argue that, as such, the government's secret services would naturally seek to target any religious or ideological organization that recruits among the wealthy and influential. Opus Dei denies its links on two fronts. Firstly, the organization contends that it recruits new members from across the social spectrum, not just from the wealthy elite, and, secondly, that it does not view itself as a political force. As such, it would not want to associate itself with a governmental body. However, if the secret service is suspicious of the Catholic group, it is likely that the US government would "place" high-ranking officers within the group to gather information and administer their own influence. The risk the CIA runs of being accused of being run (or "turned") by that organization is small, since only the deranged and truly paranoid would believe such a thing... Or so the theory goes... Again, Opus Dei continues to deny links with any political organizations, although it might not be aware of CIA agents in its midst.

Furthermore, in a country where Church–State relations are being constantly re-examined, Opus Dei's alleged presence within the political arena adds a serious undertone to State affairs, and serves up numerous theories for those seeking conspiracies. Many religious organizations lobby openly through licensed organizations, but the commonly held assertion is that Opus Dei appears to be seeking to influence policy making in a clandestine manner, hiding under its vow of never revealing the membership lists. Yet, although Opus Dei is constantly questioned about supposed members, and continues to deny that the likes of Scalia and Thomas are part of Opus Dei, the rumors and allegations continue anyway.

As a result, the question commonly asked is could some senators, representatives, cabinet members, justices, or presidential advisors be supernumeraries of Opus Dei, and ultimately taking orders from Rome? Opus Dei continues to say "No".

"In fact freedom is the key point to bear in mind when considering members of Opus Dei who are in politics," says Andrew Soane, Opus Dei's communications officer in London. "Opus Dei takes no credit for a good politician, and no blame for a bad one. That is one of the main results of having freedom. Therefore, although it could be said that the politicians active in Franco's Spain were liberalizing, this is nothing to Opus Dei—and it would also be nothing to Opus Dei if they had all been more authoritarian. There comes a point, of course, when a line is crossed, but this too must be left to conscience to decide unless the Church makes a statement on the matter. The same too applies to members of other professions (e.g. the banker above); you can only sanctify a job as long as it is an honorable one."

As yet, until there is a greater understanding of Opus Dei's works and members of the organization are more vocal in their support, Opus Dei continues to be a plentiful source for conspiracy theorists across the United States.

God's Banker Pays the Price

Bankers who hire money-hungry geniuses should not always express surprise and amazement when some of them turn around with brilliant, creative, and illegal means of making money.

Linda Davies, financial thriller writer, during a speech on the 'Psychology of Risk, Speculation, and Fraud' at a conference on EMU in Amsterdam

On June 17th, 1982, Roberto Calvi's body was found hanging beneath Blackfriars Bridge in London. Calvi had been missing from Italy for one week when a postroom clerk from the *Daily Express* newspaper, while walking to his job on Fleet Street, saw a man suspended from a scaffold under the bridge. The man was Calvi. The Italian was hanging by his neck, his feet dragging by the flow of the Thames—he had been dead for five or six hours.

After the River Police had taken him down from the scaffold, a detective noted that the dead man's cuffs and pockets were bulging with chunks of bricks and stones. When the police then went to search his body, they found, among other things, the equivalent of $15,000 in cash and a clumsily altered Italian passport in the name of Gian Roberto Calvini, aged 62.

Initially, the verdict was suicide. It seemed, at first, a probable solution as, only the day before Calvi was found dead, his secretary, Teresa Corrocher, had committed suicide in Milan by jumping off the fourth floor of the bank's headquarters. Corrocher, aged 55, had left an angry suicide note condemning her boss for the damage she said Calvi had done to the Ambrosiano bank and its employees. Further investigations into Calvi's death threw up the apparent involvement of the Masons, Propaganda Due (as previously stated, known as P2, a sinister, Italian right-wing breakaway Masonic group), the Mafia, the Vatican and, of course, Opus Dei.

Born in Milan on April 13th, 1920, Roberto Calvi was a traditional, if unexceptional, man. He went to the Bocconi University, a private institution that specializes in economic and business studies, in his home town of Milan. Then, like many Italian men of his generation, he went off to fight for Mussolini during World War II. When the war finished, he used his university degree to become a banker and, in 1947, he joined the Banco Ambrosiano in Milan.

A hard and diligent worker, Calvi climbed his way up the corporate ladder before becoming central manager in 1963. His successes at the bank meant that he was promoted again—this time to director-general before eventually becoming the chairman of Banco Ambrosiano in 1975. Under his strong leadership, Calvi transformed the Milan institution from an insignificant regional bank into a major global player.

At the height of his career, Roberto Calvi owned two large apartments in Milan; a 16th-century villa in Drezzo, which lies in the Italian lake district; a home in the Bahamas; and he had the use of an apartment in Rome. The Calvi family also had a staff of bodyguards, a couple of Mercedes, and regularly travelled across the globe. A successful career at the bank was certainly bringing rewards.

In 1978, three years after Calvi had been elected chairman, a report by the Bank of Italy on Ambrosiano concluded that several billion lira had been illegally exported—Calvi was one of the main suspects. Three years later, in 1981, Calvi was caught and arrested for illegally exporting $26.4 million out of Italy. This wasn't his only crime. Calvi was also due to be tried for alleged fraud involving property deals with the Sicilian banker, Michele Sindona, who himself was serving 25 years in the US over the collapse of the Frankfurt National Bank in New York in 1974. Convicted, but released pending appeal, Calvi returned to Ambrosiano where he resumed his position at the helm of the bank.

Calvi was initially welcomed back to his bank because, to Ambrosiano, he was a hero. He had put the bank on the world stage, and, during his tenure, it had grown to become the largest private Italian financial institution. The bank also became economically linked with the Vatican in various deals, thanks to which Calvi became known as "God's Banker".

On the news of Calvi's death, the bank virtually collapsed. A huge "black hole" in the balance sheet was revealed, amounting to

$1.3 billion in unsecured loans, and a large proportion of the missing money was later located in accounts owned by the Vatican Bank. The connections that unfolded in the wake of the Calvi "affair" linked Masons with the Mafia, implied that monks were capable of murder, and that, underlying the whole incident, was a basic and base human emotion—greed.

By all accounts, in the days leading up to his death, Calvi was a desperate man—his secretary was dead and, just 36 hours before his death, there were reports that the Vatican had refused to bail him out or offer him any support. And the Ambrosiano board had finally lost patience and removed him from his position as president, as the bank had gone into receivership. Calvi knew that an investigation into his accounts and affairs would most probably lead to a lengthy, if not life-long, prison sentence. There was nothing left for him in Italy, he had no supporters willing to help him anymore, and, as a result, Calvi fled Rome.

Calvi's movements were recorded a year after his death at a London coroner's court, which reported how, on June 15th, 1982, he had taken a private chartered flight to Gatwick from Innsbruck in Austria. When Calvi arrived in London, he moved to an eighth-floor flat at Chelsea Cloisters, a residential hotel near Sloane Avenue, in the heart of South Kensington. He was accompanied both on the flight and in the flat by Silvano Vittor, a small-time smuggler, who had been engaged by Calvi as a bodyguard and general helper.

The coroner's report stated that Vittor's employment, the arrangements for the flight from Innsbruck to Gatwick, and the accommodation in London were made for Calvi by Flavio Carboni. Carboni, a Sardinian millionaire who was formerly Calvi's right-hand man, later successfully sued the Italian makers of a film about the mystery of Calvi's death, *Banchieri di Dio* (God's Bankers). The film claimed that he was responsible for Calvi's death—he won his case against the film makers and was cleared.

According to reports, Calvi fled to England because he was frightened for his own safety in Rome. However, when he arrived at his flat in Chelsea Cloisters, his fears did not diminish. Vittor, who gave evidence following Calvi's death, claimed that Calvi was reluctant to leave his flat, would open the door only if he needed to, and was extremely wary about letting anyone in. While in the flat, Calvi spent a lot of time on the phone making clandestine calls, including a number of these on the eve of his death. However, after 11.30pm, on June 17th, 1982 (the last time Vittor saw him alive), no one saw Calvi again until he was discovered nearly 7km (4 1/2 miles) away, under Blackfriars Bridge the following morning. Quite how he got there is still a mystery.

From the moment Calvi's body was found, thoughts of the Masons were immediately invoked. "Masonic corruption was under the brightest spotlight in 1981," reported BBC journalist Jeremy Vine, 20 years later on *Newsnight*, "when a member of the infamous Italian P2 lodge, Roberto Calvi, who acted as financial adviser to the Vatican, was found hanged under the allegedly symbolically named Blackfriars Bridge in London. His pockets weighted down with, yes, masonry."

The evidence as to the Masons' involvement is as follows: Calvi was found beneath Blackfriars Bridge with bricks and stones on his body [the Bridge was designed by Robert Mylne, a Scottish Freemason]. The stones (masonry) were seen by many as the sign of P2 and, to further the claim of P2's involvement, one of the rituals of the lodge, according to writer Robert Katz, was that the men would wear black robes and address one another as "friar". To add to this, following initiation ceremonies into P2, it was said that if the new member revealed P2's secrets they would be hanged, with the corpse being washed up by the tides. Finally, before Calvi's death, he had been talking about P2 when questioned by Italian magistrates and had been threatening to talk more. The main theory behind Calvi's death was that he had to die before he revealed any further P2 or Masonic secrets. Furthermore, in 1998, Calvi's widow, Clara, gave an interview to the *Toronto Star*, admitting that her husband was a member of P2 but she stressed that he was not guilty of any wrongdoing.

Despite this "evidence", initial reports of Calvi's death were not so clear-cut. The first inquest into his death returned a verdict of suicide, although many felt there were serious flaws in the suicide scenario. Reports later showed that Calvi's jacket was buttoned incorrectly. Furthermore, he had enough barbiturates in his room to take his life painlessly twice over, so why go to the trouble of hanging himself? Calvi, as everyone could see, was a portly, unathletic sexagenarian who, according to his family, suffered from vertigo—hardly the type to go clambering up scaffolding. Then there was "the mystery of the briefcase". According to sources at the time, Calvi's suitcase, which was believed to contain all his secrets, had vanished.

Calvi's family were not satisfied with the verdict of suicide, and it was overturned the following year, 1983, with a second inquest, convened as a result of legal action by the family. The second inquest recorded an "open verdict", which meant that the new jury had not been convinced of either suicide or murder. However, by this stage, investigations had delved further into Calvi's financial dealings and it was at this moment that the Masonic group, P2, emerged as a possible major player in the story. However, to understand P2's involvement, the basic history of the case needs to be understood.

During the 1970s, Calvi had built up a close association with the Vatican, thanks to Archbishop Paul Marcinkus, the US-born priest who was also later known as the Pope's bodyguard. Marcinkus was a governor of the Vatican and head of the Vatican Bank, which also held a shareholding in Banco Ambrosiano, Calvi's bank. In a rare interview before his death, Calvi had said: "A lot of people will have a lot to answer for in this affair. I'm not sure who, but sooner or later it will come out." Many believe that Calvi was referring to the Vatican itself, a supposedly honest institution but one that Calvi, who was privy to their banking secrets and financial dealings, knew to be otherwise.

The scandal dated back to 1972, when the Banco Cattolica del Veneto (known as the "priests' bank" because the Vatican Bank owned 51 percent interest in the business and it made low-interest loans to the clergy) was sold by Marcinkus to Calvi at Banco Ambrosiano. The sale of the "priests' bank" had been an illegal transaction, which profited Calvi and Michele Sindona, the aforementioned Sicilian banker and a lay financial advisor to the Vatican. As the years rolled on, the trio continued to make illegal financial deals, using the Vatican resources and their own shady contacts to build considerable nest eggs for themselves.

While there is no suggestion that the Pope or any members of the Curia realized what was going on under their noses, it is clear that the Vatican provided the perfect foil for the trio's (and their subsequent paymasters) financial irregularities. Once their dealings were uncovered, it was time for their contacts to start covering their tracks.

The Vatican Bank, the *Istituto per le Opere Religiose* (Institute of

Religious Works, which is more commonly known as the IOR), suffered calamitous losses (some $200 million) in 1974, presumably through its problematic connections with Sindona. Opus Dei was in no way involved with this colossal exercise in mismanagement, but the theory following Calvi's death is that it was only too willing to help rescue the devastated bank.

The Italian magazine *Tiempo* reported that during the 1974 panic, Escrivá offered to provide 30 percent of the Vatican's annual costs— presumably in return for Vatican recognition. While it seems that offer (if it was indeed made) was declined, *if* this event truly did occur, it showed to commentators not only how wealthy Opus Dei was, but also what financial favors it was allegedly prepared to do. Opus Dei completely denies these allegations, stating that it never offered to bail out the bank—furthermore, if the *quid pro quo* (as the rumor had it) was Vatican recognition, Opus Dei already had it. Also, within the story there is the notion that the Pope could be bought, as it were, a premise that would insult many Catholics.

"In my capacity as counsellor of Opus Dei for Italy," wrote Father Mario Lantini at the time, "I should like to confirm what has already been communicated and published in all the press, namely that no one representing Opus Dei has ever held any connection or contact, either directly or indirectly, with Roberto Calvi or with the IOR over share transactions with Ambrosiano or in any other operation (or planned operation) of an economic/financial character of any kind or relevance. Given this absolute distancing of Opus Dei—and in order that full light may be brought to bear on this aspect—the necessity becomes apparent of knowing to which elements you are referring when you speak of Opus Dei. The intention, among other things, is to provide evidence of who could have wrongly used the name of Opus Dei or attempted to attribute false intentions to it." Opus Dei's plea fell on deaf ears; the conspiracies continue to involve the organization.

During the 1970s, while Calvi continued to climb the corporate ladder at Ambrosiano, he was constantly assisted by Marcinkus, who, incidentally, was never brought to trial following the "Calvi" affair. Instead he evaded arrest in Italy by hiding inside the Vatican City— magistrates in Milan had issued warrants, hoping to put him on trial for alleged fraud along with Roberto Calvi, but he was protected by the Vatican. In fact, Marcinkus survived as head of the IOR bank until 1992, working closely with John Paul II and never spoke of the affair again.

Marcinkus's actions did not go unnoticed by every member of the Curia, however. In 1982, Cardinal Giovanni Benelli, the former Vatican Deputy Secretary of State who was once a leading candidate for the papacy, was quoted making critical remarks about Marcinkus. "If there was any imprudence, it was because of incompetence and inexperience," Benelli told *Il Sabato*, though he did not mention Marcinkus by name. Benelli also explained how the Vatican Bank had never had any scandals under Cardinal Alberto Di Jorio, who had run the bank before Marcinkus took over in 1972. "As long as Cardinal Di Jorio was there everything was tranquil, because he was a person of great prudence," Benelli said.

According to Katz's investigations, the deal between Marcinkus and Calvi meant that when Banco Ambrosiano needed to carry out "certain operations", which had nothing to do with the IOR (Katz does not describe what these operations actually were), then Calvi was given free reign to use the bank's international facilities. In return, whenever the IOR needed to finance its own operations, Calvi and his various banks were at Marcinkus's disposal. Later, according to the magistrates, Calvi paid the IOR five-eighths of one percent commission on the amount moved out of the country.

Carlo Calvi, Roberto's son, later told journalists: "My father had many enemies within the Vatican... The Vatican was at the time effectively selling its extra-territoriality for profit." Carlo felt his father was privy to too much information, and that this was a dangerous position to be in.

Most of the missing millions had been siphoned off via the Vatican Bank (the IOR). According to some sources, it is alleged that Opus Dei lost over $50 million when Banco Ambrosiano closed. According to Calvi's family, the banker was involved in helping Opus Dei make a takeover of the IOR when he died—something that Opus Dei denies.

On October 7th, 1982, in an interview published in the Turin newspaper *La Stampa*, given while Clara Calvi, Roberto's widow, was living in Washington DC, Clara claimed that her husband had been negotiating with Opus Dei to take over the financial liabilities IOR might have as a result of its dealings with Ambrosiano. The interview quoted her as saying: "It was a risky operation, politically as well as economically. In exchange for its aid, Opus Dei was asking for specific powers in the Vatican, for example, in the determination of strategy towards the Communist countries and the Third World. In the Vatican there is a profound split between those supporting and opposing the attempts to improve Church relations within Eastern Europe."

The Vatican's response was immediate. On that same day, the Rev Romeo Panciroli, then director of the Vatican press office, dismissed her charges, saying they belonged "in the realm of pure fantasy".

Calvi's widow continued her allegations. During her husband's autopsy court proceedings she explained that: "My husband was stopped by those who didn't want him to carry to completion the Opus Dei deal." She also testified before a British court in June 1983 that her husband had sought to use Opus Dei to ward off the still-brewing Banco Ambrosiano fiasco.

A further statement from the Vatican office in October 1982 responded to Mrs Calvi's claims, saying: "The goals of Opus Dei are exclusively spiritual. Therefore it is untrue to maintain that Opus Dei took part in any economic or financial operation of whatever importance or relevance...In particular nobody on behalf of Opus Dei ever had a relationship such as that described by Mrs Calvi in her interview."

Roberto Calvi's daughter, Anna, was keen to support her mother's statements, and told journalists: "My father told me that to resolve the problem of his relations with the IOR, they had set in motion and carried forward a project that foresaw the direct intervention of Opus Dei, an organization that would have had to produce an enormous sum to cover the explosion of debt of the IOR on the balances of Banco Ambrosiano... My father added that there were, in the Vatican, certain contrary factions that were vigorously opposing the realization of the project, which, if carried to completion, would have created a completely new balance [of power] in the Vatican: that is, that Opus Dei would have acquired control of the IOR and hence a position of great prominence within the Vatican."

This conspiracy works well with other unproven rumors that there was an ongoing power struggle taking place within the Vatican between the members of the P2 Masonic lodge and Opus Dei. Furthermore, this adds to the theory that there are those within the

Curia who wish to curb Opus Dei's growing power within the Vatican and its influence on Vatican politics and policies.

Allegations also appeared in the *Wall Street Journal* in 1982, following an interview with Carlo Calvi, who was extensively quoted as saying that his father approached Opus Dei with the request. "Completely without foundation," said Opus Dei of the *Wall Street Journal* interview. "No one from or on behalf of Opus Dei ever had dealings or contacts of the kind described by Carlo Calvi in the interview."

Opus Dei continues to deny having any dealings with Calvi. "The secretariat of Opus Dei in Italy has already clearly established, several times, the estrangement of the prelature from the Calvi affair," said Giuseppe Corigliano, director of the Roman Office of Information of Opus Dei. "Never has Opus Dei had any rapport, directly or indirectly, with Mr Calvi, his family or his associates. To hypothesize the possibility of economico-financial operations between Opus Dei and the banker means to totally ignore the reality that this institution of the Church has goals and activities of an exclusively religious nature."

According to Hutchison in his book, *Their Kingdom Come*, later investigations showed that a powerful financial backer of Opus Dei, Spanish industrialist José María Ruiz Mateos, was also a treasurer of P2 and a close associate of Roberto Calvi. However, in an interview on the Spanish radio station Antena 3, on July 21st, 1983, Ruiz Mateos states that he never had the occasion to meet Calvi. Yet, according to various sources, a considerable amount of the money Ruiz Mateos pumped into Opus Dei came from illegal deals with Calvi, "perpetrated in both Spain and Argentina" argues journalist David Yallop in his book *In God's Name*. That statement too is also an allegation—Ruiz Mateos is no longer a member of Opus Dei, he left in 1985, but as a member he would almost certainly have donated some of his earnings to support apostolic works, probably ones local to Spain.

Like Yallop, the Italian government were not convinced of Opus Dei's innocence. On March 24th, 1986, four years after Calvi's death, after interrogations by both the Italian and European parliaments, Italian Prime Minister Bettino Craxi ordered a formal investigation of Opus Dei, asking for reports from the Ministers of the Interior, Defense, and Finance departments. After some protests and a petition signed by 25 parliamentarians of the Roman Catholic-dominated Christian Democratic party, it was decided that the Catholic Christian

Democrat Minister of the Interior, Oscar Luigi Scalfaro, would give the report to Parliament. His public report found no cause for legal action.

Opus Dei's name continued to be mentioned in the Calvi case, however. Prior to Calvi's disappearance from Rome, he revealed to associates that (just as his family later alleged) in exchange for 16 percent of Banco Ambrosiano, Opus Dei would help close the institution's $1.3 billion debt. However, Bishop Marcinkus, the Vatican's money man, is said to have opposed the plan, fearing—as Calvi's daughter had suggested—that the deal would require the likes of Marcinkus to be replaced with a representative of Opus Dei. Again the argument of a powerful struggle continues—in this case, this would leave the balance of power tipped in Opus Dei's favor and away from P2's men within the Vatican. Thus, goes the theory, Calvi had to be stopped.

Carlo Calvi also believes his father was murdered for the same reasons that Pope John Paul II was targeted in an assassination attempt on May 13th, 1981—to bring down Opus Dei's power. When John Paul II was appointed Pope in 1978, he turned to Opus Dei for support, and it was felt that the pontiff, by the early 1980s, had already started replacing long-serving banking officials with Opus Dei members.

"In the world of the early 1980s, it wasn't obvious that the Pope was going to be in the winning position," Carlo Calvi told the *Montreal Mirror* in an interview in 2002, "so my Dad was very much caught in the power struggle within the Vatican. I tend to think the Pope and my father were victims of the same plot. Top officials were afraid of losing their jobs and they were against the Pope's line. Meanwhile, my father was trying to align himself with Opus Dei before he was killed."

Naturally, most people remain unconvinced of the Calvi link with Opus Dei. While Father Vladimir Feltzman, a former member of Opus Dei, cannot confirm any links with the Italian banker, he asserted: "I do know that Banco Ambrosiano was the bank Opus Dei used, because when I was a member of Opus Dei I would take our money there... So the bank was definitely involved with Opus Dei." Perhaps this is where the rumors began. Opus Dei banked with Ambrosiano, but this does not mean that it was caught up in the machinations of Calvi and Markincus.

The Vatican's involvement in Calvi's case has tarnished the Vatican's global image, but what may prove far more damaging is the evidence uncovered by the magistrates, which connected IOR directly with the diversion of these funds. Katz, in his report on the affair, links the affair to two other political problems within the Vatican during this time—their financial support of the Somoza regime in Nicaragua until 1979, and the Vatican's supposed funding of the Solidarity movement in Poland. These weren't the only two events that Katz refers to—he also mentions the secret takeover attempted by Calvi and P2 of Italy's influential *Corriere della Sera* newspaper. Marcinkus, at the time, vehemently denied any part in the Solidarity funding, but it is said that when Calvi spoke to his lawyers of $50 million being diverted to the banned Polish trade union (Solidarity), he also implied there was more to come.

Not only was Calvi embroiled in deals between the Vatican, Ambrosiano, and the IOR, but, as suggested above, he was also alleged to be a *member* of P2. The secret Italian Masonic lodge was formed in 1963 with the name *Raggrumppamento Gelli—P2*. The "P" stood for Propaganda, a historic lodge dating back to the 19th century. Licio Gelli, the grand master, had initially brought retired senior members of the armed forces into the lodge, then, through them, active service heads. His web eventually covered the entire power structure of Italy to implement his aim—right-wing control, with P2 functioning as a state within a state, and only Gelli knowing the complete list of all his members.

Calvi's connections with Gelli became a particular focus of press and police attention, and caused the lodge (until then a secret organization) to be discovered. Gelli's connections with Opus Dei have never been proved (but constantly alluded to, despite Opus Dei's continual denials of involvement with P2 on both an ethical and a spiritual level), although he was a Knight of Malta, which has links with Catholic organizations. During Mussolini's rule, Gelli volunteered for the "Black Shirt" expeditionary forces sent by the Italian ruler to Spain in support of Franco and later became a liaison officer between the Italians and the Third Reich.

While in Spain, it is likely that Gelli might have met Opus Dei members, but there is no other connection between them here. However, there are those who have tried to link him to Opus Dei's history due to Gelli's close relationship with Argentina's president, Juan Perón, and the fact that Opus Dei had a strong presence in Argentina. This is the extent of their relationship, yet the conspiracies continue. As stated in Chapter Six, Gelli is alleged to have helped the leader regain his presidency in 1973, to have dealt arms in Latin America, and to have been the linkman between the CIA and Perón. Furthermore, Perón is said to have visited Rome in 1973 and was allegedly accompanied on his return to Argentina by Gelli, who was appointed honorary Argentine Consul in Florence a few months later.

P2 was incredibly influential throughout Italy, and was alleged to have a wide list of powerful members. "P-2 cut a wide swath through the upper echelons of Italian society, claiming politicians, financiers, even curial officials as members," wrote John L. Allen Jr in the *National Catholic Reporter*. "Gelli—whose international tentacles reached as far as Argentina, where he had been instrumental in bringing Juan Perón to power—was widely seen as an *éminence grise* of the Italian political scene for most of the Cold War era."

A list of adherents was found in Gelli's home in Arezzo, which contained over 900 names—it included state officers, politicians, military officers and, notably, one Silvio Berlusconi, who later became the Italian prime minister. The list also featured several characters from Argentina, including Juan Perón, the former president; José López Rega, head of the Argentine Anti-Communist Alliance, a notorious death squad; and Admiral Emilio Eduardo Massera, a member of the military junta responsible for the disappearance of 30,000 people during the "dirty war" of the 1970s and early 1980s. (The list can be viewed on the website: www.amnistia.net/news/gelli/lesnoms.htm.) P2 certainly has power in Italy, given the public prominence of its members—with regard to the Calvi case, it allegedly had another high-profile man involved in the banking world, Sindona, who also had connections to the Mafia.

David Yallop makes it clear in his book, *In God's Name*, that, by the late 1960s, Michele Sindona was a member of P2 and a friend of Gelli's—the two had a lot in common. They were both being watched by the CIA and Interpol, and Yallop also reports that Sindona was the man chosen by Pope Paul VI (Pope John Paul I's predecessor) to be the financial adviser to the Vatican.

Katz also asserts that Marcinkus's deals were "financing P2's support-hardware for Latin American fascism". Furthermore, the Milanese magistrates who were investigating the case felt that the link between Calvi and Marcinkus went "far beyond any normal relationship between two financial institutions". The Vatican Bank, they believed, was not just a passive conduit. As Katz points out, by its ownership of the Panama and other shell companies—Calvi and Marcinkus had set up other branches of Ambrosiano in places like Nassau, which served as the usual tool through which to filter money—the Vatican Bank not only knew that it was being used by Calvi to defraud the Ambrosiano, but was "actively engaged in the day-to-day deceits".

Ten years after Calvi's death, a further inquiry in London in 1992 (following Calvi's exhumation) confirmed his death as murder. The new autopsy concluded that Calvi was strangled near the bridge and then hung from it. The report also concluded that Calvi's neck bones did not show the kind of damage that would have been caused if he had hanged himself from a rope. It also found that his hands and fingernails were clean. If he had stuffed bits of brick in his own pockets and climbed a rusty scaffolding to hang himself, there would have been such traces—all this information was apparently 'missed' first time round.

Calvi's son, Carlo, had suspected that his father's death had been murder from the beginning: "This method is typical of the Sicilian Mafia," said Carlo Calvi at the time, as reported by *The Scotsman* in 2003. "This confirms that my father did not commit suicide, but was murdered on the Mafia's orders." The neck is bound to the arms and legs by slip knots joined behind the back. When the victims—known as *incaprettati* (trussed goats)—pull on the cord, they choke.

By 1997, Rome prosecutors had implicated a member of the Sicilian Mafia, Pippo (Giuseppe) Calò, in Calvi's murder, along with Carboni, the businessman who had helped Calvi escape Rome for London. Renato Borzone, Carboni's lawyer, confirmed news reports naming the other suspects as two Italians, Calò and Ernesto Diotallevi (supposedly, leader of the "Banda della Magliana", the most dangerous Roman Mafia-like association), and Manuela Kleinszig, an Austrian. Calò, identified by prosecutors as a top figure in the Sicilian Mafia, is currently serving a life sentence for a 1984 train bombing that killed 16 passengers. Another Italian linked to Calvi's death is

Mafia banker Francesco Di Carlo, who strenuously denied the allegations and has never been charged with murder.

More than 20 years after Calvi's death, the intrigue continues—yet the emphasis seems to be more on a "Mafia-style" hit rather than an Opus Dei-motivated murder. In 2002, Italian newspapers reported that police had found a safety-deposit box belonging to Calvi that could provide more clues about his death. Further evidence also emerged in December 2002, when a former Mafia boss turned *pentito* (informer) told police that Calvi had been murdered. Antonio Giuffre, the former deputy Godfather of the Sicilian Mafia, confirmed that Mafia chiefs had been angered by the way in which Calvi had mishandled the laundering of money.

Giuffre named Pippo Calò as the organizer of the murder, which others have said was carried out by Francesco Di Carlo, known as Frankie the Strangler, who was in London at the time of Calvi's death. Di Carlo denies killing Calvi and is not on the list of those to be charged. Carlo Calvi (adding to his many theories behind his father's death) opined that his father died for failing to honor mounting debts to the Cosa Nostra (a sinister Mafia organization, which had gained a strong presence in the United States) and because he knew too much about alleged links between the Mafia and the Vatican's finances.

In September 2003, the City of London Police once again reopened their investigation as a murder inquiry, and in May 2004, a London coroner involved in the 1982 inquiry into Calvi's death was robbed twice in Rome, losing information related to the case. Investigators said they suspected the files were stolen to order by organized criminals.

"City of London coroner Paul Matthews was robbed twice in a week while visiting Rome to discuss the 'God's Banker' case with Italian investigators," wrote Jeremy Charles in a report for *The Scotsman*. "Thieves first took a laptop computer with details of the investigation after breaking into Mr Matthews' hotel. Later a bag containing files was snatched as he walked through a busy station."

A spokesman for the Anti-Mafia Investigation Department in Rome said: "To have items stolen twice in a week is more than just coincidence. Once could be put down to bad luck, but twice is too much, and we firmly believe that Mr Matthews was deliberately targeted, possibly by the Mafia, while he was in Rome. He has told us that he is sure he was followed on several occasions, and the laptop and files on the Calvi case are the only items that were taken from him."

"The first theft happened while Mr Matthews was staying at the four-star Abitart Hotel in central Rome, where police said someone used a passcard to get into his room and take the computer," reported Charles. "Mr Matthews told police he had only left his room for a few minutes, and when he returned the laptop had vanished. Days later, as he walked through Rome's Termini station to catch a train to the airport for his flight back to London, his bag was snatched. Mr Matthews has been working with British and Italian police and last month the trial of three men and a woman accused of murder opened in Rome."

In March 2004, four people, including a jailed Mafia boss, went on trial in Rome, charged with Calvi's murder. Only one of the four defendants, Carboni, was in court to hear the charges. The Sardinian businessman told reporters: "I know as much about Calvi's murder as I do about the killing of Jesus Christ."

Two other people who were with Calvi on his final journey to England, Carboni's then girlfriend, Manuela Kleinszig, and a Rome underworld boss, Ernesto Diotallevi, were also charged with murder. The convicted Mafia boss, Pippo Calò, followed proceedings over a video link to his prison. According to documents leaked in 2003 (and following on from the 2002 reports), the prosecution sought to prove that Calò had ordered Calvi's murder for bungling the laundering of Cosa Nostra's funds and to stop him blackmailing powerful former associates in the Vatican and Italian society.

Eleven boxes and seven folders stuffed with new evidence were submitted to the court shortly before the start of the 2004 trial. A source close to the prosecution said it showed that Calvi had been involved in the laundering of treasury bonds stolen by the Mafia in Turin in 1982—the bonds had been passed to Banco Ambrosiano's chairman by Carboni.

The source, who remains unnamed, added that Silvano Vittor, the Trieste-based smuggler who helped organize Mr Calvi's flight to London in the days leading up to Banco Ambrosiano's collapse, had admitted lying to investigators in the past. Vittor now said it was

Carboni's decision that the group should travel to London rather than Zurich, where Calvi wanted to go. Vittor was said to have told prosecutors that on the evening Calvi disappeared, the banker left his flat in which he was staying along with Carboni. Carboni has denied seeing him that night. Confusion reigns, but one fact is clear—Calvi was murdered.

Calvi's death and links with Opus Dei may never be fully understood, especially due to the blurred evidence and many spurious theories that still abound. More importantly, however, it appears likely that Opus Dei had nothing to do with Calvi and his banking practises. Once again, this is another example of those trying to build a conspiracy theory around Opus Dei—especially considering the principal forces involved here: the Pope, the Mafia, money, murder, and intrigue.

Calvi was not the only casualty during this period. Another sinister death is also a subject of much debate—that of Pope John Paul I, who died only 30 days after he was elected Pope in 1978. His death has been linked with Calvi's, and, of course, Opus Dei's name is mentioned for good measure.

David Yallop's book *In God's Name* bills itself as "an investigation into the murder of Pope John Paul I", and argues that the precise circumstances attending the discovery of the body of John Paul I "eloquently demonstrate that the Vatican practiced a disinformation campaign". In Yallop's opinion, the Vatican told one lie after another so as to "disguise the fact" that Albino Luciani, Pope John Paul I, had been assassinated.

"When John Paul I came on the scene he was considered to be a wonderful man," remembers Father Vladimir Feltzman, an ex-Opus Dei priest. "We all read his books and there was a sort of 'Wow, this is fantastic, this is marvellous, he's what we were looking for' but he died so quickly, so that was a bit of a crisis." A crisis for the Church, but, argue some conspiracies, one that aided Opus Dei.

Yallop reconstructs the actions of Cardinal Villot and paints a suspicious portrait. It is reported that at 5am Villot confirmed the Holy Father's death. The Pope's glasses, slippers, and will disappeared. Speculation is that there may have been vomit on the slippers, which if examined would identify poison as the cause of death.

Villot (or an aide) telephoned the embalmers and a Vatican car was sent to fetch them at around 5am, asserts Yallop. Incredibly, the car was at their door at 5am. What ensued in the following hour is still a mystery. It was not until 6am that Dr Buzzonati, the deputy head of the Vatican medical service (the head, Professor Fontana, was *not* called), arrived and confirmed the death, without drawing up a death certificate. Dr Buzzonati attributed the death to acute myocardial infarction (heart attack).

At about 6.30am Villot began to inform the cardinals, and Yallop notes that, for Cardinal Villot, the embalmers took precedence over the cardinals and the head of the Vatican medical service. By 6pm, the papal apartments had been entirely polished and washed. Yallop writes that the secretaries had packed up and carried away the Pope's clothes, "including his letters, notes, books, and a small handful of personal mementos".

Villot arranged for the embalming to be performed that evening, a procedure as unusual as it was illegal. It was this action that proved questionable—why did he feel the need to rush through the embalming process, which would have rendered a post-mortem examination useless? It is also reported that during the embalming it was insisted that no blood was to be drained from the body, and neither were any of the organs to be removed. Yallop notes that "a small quantity of blood would of course have been more than sufficient for a forensic scientist to establish the presence of any poisonous substances".

"What occurred was a tragic accident," argues Villot as to the circumstances of Pope John Paul I's death, as reported in a press clipping from the *Ouest-France* press agency. "The Pope had unwittingly taken an overdose of his medicine. If an autopsy was performed it would obviously show this fatal overdose. No one would believe that His Holiness had taken it accidentally. Some would allege suicide, others murder. It was agreed that there would be no autopsy."

Official accounts put out after the Pope's death suggested he had a history of illness, including a weak heart, and said the strain of high office had proved too much for a "quiet and holy man". Yet, one of Pope John Paul I's supporters, Cardinal Lorscheider, who together with other Latin American cardinals was instrumental in securing John Paul I's election, said suggestions that the Pope had been in poor health were nonsense. "I never heard anything negative about his health," he told the Catholic magazine *Trenta Giomi*.

"In my family almost no one believes it was a heart attack that killed my uncle," said the Pope's niece in 1978. "He never had heart trouble or any illness of that kind." The *San Juan Star* reported in 1978: "John Paul's brother Edoardo, in Australia on a trade mission, reported that the Pope had been given a clean bill of health after a medical examination three weeks ago. He was frail in health as an infant and as a young priest, but there were no reports of heart trouble."

"The Pope has never spent 24 hours in bed, nor a morning or an afternoon in bed," said John Paul I's personal doctor, Dr Da Ros. "He has never had a headache or a fever that forced him to stay in bed. He enjoyed good health; no problem of diet, ate everything put in front of him, he had no cholesterol or diabetes problems; he had only low blood pressure."

However, if Pope John Paul I was murdered—why did he have to die? Theories abound and the likes of Opus Dei, P2, the Mafia, Calvi, and Banco Ambrosiana are all named in numerous fantastical conspiracy theories.

According to detractors, Opus Dei and Albino Luciani (Pope John Paul I) disagreed on certain doctrinal issues. Luciani's two greatest concerns at the outset of his pontificate were to revise *Humanae Vitae* and to convince Giovanni Benelli to become his Secretary of State. There have been theories that Archbishop Benelli was mildly hostile towards Opus Dei. For example Professor Estruch, in her book *Saints and Schemers: Opus Dei and Its Paradoxes*, has a theory that Archbishop Benelli was cool towards Opus Dei and somehow blocked access by St Josemaría to Pope Paul VI. Estruch makes quite a convincing case of this particular point, stating that while Benelli was Substitute Secretary of State Escrivá had no audiences with the Pope (in contrast with before and after). However, Benelli never showed any hostility in public, so this is speculation. On Escrivá's death he visited the chapel where his body lay and prayed there a while (something noted by several authors, including Estruch).

Commentators at the time noted that Benelli's return to the Curia would have meant greater Vatican conciliation towards the Communist bloc and an easing of its stance against artificial birth control: two issues that the more conservative cardinals opposed. It was felt that Luciani's views would have brought him into opposition with Opus Dei and, had he lived, the theory here is that Luciani's papacy and religious reforms would have undermined Opus Dei's stringent practises, beliefs and, more importantly, its supposed power base.

"When I hear it said that he [Pope John Paul I] would have instituted reforms that would have undermined Opus Dei, I am always left wondering what is meant," says Andrew Soane from the Opus Dei communications office in London. "If it means 'reining in' of some sort, it should be noted that he supported Opus Dei in one of his writings. If on the other hand it means some kind of doctrinal statement that would leave Opus Dei out on a limb, I think that is wishful thinking on the part of those who say it—they had similarly high hopes when Pope John Paul II became Pope. I do not think the Church works like that, and in any event Opus Dei will always follow Church teaching."

As it happens, Luciani was a public supporter of Opus Dei. Just one month before his election to the papacy, Luciani wrote an appraisal of the Catholic group saying: "Newspapers give [Opus Dei] a lot of coverage, but their reports are frequently quite inaccurate. The extension, number, and quality of the members of Opus Dei may have led some people to imagine that a quest for power or some iron discipline binds the members together. Actually the opposite is the case: all there is is the desire for holiness and encouragement for others to become holy, but cheerfully, with a spirit of service and a great sense of freedom." However, while Luciani eloquently praised some of the basic spiritual concepts of Opus Dei, some have commentated that Luciani was discreetly silent on the issues of self-mortification and the movement's potent fascist political philosophy—but due to his secret feelings there is no proof of his distaste and disgust at this moment in time.

When Luciani was elected Pope, he stated that he was on a mission to reverse the Church's position on contraception, clean up the Vatican Bank, and dismiss Masonic cardinals. Both Hutchison and Yallop agree that in September 1978, Luciani told Cardinal Villot that, as well as removing Marcinkus from his post, he also intended to send Sebastiano Baggio to Venice while the Vicar of Rome, Ugo Poletti, was to be sent to Florence. Another member of the Curia whom Luciani allegedly wanted to replace was Villot himself. Hutchison also brings in the theory that these four prelates were "essential to the success of Opus Dei's intentions". These "intentions", maintains Hutchison, were getting Escrivá canonized, winning the status of Personal Prelature, and, finally, gaining control of the Vatican finances.

Twenty years after John Paul I's death, Cardinal Aloisio Lorscheider of Brazil, a strong supporter of John Paul I who had helped elect him, said he had decided to speak out to "record with sorrow" that the official version of John Paul I's death was open to question.

As noted, the new Pope was intending to make a series of dismissals and new appointments to remove those accused of financial and other misdeeds. A new Pope's investigation into these financial irregularities would have upset the likes of Marcinkus and Calvi's monetary scams. Furthermore, the Vatican Bank (IOR) was personally owned and operated by the Pope and made loans to religious projects all over the world. It was discovered that the bank exploited its high status and engaged in risky speculation and illegal schemes, including money laundering. Again, these were the actions perpetrated by Calvi and his friends and had nothing to do with the Curia itself.

Pope John Paul I wasn't the only death connected with IOR or Ambrosiano during this period. Judge Emilio Alessandrini, a magistrate investigating the Banco Ambrosiano activies, was murdered. Alessandrini was just about to issue a warrant for Calvi's arrest, but while driving along the Via Muratoni one evening, the judge stopped at red traffic lights and was shot dead.

Mino Pecorelli was another victim. He, too, was shot dead in his car on a Rome street, in March 1979. An investigative journalist, he was working on exposing the membership and dealings of P2 and, as editor of the weekly magazine *Osservatore Politico*, he had access to a startling quantity of confidential information. "Some observers believe the journalist [Pecorelli] was killed because of his tendency to use that information," wrote Philip Willan in the *Guardian*, "often provided by contacts in the secret services, to blackmail politicians and businessmen in order to keep his struggling organ afloat. Others say he was a victim of his own crusading verve, which led him to publish sensitive material that other media would not handle, out of a romantic sense of the investigative journalist's mission." However, the Perugia appeals court appears to have accepted the testimony of a number of Mafia turncoats, who claimed that Pecorelli was killed by the mob in order to prevent him from publishing material that could have seriously damaged former Italian prime minister (and another alleged Opus Dei member), Giulio Andreotti's career.

Further deaths during this period include that of Lt Col Antonio Varisco, head of Rome's security service, who was also investigating P2's activities. Varisco's assassination took place on July 13th, 1979—both he and his chauffeur were killed following four shots from a sawn-off shotgun. Just prior to Varisco's murder, Giorgio Ambrosoli, an Italian prosecutor, was killed thanks to four bullets from a P38. Finally, it turned out that Ambrosoli had also spoken to the head of the criminal section in Palermo, Boris Giuliano. On leaving the Lux Bar in Palermo one day, Giuliano was assassinated, and replaced by Giuseppe Impallomeni, a member of P2. Then, on April 27th, 1982, Robert Rosone, the general manager of Banco Ambrosiano, who was trying to clean up the bank, was the victim of an assassination attempt. The attack failed, leaving Rosone with wounds in his legs.

Theorists conclude these men were all victims of a plot involving the Mafia, the Vatican Bank, and P2. As stated, those with the most to lose from the new Pope's potential inquiries included Bishop Paul Marcinkus, then head of the Vatican Bank; Roberto Calvi, head of the Banco Ambrosiano of Milan, and Licio Gelli, the head of P2.

But what of Opus Dei? Was it involved? It seems highly unlikely. The main problem with Pope John Paul's death has been the blurring of facts from the Vatican, which has managed to raise suspicion. "I've heard that he [Pope John Paul I] died reading a novel and was discovered by a nun," says former Opus Dei member Feltzman. "But you can't have a holy man reading a novel or discovered by a nun in case people assume he was doing something naughty. So, it became that he was reading some holy book and was discovered by his private secretary. Now, when you start analyzing where his private secretary was, it just doesn't fit. So, you can say it's a lie, a pious lie, but still a lie and something that is left open to interpretation and various theories. Had Opus Dei been involved, I don't think they would have cocked it up. They are more professional."

Feltzman's comments are slightly tongue in cheek here. While he strongly disbelieves that Opus Dei was involved in a "plot to kill the Pope", which has shades of the Robbie Coltrane film *The Pope Must Die*, he has a point. Opus Dei is an organized strong movement, yet it is precisely its strength (in both belief and will) that appears to threaten those outside the organization. Conspiracy theories allege that with, Pope John Paul I conveniently out of the way, the path was clear for Opus Dei to continue its financial involvement with Banco Ambrosiano and enjoy the patronage of Karol Wotjyla, who took the name John Paul II in tribute to his predecessor, following his election on October 16th, 1978. The rumors, nevertheless, continue and have led to further tales of Opus Dei's supposed takeover of the Vatican itself. The conspiracies refuse to die down and, as the years roll on, appear to evolve into further sinister tales with no basis in fact—especially when you begin to analyze the actual extent of Opus Dei's "hold".

At the Heart of the Vatican

I know some people talk about Opus Dei's "lobby" and its influence on John Paul II. But I think it's simply that the Pope has a lot of confidence in some of the new institutions in the Church. Opus Dei is one of them, but not the only one. John Paul II's sympathy towards the theology of work at the base of St Josemaría Escrivá's teachings predates his papacy. Opus Dei for its part owes the Pope fidelity and obedience to his teachings. It's clear to me that the faithful of the Prelature try to help him with their prayer and mortification, which today hardly anybody talks about. But one has to know how to carry the cross with grace, as John Paul II does.

Cardinal Julián Herranz, interviewed in El Mundo, *October 2003*

At 6.18pm on October 16th, 1978, a puff of white smoke appeared from the small chimney of the Sistine Chapel—a new Pope had been elected. Nearly half an hour after the smoke, Cardinal Pericle Felici appeared on the central loggia of St Peter's Basilica and announced the election of Pope John Paul II to the See of Peter with the words: "*Annuntio vobis gaudium magnum Habemus Papam Carolum Wojtyla, qui sibi nomen imposuit Ioannem Paulum II.*" The first non-Italian Pope since the 16th century, Karol Wojtyla, had arrived; everyone was surprised.

When Felici announced Wojtyla's name to the gathered crowd there was a stunned silence—a non-Italian pope? John Paul II, Cardinal Karol Wojtyla, Archbishop of Cracow, was elected as the 264th Pope by the other 109 cardinal electors on the second day of the second conclave of 1978. Six days later, on October 22nd, 1978, his pastoral ministry was inaugurated. At the same time Opus Dei began to consolidate its position within the Vatican and Vatican politics.

The conclave itself had been divided between two strong candidates: Giuseppe Siri, the conservative Archbishop of Genoa, and Giovanni Benelli, the liberal Archbishop of Florence and close associate of Pope John Paul I. In early ballots Benelli came within nine votes of victory. Wojtyla, however, secured election as the compromise candidate, in part through the support of liberal cardinals such as Franz König, and conservatives who had previously supported Siri.

Nearly an hour after his election, at 7.15pm, the new pontiff, clad in the traditional papal white, appeared on the same balcony and spoke in Italian the words now familiar to tens of millions of people around the world: "Praised be Jesus Christ!" He continued: "The most eminent cardinals have called a new Bishop of Rome. They called him from a faraway country, ...far, but always near in the communion of faith and the Christian tradition. I was afraid in receiving this nomination, but I did it in the spirit of obedience to Our Lord and with total trust in his Mother, the Most Holy Madonna."

According to the late Penny Lernoux, matters in the papacy "changed radically" when John Paul became Pope because he was "close" to Opus Dei. As a cardinal, Karol Wojtyla (as he was then) had been invited to speak at Opus Dei centers and, when he was in Rome for the funeral of John Paul I, he had visited Opus Dei's center to pray at Josemaría Escrivá's crypt—Escrivá had died three years earlier in 1975. Following Escrivá's death, Msgr del Portillo had taken over as the spiritual leader of Opus Dei and had become a frequent visitor to the Vatican—a move seen by Opus Dei critics as threatening.

Wojtyla's appointment as Pope was a ground-breaking move by the Catholic Church. The first Polish pontiff and the first non-Italian pope in 455 years, he was also, at 58, the youngest pope of the 20th century. Wojtyla had risen swiftly through the ranks of Catholic clergy to become Archbishop of Cracow, and his career, although rapid, was not spectacular. He was respected but unknown outside Vatican circles, and few experts had tipped him to be Pope John Paul's successor. As a result, he needed a competent, strong, supportive team behind him. Enter Opus Dei. It is at this point, argue conspiracy theories, that Opus Dei truly consolidated its position within the Vatican.

According to ex-Opus Dei member Father Vladimir Feltzman, the relationship between Opus Dei and the new Pope first began in the 1960s, when the young bishop visited Rome from Poland. It was a bond that was to serve Opus Dei well. "When he became Pope," says Feltzman, "he said: 'Who can I support? Who can support me? Who can I rely on? Who can I trust? Who has the competence? Who knows banking? Who knows public relations?' Naturally, he turned to Opus

Dei who popped up going 'Here we are, Holy Father'." With Opus Dei by his side, John Paul II had a corps of well-educated, disciplined, profoundly committed Catholics who, as laity in ordinary jobs, could penetrate society in ways that priests could not.

Soon after his election, in 1979, John Paul II addressed members of Opus Dei, saying that: "Opus Dei anticipated the theology of the laity in the Second Vatican Council." The Pope was an admirer of Opus Dei and he, and the movement, shared similar outlooks on doctrinal and spiritual matters.

Furthermore, the Vatican stated: "The headquarters of Opus Dei were fixed in Rome, to emphasize even more clearly the aspiration which is the guiding force of all its work, to serve the Church as the Church wishes to be served, in close union with the See of Peter and the hierarchy of the Church. On several occasions, Pius XII and John XXIII sent Blessed Josemaría expressions of their affection and esteem; Paul VI wrote to him in 1964 describing Opus Dei as 'a living expression of the perennial youthfulness of the Church'." It seems the admiration between Opus Dei and the Vatican went both ways.

The Pope's concepts of obedience, orthodoxy, and fundamentalism were also very similar to those of Opus Dei—John Paul II was considered a conservative on issues relating to birth control and the ordination of women. He too, like Opus Dei, was critical of liberation theology, and those who regarded themselves as Catholics, while questioning the Church's teachings on faith and morals. Nearly 20 years after his election to the papacy, John Paul II published the encyclical *Evangelium Vitae* (The Gospel of Life) in which he reasserted the Church's condemnation of abortion, euthanasia, and capital punishment, calling them all a part of the "culture of death" that is pervasive in the modern world.

Opus Dei and John Paul II had plenty more in common. While Opus Dei rallied against Communist forces, according to Father C. John McCloskey, a leading Opus Dei priest in the United States: "Pope John Paul II played a crucial, if not pre-eminent, role in the downfall of Communism in Eastern Europe. He now views his final struggle as to rescue the formerly Christian West from a hedonistic materialism that threatens civilization as surely as Godless Marxism. The ideology of the Bolshevik Revolution having collapsed, the ideological excesses of the French Revolution must be the next to go."

Furthermore, adds the Opus Dei priest: "The Pope has defined work, as 'anything useful to man'. This is the hinge on which the spirituality of Opus Dei is based."

Opus Dei, and the rest of the Catholic world, suffered a scare three years into John Paul II's papacy when an attempt was made on the pontiff's life. On May 13th, 1981, the Pope was shot and nearly killed by Mehmet Ali Agca, a Turkish gunman, as John Paul II entered St Peter's Square to address a general audience. His closest colleagues say that John Paul believed his survival then was a direct hint from Providence.

Naturally, the motives for killing the Pope led to more conspiracy theories. One unproven speculation, explored by Edward S. Herman and Noam Chomsky in their book *Manufacturing Consent*, was that the assassination was ordered by the Soviet Union; the KGB, however, categorically insists that it had no involvement in the attempt on the pontiff's life. Another far-fetched explanation for the assault on the Pope is alleged to have come from Agca himself, who claimed that forces within the Vatican itself hired him to attack the pontiff.

One theory that has cropped up on the internet is that the assault on the Pope in 1981 "paved the way for Opus Dei to achieve its current hegemony over the Church". The reasoning behind this suggestion comes from the fact that Agca failed to hit his target although he was an expert marksman and was firing at a point blank range of less than 4m (4yds). The theory contends that he was intending merely to wound and not kill the Pope, and the latter, feeling under threat, would lean more on his friends in Opus Dei. This theory, however, has been viewed by nearly everyone as too ridiculous to be given any credence.

Following the attack on the Pope in 1981, it was felt by some commentators that Opus Dei had replaced the Jesuits as the Pope's intellectual and diplomatic arm within the Vatican. The Jesuits have a large number of supporters across the globe and a history of papal association over a 442-year span, but lost out to the Opus Dei organization, which, ultimately, has an incredibly small representation within the Curia. "What really scares the Js, [Jesuits]" said the editor of a Catholic newspaper, "is that as the Church's elite troops, they now have a Spanish competitor."

As John L. Allen Jr points out in *National Catholic Reporter*: "Opus

Dei does seem disproportionately represented in the Roman Curia. To take one point of comparison, Opus has the same number of clergy working in Vatican congregations and councils as the Jesuits (five priests and one archbishop), despite the fact that there are over eight times as many Jesuit priests to choose from (14,852 to 1,763)."

"Will the Jesuits survive another 450 years?" asks Jamie Buchan in the *Independent*. "It's impossible to answer. They seem haunted by the prospect of suppression. Two Jesuits in different places described the same dream. This is the better version: We are in Rome. From the doors of the Vatican, Cardinal Casaroli emerges, crosses Bernini's great piazza, avoiding tourists and pigeons, and comes into the cool and quiet of the Borgo Santo Spirito. He reaches No 5, is shown in and rides up in the lift to the Superior General's office. With him, he carries a letter, which he reads out. He comes to the passage which says that the Holy Father, for reasons he must keep locked in his heart, has resolved that the Society of Jesus should at once—without excuse or expenses—vacate these commodious buildings and hand them over to the President General of Opus Dei. In the dream, Peter-Hans Kolvenbach bows his head and says: 'I accept the Holy Father's command!'" It has been rumored that the Jesuits fear this dream may yet become a reality...

Opus Dei's real *coup* within the Vatican was gaining its unique Personal Prelature status, the first and, as yet, only one of its kind, which was mooted initially as a concept during the Second Vatican Council. The year was 1982 and the Personal Prelature granted by John Paul II gave Opus Dei unusual independence from the normal Church hierarchy. The process had begun in 1979, when John Paul II began the background information search required before he could formally initiate the process necessary to recognize Opus Dei as a prelature.

The Pope got an impressive answer. Among other things, the relevant document stated that there were 72,375 members in 87 different countries, forming a kind of "mobile corps," ready, like a religious army of sorts, to go wherever they were needed. At this stage, Opus Dei was involved with a total of 479 universities and high schools on five continents, and had a hand in 604 publications, 52 broadcasting stations (radio and TV), 38 press and publicity agencies, and 12 film production and distribution organizations. Even without Personal Prelature status, Opus Dei had made some impressive strides.

According to canon law, a Personal Prelature consists of secular priests "presided over by a prelate as its proper ordinary, who has the right to erect a national or international seminary, to incardinate the students, and to promote them to orders... [A Personal Prelature may be] erected by the Apostolic See, after consulting with the conferences of bishops involved..." Personal Prelatures are made up of a pastor, a presbyterate consisting of secular priests, and men and women lay faithful. The prelate, who may be a bishop, is appointed by the Pope, and governs the prelature with power of governance or jurisdiction.

For Opus Dei, this Personal Prelature status was merely in keeping with Vatican Council II. For its critics, it elevated the Catholic movement to a "church within the Church", an autonomous battalion in the Pope's divisions bearing allegiance to Opus Dei's head office in Rome and not to a local bishop. In short, this is interpreted as "power". Opus Dei, in critics' eyes is answerable to no one—save the Pope himself.

"From its beginnings," said Pope John Paul II in Ut Sit, the Apostolic Constitution, which awarded the Personal Prelature status, "this Institution has in fact striven not only to illuminate with new lights the mission of the laity in the Church and in society, but also to put it into practise; it has also endeavored to put into practise the teaching of the universal call to sanctity, and to promote at all levels of society the sanctification of ordinary work, and by means of ordinary work. Furthermore, through the Sacerdotal Society of the Holy Cross, it has helped diocesan priests to live this teaching, in the exercise of their sacred ministry."

The final statement in Ut Sit declared: "The central Government of the Prelature has its offices in Rome. The oratory of Our Lady of Peace, which is in the central offices of the Prelature, is erected as a prelatic church. The Most Reverend Monsignor Alvaro del Portillo, canonically elected President-General of Opus Dei on September 15th, 1975, is confirmed and is appointed Prelate of the Personal Prelature of the Holy Cross and Opus Dei, which has been erected. Finally, We designate the Venerable Brother Romolo Carboni, Titular Archbishop of Sidone and Apostolic Nuncio in Italy, for the opportune execution of all the above, and confer on him the necessary and opportune faculties, including that of sub-delegating—in the matter in question—in any ecclesiastical dignitary, with the obligation of sending, as soon as possible, to the Sacred Congregation for Bishops, an authentic copy of the act which testifies to the fact that the mandate has been carried out." Opus Dei now had an established, ratified, papally recognized power base in Rome—where better, it was felt, for Opus Dei to lobby the center of the Catholic Church than at the very heart of its operations?

"I know some people talk about Opus Dei's 'lobby' and its influence on John Paul II," said Opus Dei member Julián Herranz in an interview with *El Mundo*, following his appointment to cardinal. "But I think it's simply that the Pope has a lot of confidence in some of the new institutions in the Church. Opus Dei is one of them, but not the only one. John Paul II's sympathy towards the theology of work at the base of St Josemaría Escrivá's teachings predates his papacy. Opus Dei for its part owes the Pope fidelity and obedience to his teachings. It's clear to me that the faithful of the Prelature try to help him with their prayer and mortification, which today hardly anybody talks about. But one has to know how to carry the cross with grace, as John Paul II does."

Pope John Paul II showed his further approval of Opus Dei just two years later, in 1984. "Clad in simple white albs," reports *Time* magazine, "77 candidates for the priesthood prostrated themselves before the high altar of St Peter's Basilica last week as the Supreme Pontiff invoked the blessings of the saints in heaven. Then, while the group knelt in four neat rows, Pope John Paul [II], followed by Monsignor Alvaro del Portillo, laid hands on the candidates' heads to convey to them the powers of priesthood."

The Pope's presence marked a rite of special significance. Thirty of the newly ordained priests were destined to serve exclusively for Opus Dei, and the pontiff's attendance at the ordination demonstrated how highly he valued the movement. Only earlier that year, John Paul II had had his first formal audience with del Portillo, the Prelate of Opus Dei, and the Pope's first pastoral visit that year was to an Opus Dei center in Rome. Furthermore, every Easter evening since his election, the Pope would relax by having Opus Dei students drop by to sing songs and read their poems.

Opus Dei had further cause to celebrate John Paul II—its founder Josemaría Escrivá was first beatified in 1992, then canonized in 2002. During his reign, Pope John Paul II beatified and canonized far more candidates than any other previous pope in history. By October 2004, he had beatified 1,340 people. Whether he canonized more saints than all his predecessors put together, as is sometimes claimed, is difficult to prove, as the records of many early canonizations are incomplete or missing.

"It is no secret that while all the Roman pontiffs whose reigns have coincided with the growth and development of Opus Dei since 1928 have highly approved of its message and mission, John Paul II, perhaps as a result of his varied work and educational background, has grasped its importance in a deeper fashion," writes Father C. John McCloskey. "The Pope has played an essential role in encouraging its development through granting its definitive juridical status a Personal Prelature, establishing the Pontifical University of the Holy Cross, and finally canonizing its founder, Saint Josemaría Escrivá."

A sainthood for Escrivá would vindicate the movement's creation under "divine inspiration" as the Pope described it, since Escrivá's personality, words, and works are the essence of Opus. Under del Portillo, and his successor Javier Echevarría, Escrivá's closest collaborator, every Opus action still conforms to "the Founder's" intentions.

The idea of Escrivá as Saint had certainly been mooted in Vatican circles before his death. Del Portillo describes the last meeting between Karol Wojtyla and Escrivá's (before the founder's death), on June 25th, 1973. Del Portillo reports that Escrivá spoke to Wojtyla about supernatural matters, and explained how Opus Dei had developed over the last few years: "The Holy Father was very pleased with what he heard. From time to time he would interrupt with some words of praise or simply to exclaim, 'You are a saint'. I know about this because I couldn't help noticing afterwards that the Father had a very pensive, almost sad look on his face. I asked him why. At first he refused to answer me. Then he told me what Pope Paul had said to him, and he said he had been overcome with shame and grief for his own sins, so much so that he had made a filial protest to the Pope: 'No, no! You do not know me, Your Holiness—I am just a poor sinner.' But Pope Paul had insisted, 'No, no—you are a saint'. At this the Founder, full of emotion, had replied, 'On this earth there is only one saint—the Holy Father'!"

Two years later, on March 28th, 1975, Escrivá had completed 50 years of priesthood. He spent the day, which fell on Good Friday, in prayer. "Fifty years have gone by, and I am still like a babbling child," wrote Escrivá. "I am just beginning, beginning again, as I do each day in my interior life. And it will be so to the end of my days? A glance backwards... What an immense panorama, so many sorrows, so many joys. But now all is joy, all joy...because experience teaches us that sorrow is the chiselling of the divine artist, who is eager to make of each one of us, of this shapeless mass that we are, a crucifix, a Christ, that *alter Christus* each one of us is called to be."

Three months later, Escrivá got up early as usual, made the usual half hour of prayer and celebrated Mass at about eight o'clock. About 9.30am he left for Castelgandolfo where he was due to hold one of his informal, family-style meetings at the Roman College of Our Lady. It was a hot day and during the ride Escrivá and his companions prayed the rosary but, shortly after arriving at their destination, Escrivá felt ill and they decided to return to Rome. When they arrived back at the Villa Tevere, Opus Dei's Roman headquarters, Escrivá entered the house and is said to have turned to Father Javier Echevarría saying: "Javi? I don't feel well." With those words, he collapsed on the floor and died peacefully beneath an image of the Madonna.

Msgr Alvaro del Portillo succeeded Escrivá in September 1975 and was received in audience by Pope Paul VI on March 5th, 1976. The former Giovanni Battista Montini declared that he was convinced he had known a saint. He also told del Portillo that he considered the founder of Opus Dei "one of the individuals in the history of the Church...and who responded to the gifts given by God with the most generosity". In another audience, on June 19th, 1978, he repeated these ideas and added that he had realized the extraordinariness of this figure in the history of the Church from the day he had first met him, in 1946.

Since Escrivá's death, at most hours of the day and evening, worshippers sit or kneel by the dark green marble slab of his tomb in a crypt under Opus Dei's headquarters at the Viale Bruno Buozzi. The inscription simply reads "El Padre" with a cross and his dates "Jan. 9, 1902" and "June 26, 1975". The worshippers bend to kiss the marble and place rosaries, crosses, or cards with Escrivá's portrait or a prayer for his intercession with God on their behalf. Following Escrivá's death, the cards were issued by groups devoted to advancing the cause of Escrivá's sainthood, a procedure officially opened by the Vatican in 1981, only six years after "El Padre's" death. Just 17 years after his death, the Opus Dei founder was beatified on May 17th, 1992.

On the day, Opus Dei marshalled a record crowd of nearly 300,000 (including 200 bishops) for the beatification. All of Rome's 60,000 hotel beds were booked months in advance, while two "floating hotels" were chartered to ferry wealthier members of Opus Dei from Spain, Escrivá's homeland. "With supernatural intuition," said Pope John Paul II in his homily, "Blessed Josemaría untiringly preached the universal call to holiness and apostolate."

Beatification makes a person a saint, and is the final step before canonization, which guarantees a place in paradise. Canonization can proceed quickly or take centuries, but, within the Catholic faith, beatification automatically draws a cult of sanctity. Until 19 October 2003, when Mother Teresa of Calcutta was beatified, Escrivá held the Vatican record for the quickest beatification for five centuries.

Accusations of favoritism towards Opus Dei were rife, following Escrivá's swift acceptance by the Vatican state. Normally, to assess a potential saint, the Vatican appoints "consultors" who come from the candidate's homeland. According to Woodward in *Newsweek*: "Eight of Escrivá's nine judges were Italian—a sign, say critics, that the congregation wanted to avoid Spanish theologians, many of whom are known to oppose Opus Dei. Also, Opus Dei has been accused of refusing to let outsiders see the material on which Escrivá's 'heroic virtues' were judged—an unprecedented act of secrecy, say priests familiar with the process."

Naturally, Opus Dei members are highly defensive when charges of favoritism are levelled against them. An important point to note is that, as regards the beatification and canonization of Escrivá, Msgr Carlo Colombo, a theological advisor and close friend of Pope Paul VI, has testified that Paul VI himself encouraged him (Colombo) to write a letter petitioning for the opening of the cause of beatification and canonization of the founder of Opus Dei. Furthermore, the success of Opus Dei in recruiting new members to the faith, compared with other movements that have not been quite as fruitful in recent years, would, naturally, lead senior Catholic leaders to want to progress Opus Dei's cause.

During the 20th century, the Catholic Church was in retreat

throughout the developed world. Opus Dei was one of the few organizations in that period to reverse the trend—not only among the traditional, poorer social groupings, but across the board, as Opus Dei managed to bring wealthier and educated, lapsed Catholics back into the fold as well. Any ruling power, in this case the papacy, would be foolish to ignore the results and influence of a section of its Church, which was proving successful where traditional or current ways of operating were falling. The Roman Catholic Church is a business like any other, but it collects souls as well as money for its cause. With Opus Dei proving the most successful Roman Catholic worldwide organization at present, it stands to reason that it should be rewarded—especially as its message is a traditional Roman Catholic one. Why ignore the message of Opus Dei?

In 1992, Postulator-General of Opus Dei, Flavio Capucci, wrote a stern letter to *The Times* (London) newspaper: "The forthcoming beatification of Opus Dei's founder, the Venerable Josemaría Escrivá, cannot be interpreted politically as a sign of Opus Dei's influence on the Holy See. Applying the logic of politics to this ecclesiastical act reveals a misunderstanding of the nature of the act itself... You give a misleading account of the background to the forthcoming beatification. Although the progress of the cause has been swift, this is principally because the case was remarkably clear, in 11,000 pages of evidence, including all the objections against the cause. Moreover, it is quite wrong to suggest that there was special influence in the Vatican. In fact, the cause of Msgr Escrivá was supported by the widest range of senior church figures of many nationalities, including, for example, Cardinal König of Austria, Cardinal Sin of the Philippines, and the late Archbishop Romero of El Salvador."

The Times was not the only newspaper receiving letters of indignation from senior Opus Dei figures. In a letter to the *International Herald Tribune* in 1992, Giuseppe Corigliano, the communications director of the prelature in Rome, told readers that there were over 6,000 letters backing Escrivá's candidature, including recommendations from 69 cardinals, 241 archbishops, and 987 bishops, more than one-third of the worldwide Catholic episcopate. "The process of beatification has heard 92 witnesses," he continued, "who testified under oath. They were selected by two tribunals appointed by church authorities. Not one member of Opus Dei formed part of these courts.

The majority of the 92 witnesses, who included four cardinals, four archbishops, and a good number of priests and religious leaders, did not belong to Opus Dei."

Humble individuals, all Opus Dei members, who came forward to report to the Vatican and describe some of Escrivá's "miracles", also helped these senior church figures. One such person was Spanish surgeon Manuel Nevado. In 2001, aged 69, Nevado assured the Vatican that his hands were crippled by overexposure to X-rays in the days when Spanish clinics were short of protective equipment. According to a report delivered to Vatican authorities, those hands were miraculously cured after he prayed for help from Escrivá. Nevado told the Vatican investigators that within 15 days of praying to Escrivá, his illness was cured. "The wounds disappeared and the hands were completely cured," he said. That cure, claimed Opus Dei at the time, provided some initial proof that Escrivá should be canonized.

In order to "win" canonization, the saint-to-be needs two miracles under their belt. The first, Nevado's hands, occurred in 2001, but then Opus Dei followers discovered another Escrivá miracle—this one occurred in June 1976. Members of a family of a Spanish Carmelite nun prayed for his heavenly intercession to cure her. "Sister Conception Rubio was on the verge of death," reports one Opus Dei member. "The Carmelite nun suffered from large tumors (one of which was the size of an orange) and other health complications: haemorrhages, ulcers, and hernias. One morning, however, after having prayed for Escrivá's intercession, she awoke completely cured, with no trace of the tumors anywhere in her body."

The Vatican states that on January 21st, 1982, "another tribunal to document a miracle attributed to the intercession of the Servant of God was created and presided over by Cardinal Enrique y Tarancon. The miracle had occurred in 1976 with the sudden cure of a Carmelite nun suffering from terminal cancer. On April 3rd, this tribunal was concluded and a certified copy of the proceedings was sent to the Congregation for the Causes of Saints in Rome."

"I lived with him for 22 years, and from the first day I met him, I could see that he was a saint," said one of his cardinals, Julián Herranz, following Escrivá's canonization in an interview in El Pais. "Perhaps that sounds too strong, too certain. But I saw repeated examples of his heroic faith and continuous union with God. The day

I met him, a young man who was living in our residence had died. He came into the room with all the sorrow of a father who had just lost his son. The suffering was reflected on his face. He got on his knees and kissed the young man on the forehead. We prayed a Response for the Dead, and, then, going out of the room, his face was transformed and he began to smile. And he said: 'I smiled because your brother has won the last battle. He has finished his life fulfilling the will of God.' His life reflected the human and divine dimensions of Christ, and made you fall in love with the humanity of Christ: '*perfectus Deus*' and '*perfectus homo*', perfect God and perfect man."

Escrivá's canonization was set for Sunday, October 6th 2002, in St Peter's Square. More than 350,000 people packed the square and the Via della Conciliazione for the proclamation. Among the gathered crowd, there were nearly 50 cardinals, archbishops, and priests, including Cardinal José Saraiva Martins, Prefect of the Congregation for the Causes of Saints; Cardinal Angelo Sodano, Vatican Secretary of State; Cardinal Antonio María Rouco Varela, Archbishop of Madrid; Cardinal Camillo Ruini, Vicar for Rome; Cardinal Joachim Meissner, and Cardinal Roger Etchegaray.

During Pope John Paul II's homily, he recalled that Josemaría Escrivá "allowed himself to be docilely guided by the Holy Spirit, convinced that the will of God could be accomplished only in this way... Basic Christian truth was a recurring theme in his preaching. He never ceased to invite his spiritual children to invoke the Holy Spirit so that...their relationship with God and their family, social and professional life were not separated but constituted one existence, 'holy and full of God'."

Following Mass, John Paul II greeted the pilgrims in the square in Italian, French, German, English, Spanish, Portuguese, and Polish. He then made his way across St Peter's Square and drove slowly down the Via della Conciliazione in an open car in order greet the travellers, who had come from more than 80 countries to see Escriva's canonization.

Despite Opus Dei's celebration of Escrivá's beatification and subsequent canonization, it was not a universally popular choice, and, unsurprisingly, caused some bitter conflicts within the Vatican. The Jesuit order is said to have mounted a fierce opposition campaign, while others alleged that evidence against the beatification was suppressed. The saintly leader known to many as "El Padre" or "The Founder" has been accused of vanity (reports allege he added "de Balaguer" to his name out of snobbery), fascism (due to his remarks about the Holocaust as well as his allegiance to Franco's regime), arrogance, and ambition.

Furthermore, there were reports that following Vatican II, Escrivá's hatred for the liturgical changes saw him consider a move into the Greek Orthodox Church. Reports allege that following Vatican II, Escrivá and his successor, Bishop Alvaro del Portillo, together with Father Echevarría, all went to Greece in 1966 to see whether he could bring Opus Dei into the Greek Orthodox Church. "When he came back from Greece," reported one of Escrivá's associates, "he told me the Orthodox were not for us as the congregations and the churches were very small." Flavio Capucci, Postulator-General of Opus Dei, does acknowledge Escrivá's trip to Greece, but says the Father had no intention of abandoning Rome (see Chapter Five).

These accusations contrast vastly with the image of Escrivá portrayed by his promoters: that of a combination of spirituality, charity, and temperance with a deep understanding of the problems of coping with a materialistic society.

Father Vladimir Feltzman had been a close friend of Escrivá, who became a father figure to him when Feltzman lived with him in the Opus Dei center in Rome, but even he felt the time wasn't right to turn his former mentor into a saint. "He was a wonderful man," said Feltzman of Escrivá, "and a very complicated man in many ways. Passionately committed to what he believed. Very strong in many ways and yet very affectionate... I was the spoilt one, you know, the kid, so I spent a lot of time with him in Rome."

However, Feltzman continues: "I became enemy number one because I said it's not the right time to do it [the beatification] because given his [Escrivá's] culture, given his approach to Hitler, who he couldn't really believe was as bad as he was...I mean he is right-wing politically in almost everything. I didn't think it was a great idea to canonize a guy like that who could be used by the Croatian extremists as a hero in what he did. Give it 50 years."

Msgr Luigi de Magistris, Titular Archbishop of Nova, at the Chiesa di S. Michele, agreed with Feltzman saying: "It seems to me totally ill advised to assume the responsibility of assessing his heroic virtue at a distance of only 14 years." He advised that "several decades" should pass to let passions cool.

Although Feltzman still praises Escrivá, in 1991 he wrote to Archbishop Luigi Barbarito, papal pronuncio in London, with a first-hand account of life with Escrivá. Two days later, Barbarito thanked Feltzman for his letter, promising he would forward it to "the competent authorities in Rome". Feltzman heard nothing back from Rome.

There are other former friends and colleagues who wanted to testify to the beatification committee about Escrivá's less attractive side. Miguel Fisac, an early Opus Dei numerary who joined in 1936 and left nearly 20 years later, remembers a man who "spoke well of no one," and who had so exalted a view of his mission that he was "completely convinced that he had been chosen by God to reform the Church". Fisac recalls that Escrivá spent millions of pesetas on luxuries in Opus Dei's central Roman home and comments: "During the time I knew him, I never saw him with any poor people." Fisac discovered that his anti-Escrivá testimony was ignored. "They knew my appraisal was going to be first hand and completely objective," said Fisac, "and I was not going to stop to think whether what I said favored or hindered the case."

Kenneth Woodward, the religious editor of *Newsweek* and Opus Dei critic, claimed that Opus Dei had sufficient influence on the tribunal to prevent any critics from testifying. "It seemed as if the whole thing was rigged. They [Escrivá's supporters] were given priority, and the whole thing was rushed through." Woodward also accuses Escrivá of being an "unexceptional spirit", "derivative" and often "banal" in his thoughts.

Woodward continues this disappointment in Escrivá's beatification in *The Helpers of God: How the Catholic Church Makes Its Saints*, where he describes how he had appealed to John Paul to stop Escrivá's beatification, and claims that the Pope had not been informed that, firstly, two negative votes out of the nine cast by the Vatican court handling the beatification process were never presented to him, and that, secondly, while 1,300 bishops and cardinals from all over the world had written to the Vatican with positive statements about Escrivá, only 128 of them had actually met him in person. Woodward further reported that Opus Dei members had put hundreds of bishops under financial pressure, threatening a cut-off of Opus Dei funds unless they submitted positive testimony. Opus Dei denies all these claims.

Another witness was Maria del Carmen Tapia, who worked with Escrivá in Spain before going on to run Opus Dei's female section in Venezuela. She, too, had reasons to complain about Opus Dei. Tapia had been summoned to Rome in 1965 for breaching discipline (this included allowing women to go to the Opus Dei priest of their choice), and was kept in Rome with no contact with the outside world. At her hearing, Tapia claims Escrivá shouted: "You are a wicked woman! A lost woman! Mary Magdalene was a sinner, but you? You are a seductress! Leave my priests alone! Hear me well! Whore! Sow!"

Tapia's book, *Beyond the Threshold: A Life in Opus Dei*, was originally published in Spanish, and has been translated into German, French, Portuguese, English, and Italian, but Opus Dei's leadership has forbidden even the mention of her book within the Work.

Another ex-Opus Dei member, John Roche, also had complaints about Opus Dei. In a paper Roche wrote in 1982, while at Linacre College, Oxford, UK, he claimed that: "the ethos of Opus Dei was entirely self-centered, sectarian, and totalitarian, and that it was misleading the Church about important aspects of its character."

Also in 1982, the leader of the Catholic Church in England, Cardinal Basil Hume, issued public guidelines for Opus Dei in his diocese. Disturbed about Opus Dei's recruitment methods and secrecy in Westminster, he instructed Opus Dei not to recruit anyone under 18, to ensure that parents were informed when young people joined, not to exert pressure on people to join, to respect the freedom of members to leave, and to allow members to choose spiritual directors freely. He also required Opus Dei's activities to carry a "clear indication of their sponsorship and management". Hume was a rarity, proving to be one of the few cardinals across the globe to produce such guidelines.

"It's not simply that Escrivá and Opus Dei have a legion of critics and a history of dubious practises," writes John Martin in *The Remnant* newspaper, "it's the startling pace John Paul II has followed in exalting this mysterious shepherd and his multinational flock through a series of breathtakingly honorific ten-year milestones—granting Opus Dei Personal Prelature status (1982), beatifying Escrivá (1992), and now (2002) declaring this dynamic, but disturbing son of Spain worthy to rub elbows with such giants as John the Baptist, Peter and Paul, Joan of Arc, Thomas More, Therese of Lisieux, and Christina the Astonishing. And truly, if there's anything more astonishing than St Christina, who climbed trees, hid in ovens, and even flew into the rafters of a church to avoid sinful human contamination, it's the record speed with which Escrivá (1902–75) will have won his heavenly spurs: a mere 27 years from coffin to choir."

Some Opus Dei sympathizers, reports Kenneth Woodward in *Newsweek*, like retired Cardinal Silvio Oddi who served the Vatican for decades in key posts, believe the push to make Escrivá a saint has done Opus Dei "more harm than good". Although bishops are reluctant to criticize Opus Dei openly, says Oddi, many are "very displeased" by the rush to judgement, and see "no need for the immediate beatification of their founder". Again, the alleged conspiratorial nature of Escrivá's canonization mean that attacks and accusations that Opus Dei continues to seek power and influence is still occurring—can the organization defend itself?

"The spotlight always falls on those who have prominent positions in society, business, politics, or academia," argues Cardinal Julián Herranz in an interview with *El Pais*. "It never falls on the multitude of members of Opus Dei whose activities are unremarkable: professionals, artists, workers, farmers. The second reason is that some people don't understand the political and professional independence of the members of the Prelature. I have always found the diversity of political views in Opus Dei remarkable... In Opus Dei there is great freedom in everything, which is a matter of opinion. Yes, there is a common denominator shared by all the members of Opus Dei, but the common denominator is something John Paul II has emphasized greatly: the mandate of the Church's social teachings to defend life, marriage, freedom of education, the rights of parents, ethics in economic affairs, and the equality of persons. There we all must agree— but not just members of Opus Dei: all Catholics."

Despite Herranz's valiant defense of his Church, there are still others who fear Opus Dei's strength within the Vatican. "Opus Dei's real power is inside the Vatican bureaucracy," writes Kenneth Woodward in *Newsweek*, "where it has replaced the Jesuits in political, though not intellectual, leverage. Several ranking cardinals, and at least one of the Pope's personal secretaries, Father Stanislaw

Dziwisz, from Cracow, are either Opus Dei card-carrying 'cooperators' or, like the Pope himself, strong sympathizers of Opus Dei. Opus Dei is well represented in the Vatican's public-relations apparatus. John Paul II's press spokesman is a member. So are the officials who supervise the media-conscious Pope's liaisons with TV." Dziwisz, incidentally, is definitely not a member of Opus Dei.

Accusations across the internet are often harsh and vitriolic in their criticisms of Opus Dei, calling the movement a "malevolent force…vying for control of the Church", and charging Opus Dei with being part of a silent *coup* and "seizing control of key departments, controlling beatifications, appointment of bishops and press/public relations". These are strong charges and completely unproven ones at that. Yet, according to Opus Dei, the only members of Opus Dei in the Roman Curia at the time of writing are as follows:

- Mr Joaquín Navarro-Valls (Papal Spokesman)
- Cardinal Julián Herranz (President, Pontifical Council for Interpretation of Legislative Texts)
- Mr Gió María Poles (Personnel Manager of the Vatican)
- Fr José Luís Gutiérrez (Relator, Congregation for the Causes of the Saints)
- Fr Miguel Delgado (Pontifical Council for the Laity)
- Fr Francesco di Muzio (Congregation for the Evangelization of Peoples)
- Fr Osvaldo Neves (official, Secretariat of State)
- Fr Stefano Migliorelli (official, Secretariat of State)
- Fr Mauro Longhi (Congregation for the Clergy)
- Fr Ignacio Carrasco (Chancellor, Pontifical Academy for Life)
- Mgsr Celso Morga Iruzubeita (Congregation for the Clergy)

Of these men, only the first three, Navarro-Valls, Herranz, and Poles are in high-profile jobs (though it should be noted that within the Church, "personnel" is not deemed as particularly important). Looking at the facts, in total there are only ten policy-level members working in the Curia out of 500 such posts. This means that Opus Dei "commands" only two percent of the Curia—hardly the act of a group that is supposedly "vying for control" and achieving its aims. Furthermore, the total number of those working in the Curia is approaching 2,700.

As Andrew Soane, from the communications office in London, said: "No member of Opus Dei is currently a superior or decision maker within any of the 'Congregations'."

An *Irish Times* article headlined "This Is Why the Holy Father Receives No Negative Information" pointed out that, along with Navarro-Valls, Msgr Celso Morga Iruzubeita (Congregation for the Clergy), Msgr Julián Herranz (President, Pontifical Council for Interpretation of Legislative Texts), Msgr Fernando Ocariz (Consultor with the Congregation for the Doctrine of the Faith) and Msgr Cormac Burke (Sacra Rota) were all Opus Dei members. Of these five, Ocariz is not actually in the Curia but a Consultor who is brought in from time to time, Burke returned some years ago and lives in Kenya and, while Navarro-Valls, Herranz and Morga Iruzubeita are confirmed members.

Those who mistrust Opus Dei feel that its influence within the Curia is still growing, thanks to the generous nature of Pope John Paul II. In the first 19 years of his papacy, he held six consistories in which he created 137 cardinals. One of these consistories, on November 26th, 1994, saw Pope John Paul II create some 30 cardinals. As of 2004, there were 147 members of the College of Cardinals, 114 of whom were created by John Paul II, and from the start of his pontificate to 2004, the Holy Father named over 2,500 of the world total of nearly 4,200 bishops. Yet, as stated earlier, Opus Dei makes up only two percent of the Curia and has only two cardinals within the College of Cardinals— Cardinal Juan Luis Cipriani Thorne of Lima, Peru, and Cardinal Julián Herranz (who works in the Curia—see above).

On March 14th, 2004 John Paul II's pontificate overtook that of Leo XIII as the longest in the history of the papacy, other than Pius IX and St Peter. His death in April 2005 was hardly a surprise; nor was the cardinals' choice of successor—Cardinal Joseph Ratzinger of Germany, who chose to be known by the name of Pope Benedict XVI.

In the lead-up to the vote within the Curia, conspiracy theories abounded that Opus Dei would assert its influence to get a candidate who would be "one of its own". Jeff Israely, in *Time* magazine, wrote "Opus Dei, which boasts a core group of highly accomplished lay professionals and well-placed clergy, is known to have the access to privately influence scarlet-clad princes of the Church". And, according to Giancarlo Zizola, a Vatican political commentator:

"Opus Dei is the only group well organized enough, working within the power structure of the Roman Curia, that can 'make a difference' in how cardinals vote."

The question of Opus Dei's influence within the new papacy will, no doubt, soon become apparent in the coming years. Once again, however, Zizola's theory assumes that members of Opus Dei all think the same way and are somehow conspiring in something. Again, this relates back to the issue of "freedom" discussed earlier in the book—Opus Dei insists that its members are free, and it appears that the influence of Opus Dei among the cardinals is consistently exaggerated. Church secrecy renders a precise answer unknowable.

Furthermore, all the cardinals who voted in the conclave to select their new Pope were bound by a vow of silence on all matters related to their choice before, during, and after their sequestered election inside the Sistine Chapel. Any devices that could record or transmit audio or video are forbidden during the conclave: "It is specifically prohibited to the Cardinal electors, for the entire duration of the election, to receive newspapers or periodicals of any sort, to listen to the radio, or to watch television," say the Vatican statutes.

Although predicting Opus Dei's influence is hard to gauge under the new regime, the signs are that it is business as usual. Under Pope John Paul II, Ratzinger was Prefect of the Congregation for the Doctrine of Faith for nearly 25 years, which meant that, in effect, he served as the guardian of orthodoxy. Ratzinger also had the broad authority to punish wayward theologians and to rule on a number of aspects of church life. The German-born prelate was viewed as John Paul II's right-hand man—the defender and promoter of an increasingly unbending orthodoxy, and known as "God's Rottweiler".

As the new Pope stood on the balcony at St Peter's Basilica in the Vatican, in front of the crowds, he said: "The Cardinals have elected me, a simple, humble worker in the vineyard of the Lord. The fact that the Lord can work and act even with insufficient means consoles me and above all I entrust myself to your prayers."

Twenty years ago, in February 1985, an article on the papacy in *Time* magazine stated: "Without doubt the most influential man in John Paul's Curia is Joseph Cardinal Ratzinger, 57, the German-born prefect of the Congregation of the Faith and the Pope's theological watchdog. Though Ratzinger and John Paul are not close personally, they see eye to eye on theology othordoxy, and the Pope respects the one-time professor's intellectual skills. Extremely hard working, articulate, and reserved, Ratzinger was a progressive adviser at Vatican II. Disillusioned with its aftermath, he turned conservative, and now says, 'Not all valid councils have proven, when tested by the facts of history, to have been useful.'"

His stringent views are ones that are echoed within Opus Dei, which means that the organization will continue to be accepted within the Catholic Church and, more importantly, will continue to have papal support under Ratzinger's papacy. However, Ratzinger's elevation to Pope is seen by many as a temporary measure to fulfil the desire for a brief pontificate. It is felt that, at 78, he will not hold the title for years to come, like his predecessor. When his prelate ends, a newcomer could change the political balance of power within the Vatican, but, for now, it appears that there will be few changes.

"In my name, and with the certainty that I am expressing the sentiments of the men and women who make up the Prelature of Opus Dei," said Bishop Javier Echevarría, the Opus Dei Prelate on hearing the result of the papal election, "I assure Benedict XVI of our fullest union both with him and with his teachings: a deep communion. The new Pope is well acquainted with the Prelature's mission and knows he can count on the cheerful efforts of the priests and lay people who form part of it in order to serve the Church, which was St Josemaría Escrivá's only ambition. Along with our union with him, I also want to transmit to him my deep filial affection, joined to the prayer and affection of all the faithful of Opus Dei... I am also struck, as is only natural, by the Church's marvellous continuity, so clearly reflected in the joy of the People of God at the election of Peter's new successor."

Before Ratzinger's election, those who believed that Opus Dei would make its influence felt also believed that Pope John Paul II's successor would come from an Opus Dei "stronghold" like South America. It was not to be. Again, the theorists who insist that Opus Dei runs the Vatican and controls papal elections have been proved wrong. The conspiracy theories have again been disproved.

No matter how strong Opus Dei's influence within the Curia is believed to be, it was up to the 120 or so voting-age (under 80 years old) cardinals alone who elected the new Pope. When the conclave appointed Pope Benedict XVI to lead the world's 1.1 billion Catholics,

John Paul's influence was still considerable. The former Pope had appointed 115 of those 120 cardinals eligible to elect the new Pope, all with an eye to enforcing his conservative stance on issues like abortion, the role of women in the Church, homosexuality, and bioethics. Ratzinger proved the worthy candidate in one of the fastest conclaves—it lasted just under 24 hours.

Before Pope John Paul II's death, Father John Wauck, a Chicago native and Opus Dei priest (and the brother-in-law of KGB spy and Opus Dei member Robert Hanssen—see Chapter Seven) stated that Opus Dei was not lobbying for a particular candidate. However, he did concede that the group's members, like the other church factions, would use their access to cardinals to push their agendas. "Whether you want to call it politics or not, Opus Dei would have influence in that way," Wauck says. "If you're a cardinal and you think highly of Opus Dei, their approval of someone will be a point in his favor."

John L. Allen Jr, writing for the *National Catholic Reporter* stated: "Opus Dei is theologically and politically conservative, and hence in favor of today's Church. Stop. *Nec plus ultra*—there's no more beyond, no conspiracy, no dark plot." So how does Allen explain the rise of Opus Dei? "They're hungry. Opus is in a stage of development of every new movement in the Church in which signs of favor are important, and hence (consciously or not) they hustle after them in ways that most established communities don't... They're filling a vacuum. I know people who have turned down offers to work in the Curia, in part because they have bigger fish to fry, in part because they don't want to investigate their colleagues... It's part of the larger phenomenon of disengagement from the institution on the Catholic left; disenchanted progressives too often like to pretend that the Vatican doesn't exist, preferring to 'do their own thing'. It's understandable, but this retreat creates a void that groups such as Opus Dei and the Legionaries are only too happy to fill."

Allen dismisses the Jesuits' fears as no more than paranoia and concludes that "rather than demonizing Opus Dei, progressives need to deepen their theological reflection on the key issues facing Catholicism. They need to stay engaged with institutional politics, however distasteful and discouraging the effort may sometimes be. The battle for public opinion in the Church will be won with arguments, not accusations."

Allen cannot win everyone over. A letter to *New Oxford Review* by Grover Corcoran, whose son-in-law was a member of "The Work", said: "Opus Dei is not a conservative organization, it is a chameleon organization. Opus Dei people are conservative when they are among conservatives, but liberal when among liberals—whatever serves Opus Dei's purpose of garnering influence, favorable publicity, money, and power."

No matter what Allen argues, there is no denying that Opus Dei had close ties with John Paul II's papacy. Both strongly suggested a hankering after the absolutes of times past with their unequivocal one-true-Church certainties in practise and belief. "The 1980s marked a historic turning point for Roman Catholicism," comments Connor Cruise O'Brien in *The Times* (London). "Beneath all of the gloss and spectacle of the papacy, beyond the wealth, power, and influence of the Holy See, a profound struggle is taking shape, one that is of crucial importance to the Church's 810 million members—and to many not in its fold. At stake is the future direction of a strong, dynamic, yet deeply perturbed institution." Now, this institution with Pope Benedict XVI continuing Pope John Paul II's work, is still one that Opus Dei is at the heart of, but, contrary to the beliefs of many conspiracy theorists, it is not one that Opus Dei is in control of.

Murders at the Vatican—the Power Struggle Continues?

Opus Dei has refused to comment publicly on the deaths, or Estermann's involvement with them. It seems evident, however, that despite his denials Estermann was an Opus Dei member, given his recruitment efforts, his wife's close relationship with Opus, and the unanimous belief among the Guard that Estermann belonged to Opus. An insider said that this caused Estermann's promotion to Commander to be blocked: "Many people in the Vatican feel that Opus Dei has got its finger in too many pies. There's so much intrigue in the Vatican, so many factions..."

Mark Fellows, The Catholic Family News, *November 3rd, 2003*

Myths concerning Opus Dei and Vatican politics continue to rumble on, as the accusations of Opus Dei being part of a conspiracy to control the Holy See have become wilder and more far-fetched. One such case was "The Estermann Affair," which sought to prove that Colonel Alois Estermann's murder was not, as was generally decided, the murderous act of Cedric Tornay, a disgruntled Swiss Guard, but instead—attributing a more sinister undertone—part of the power struggle between Opus Dei and its rival "forces" within the Vatican. So, what really occurred?

On May 4th, 1998, Estermann was appointed commander of the Swiss Guard, the Pope's personal army. The Swiss German, and alleged Opus Dei member, told his friends that he detected the hand of God in his promotion, despite a mysterious seven-month decision-making delay following the retirement of the previous chief. During that seven-month period Estermann had been acting commander.

"It's an honor," Estermann had told the Swiss newspaper *Le Matin*. "These are big responsibilities. But behind this choice, I see the will of God, who will help me accomplish my service well...My wife is happier than I am because she doesn't have to do the work." Estermann joined the Swiss Guard in 1980, and had come to Pope John Paul II's notice when, during the 1981 assassination attempt on the pontiff, legend has it that Estermann jumped onto the moving Pope mobile and shielded him with his own body. However, later reports have stated that the shooting happened too quickly for anyone to shield the Pope—yet the fable remains.

An elite force, Swiss Guards must be Roman Catholic males of Swiss nationality, who have completed basic training with the Swiss military to obtain certificates of good conduct. Furthermore, in order to join the organization, all recruits must be aged between 19 and 30 and at least 174 cm (5ft 9in) tall. While much of the work of the present-day guards is ceremonial, the Swiss Guard is responsible for the security at the Apostolic Palace, the papal apartment, and the four main entrances to the Vatican. They are also in charge of the Pope's physical safety when he travels outside Vatican City.

The newly appointed chief, Estermann, was an 18-year veteran of the force and one of the few non-noblemen to head the 100-member Swiss Guard. He lived with his wife, Gladys Meza Romero, herself notable for being Venezuela's first policewoman. The pair had met at the Dante Alighieri Institute of Rome, where they both studied Italian and, by 1998, were celebrating 15 years of marriage. However, Estermann's jubilation at being appointed commander was to be short-lived.

Hours after Estermann's appointment, shortly before 9pm, Pope John Paul II was resting in his nearby quarters when the sound of gunshots rang out in the Vatican. A wife of one of the Swiss Guards heard the noises coming from the Estermann's Vatican apartment and swiftly raised the alarm.

The scene was one of unexpected carnage. The colonel was discovered stretched out on the stone floor, blood seeping from a hole in his left cheek; next to him, a telephone handset swung slowly on its chord. Gladys was slumped against a wall. A few feet away lay Cedric Tornay, a young French-speaking vice-corporal. Blood trickled from his mouth and the back of his head. For everyone at the Vatican, the scenario was clear. The killer, Tornay, 23, one of Estermann's subordinates, had shot the Estermanns before turning the weapon, a Swiss-made 9mm, on himself.

Msgr Alois Jehle, the Swiss Guard chaplain, left the Estermanns' flat to inform the Pope, but due to Vatican immunity, the crime scene was never inspected or examined by members of the Italian police. The affair was then passed over to Cardinal Angelo Sodano, the Vatican Secretary of State.

Speed and utter secrecy characterized the removal of the bodies from the flat. Disguising the bodies as patients, the Estermanns were transported to the Vatican Gemelli hospital in a white ambulance bearing the Vatican number plate SCV 424. SCV stands for "State of Vatican City"—those in Italy with a penchant for Vatican humor refer to SCV as "*Se Cristo Vedesse*" ("If Christ could see…").

Within 12 hours, Vatican spokesperson Joaquín Navarro-Valls held a press conference: "We are still waiting for the autopsy results, but with what we already know we can begin to put together what happened. A few minutes after 9pm a woman, the wife of a Swiss Guard, heard strange noises in the apartment of recently appointed Commander Alois Estermann. She entered the hallway, saw the door half-opened, entered, and discovered the bodies of Estermann, his wife Gladys, and corporal Cedric Tornay. Terrified, she immediately sounded the alarm and called an ambulance. The authorities of the Holy See immediately sent two doctors to examine the bodies. The investigators found one only firearm, under Tornay's body. It was a regulation weapon belonging to Tornay and registered in his name, a 9-calibre Stig 75 that holds six bullets, five of which had been discharged. We do not know in which direction the shots went off; we are still waiting for the results of the autopsies and the ballistics study. The one thing we do know is that two bullets were found in Estermann's body and another projectile with some parts of human material was lodged in the ceiling."

The Estermanns' coffins were placed in front of a high altar in a packed St Peter's Church in the Vatican Basilica—a rare honour for laymen (and women). For anyone wishing to pay their condolences, it was a dramatic scene, thanks to the ancient church's awesome size and the pervasive golden light that bathes every corner of the sanctuary. Here, Estermann's Swiss Guard emblems, his sword and white-plumed silver helmet, rested on his casket as Sodano conducted the service in front of all the assembled dignitaries who had come to honor Estermann. In his homily, Sodano said: "In times like these, we feel above all the need to be silent." Prayers for the repose of the pair's souls in purgatory continued for several days.

In contrast, Tornay's coffin was denied any of his Swiss Guard military regalia and was privately sent off to a lowly chapel, the small church of St Anne, in a dark corner on the border of Vatican City. Inside, a line of Swiss Guards, some of them visibly emotional, allowed a gap for the space where Tornay usually stood. Outside, there was an overflow crowd of confused and mourning friends. The Pope's only fleeting public reference to Tornay during this time was to his coming appearance before the Lord on the Day of Judgement, "to whose mercy" he entrusted him.

On February 8th, 1999, one year after the murders, lawyer Nicola Picardi, the Vatican's promoter of justice, presented the "facts" to examining Judge Gianluigi Marrone. The Papal See insisted that on May 4th, 1998, Tornay arrived at the Estermann flat in the Swiss Guard barracks in Vatican City, carrying his regulation gun. He entered the flat and shot Commander Estermann twice while he was on the telephone. Then, turning to Gladys Romero, he fired a third shot, which missed, but he killed her with the fourth. He then knelt down and turned the gun on himself. The Vatican then announced the matter "closed".

"The most probable hypothesis, and already more than a hypothesis, is that of a gesture of madness born in the mind of a person who was convinced of not being sufficiently considered in the guards," Navarro-Valls told the gathered journalists at the time.

The Pope's spokesman went on to suggest that this "moment of madness" was caused by Tornay's fury at being passed over for a decoration. Furthermore, Navarro-Valls added, Tornay, who had been on the force three years, was bitter about a written reprimand from Estermann on February 12th for not having returned to barracks by the midnight curfew. Navarro-Valls also reported that Tornay had recently broken up with his Italian girlfriend, and had complained on the previous Monday about not being among the guardsmen, who were to be honored by the Pope in a ceremony for three years' service in the Guard.

However, it has been alleged that a host of testimonies about the personality of Tornay has been misrepresented to fit the Vatican story of "madness". Even Colonel Buchs, Tornay's commander before Estermann, said to journalists at the time, "this action [of Cedric] remains incomprehensible, so much the more that he was a young man full of vitality and interests, in harmony with his colleagues, and who found Rome to his liking..." Yet, despite Buch's testimony, Tornay was branded an insane killer.

If Tornay was insane, or indeed a drug addict (much has been made of the traces of marijuana found in his body following his post-mortem), his promotion to vice-corporal within the Swiss Guard is difficult to explain. Tornay had served in the Guard for over three years, and his responsibilities as vice-corporal included being in charge of all the guards deployed in the Apostolic Palace and monitoring St Anne's gate, the key entry point into Vatican territory. Whatever the truth about Tornay's character, it is unlikely that anything will be discovered as the Vatican forbids current members of the Swiss Guard to discuss Estermann, Tornay, or the murders.

Navarro-Valls went on to describe how John Paul II, whose official apartments are in a building about 100m (100yds) from the living quarters occupied by the Estermanns, was awake when the shootings occurred. The Pope was informed almost immediately, explained Navarro-Valls. "You could see that he was touched, he was visibly sad," the spokesman said. "The Holy Father loved him [Estermann] particularly. He remembered the famous 13th of May, 1981 [the date of the attempted assassination on Pope John Paul II]."

"The speed with which Navarro presented the Vatican's version of events led some to charge a rush to judgment," argues John L. Allen Jr at the *National Catholic Reporter*. "It should be recalled, however, that in September 1978, when Pope John Paul I died suddenly, the Vatican came under heavy criticism for not offering an explanation quickly, and Navarro obviously wanted to be more responsive. Nevertheless, rumors spread about Opus Dei connections, of a homosexual affair gone wrong, even of Estermann being a former spy for the Stasi, the East German secret police."

The reason for the media speculation came not only from Navarro-Valls' swift response when he reported to the journalists, but also from inconsistencies that the media were slowly discovering and discussing. There were unanswered questions. Were the murder victims both Opus Dei members? Was this a lovers' tiff and, if so, who were the lovers? Gladys and Tornay? Estermann and Tornay? Also, thanks to Vatican protocol, the Italian police were denied access to the scene, and the Vatican allegedly refused to accept help from

Italian investigators. Forensic experts did the autopsies in secret after first swearing never to speak of it again. With information and facts "blocked" by the Vatican, the media were naturally curious, and conspiracy theories were swiftly developed.

Post-mortems were quickly carried out by Vatican pathologists and the "closure" report, *Bollettino* 55/99, made much of traces of a cannabis metabolite present in Tornay's urine but not in the blood. This, it was claimed, led to "loss of insight", giving Tornay another motive, although the amount was far too small to indicate a large intake of cannabis and the effect, if any, would have been to calm aggressive impulses.

As a result of the Vatican's secrecy, journalist John Follain, who covered the Vatican for Reuters News Agency and was also the *Sunday Times* correspondent in Rome, was encouraged to try and bypass Navarro's stonewalling to investigate further. In so doing, Follain felt he had discovered some suggestive facts. For example, he claimed that a murderous hatred exists between German and French speakers in the Swiss Guard, and asserted that Tornay was a jilted lover of Estermann, who had moved on to another guard. Follain also said that Pope John Paul II had delayed the commander's appointment for several months because he was aware of Estermann's homosexual tendencies.

Follain's investigation inferred that Estermann had married early in his career (the implication being that had he remained unmarried he would never progress in the Swiss Guard). Follain went on to imply that Estermann was a promiscuous sodomite who preyed on the young soldiers and had a two-year affair with Tornay before ending it. There is no proof of these allegations.

Follain also alleged that Estermann wasn't the only bully within the Swiss Guard and claimed that young soldiers were regularly preyed upon by senior Vatican priests. Massimo Lacchei, an Italian writer of many fictitious novels, is quoted as saying: "I see the Swiss Guard as a kind of hot-house, whose flowers are picked by homosexual bishops and cardinals. People in the Vatican tell me that's how the Guards supplement their tiny wages."

Naturally, not only is this unproven, but it was also a story the Vatican were not keen to propagate. Off the record, according to journalist Peter Stanford: "they [the Vatican] tell of anything but a loyal and faithful servant of the Pope. Tornay was undisciplined, kept late hours, used soft drugs, and screwed around..."

The version of a heterosexual Tornay differs wildly with Fabio Croce's theory, who follows Follain's path of a homosexual affair being at the root of these deaths. Croce, a publisher, writer, and gay-rights activist in Rome, has written an account of the affair in his book *Delitto In Vatican: La Verita (Crime in the Vatican: The Truth)*. The book details a long affair between Tornay and Estermann, which Croce claims started soon after the two met, in August 1995. Once Tornay joined the Guard, he became Estermann's lover, as Mrs Estermann was away in her native Venezuela much of the time.

Croce theorizes that problems arose in 1997 when Estermann was in line to succeed Colonel Ronand Buchs as the commander of the Guard. The reason behind the seven- to eight-month delay in Estermann getting the post was because the Vatican had told Estermann to dump Tornay. Unable to live with this rejection, Tornay committed the murders and then killed himself, according to Croce.

Croce's allegations fail to take into account the "suspect" suicide note Tornay supposedly sent to his mother. Those investigating the crime pointed out that not only did the suicide note include a precise, but incorrect, reckoning of the time he had spent in the Swiss Guard but also, for the first time ever, he had addressed her by using her maiden name.

These weren't the only discrepancies. Tornay used different paper from usual; he had dated the letter "4.05.98", yet he usually wrote the month in full and, according to sources, never used a zero to delineate the first nine months of the year. He refered to Estermann as "Lieutenant Colonel" when he must have known Estermann was now Colonel—if, of course, he was really writing a suicide note hours before taking his life. Furthermore, he called his sister "Melinda" when he always referred to her as "Dada". Finally, to confirm all these suspect suicide note theories, writing experts engaged by Tornay's mother confirmed that her son did not write the letter.

As a result, experts concluded the note was a forgery and part of a cover-up, but, strangely, the note also referred to an investigation which Tornay was carrying out into the activities of Opus Dei. This seems a strange footnote.

According to Peter Stanford, in the *Independent on Sunday*:

"Estermann attended its meetings [Opus Dei] and some suggest that he was the close friend and protégé of Navarro-Valls, another pawn in Opus Dei's ambitious plan to have its men (it is an organization with little time for strong-minded women) in all key Vatican posts. So why would a Vatican cover-up of the deaths point an accusing finger at Opus Dei? Might it be that there are two opposing camps within the Holy See—the gay priests having a swinging good time and the austere Opus Dei operatives trying to purge them? Each could have seen an opportunity to disgrace the other in the deaths of Tornay and the Estermanns."

This theory ignores a further allegation, first suggested by the *Berliner Kurier* newspaper, which claimed that Estermann was a Stasi spy, planted in Rome in the 1980s by the East German spymaster, Markus Wolf. Naturally, Navarro-Valls was called upon to comment on the accusations: "The hypothesis is not even being considered." He added: "This is not the first time untruths have been aired about an honest man." The Vatican and Navarro-Valls' statement did little to quell the debates and issues being raised, as conflicting reports from a whole host of former secret agents raised as many questions as they cast doubts. As yet, nothing has been proved with regard to the *Berliner Kurier*'s allegations.

The consensus for many conspiracy theorists seems to be that the deaths of the Estermanns and Tornay was indeed due to a power struggle between all the various factions within the Vatican.

One faction was within the Swiss Guard itself. In his article "Bloody Lies in the Vatican", which was posted on the European Institute for Protestant Studies website, Protestant historian Dr Clive Gillis discusses the divisions within the Swiss Guard between the French and German contingents, which Follain had also identified. The French Swiss, like Tornay, were considered "inferior bumpkins," and Gillis infers that the French were "ruthlessly" discriminated against, given extra duties and unpleasant tasks, and the worst deals on duty rosters.

John Cornwell, a Vatican expert and journalist for the *Sunday Times* surmised: "It appeared that the two men [Estermann and Tornay] were in a sexual relationship and that the elder, Col Estermann, was a bullying and proselytizing member of Opus Dei who wanted to turn his charges into 'soldier monks'." But was Estermann truly a member of Opus Dei? All the theories surrounding Tornay and Estermann appear to depend on Estermann's involvement in the organization.

Ex-Opus Dei member Father Vladimir Feltzman said in one interview: "Estermann would be of great interest to Opus Dei. Escrivá's view was that if you had the head of an organization, you had everything. With Estermann in its grip, Opus Dei would have been able to find out how the Pope was, and who he saw from day to day. It would be privy to quite a few secrets about the cardinals, their health, that kind of thing. And among the cardinals is John Paul's successor. Never forget that, for Opus Dei, knowledge is power. It would be able to get anyone into the Vatican; the guards wouldn't breathe a word. You have access, you have freedom." Yet Opus Dei denies Estermann was a member.

Division within the Vatican was also suggested by a group of disaffected priests from within the Vatican, just one year after the murders, in 1999. The claims were printed by a small Milan publisher in a book entitled *Blood Lies in the Vatican*, and the authors identify themselves anonymously as "the disciples of truth"—their identities are still not widely known. Within the book, the authors allege that evidence was tampered with in order to fit the hypothesis that the killings were the result of Tornay's "moment of madness".

This conspiracy theory also brings Opus Dei into the frame—again making much of the supposed power struggle between Opus Dei and other factions within the Vatican. A report by Philip Willan in the *Guardian* in 1999 describes the book, explaining how, according to the anonymous group, "Estermann was the victim of a struggle for control of the Swiss Guard—which had been in charge of papal security for the past five centuries—between the secretive, traditionalist Catholic movement Opus Dei and a Masonic power faction ensconced in the Curia."

"In the Vatican, there are those who maintain that vice-corporal Tornay was attacked after coming off duty and dragged into a cellar," the book claims. Tornay was then "suicided" with a silenced 7mm pistol, and his duty revolver was allegedly used to kill the Estermanns in their Vatican apartment. Following the murder, his body was said to have been dumped in the Estermann's flat to make the triple killing look like a murder-suicide. Further rumors brought up in the book insist that all three victims were killed by a commando unit of three people: a killer and two accomplices. The book also claims there is a witness, who saw the commando unit, but who refuses to testify. All this makes for a best-selling novel, and is, as yet, unproven.

Blood Lies in the Vatican also alleges that both Estermann and his wife, who worked at the Venezuelan embassy to the Holy See, were actively engaged in secret international financial deals for the benefit of Opus Dei. The book argues that the Vatican's investigation was superficial and tailored to coincide with the reconstruction offered immediately after the event by Navarro-Valls, himself a member of Opus Dei. A book filled with theories, it also examines the financial scandals that have tarnished the Vatican's reputation and explores the 1982 Banco Ambrosiano affair. It claims that the arrest warrant for Archbishop Paul Marcinkus was also a part of the power struggle between Freemasons and Opus Dei, which came back to haunt Estermann and cost him and his wife their lives nearly two decades later.

The case refuses to go away. As of 2005, the French lawyer Jacques Verges and his colleague Luc Brossollet, acting for Tornay's mother, insist that they will file the murder claim in Switzerland. "We have faced years of stubborn deafness from the Vatican," Brossollet told the *Observer* newspaper in January 2005. "Cedric Tornay was Swiss, so it is proper to bring the case before a court in Switzerland." Once Verges has filed the murder claim in Martigny, Switzerland, where Tornay is buried, a judge will set a date, probably before the summer of 2005, for a hearing.

So far, Opus Dei has not commented publicly on the deaths, or on Estermann's involvement with them—apart from to stress that Estermann was not a member of Opus Dei; even though he attended the occasional prayer meeting, the organization emphasizes that this did not mean he was a full member. Furthermore, there is no reason for Opus Dei to comment on the deaths of Estermann and Tornay— as giving a statement could give some kind of credence to these ludicrous claims of commando units within the Vatican. The theories about Estermann continue—he is a convenient pawn in the conspiracist's chessboard. By claiming him as Opus Dei, the theories behind his death and Cedric Tornay's involvement are given a new meaning. To the critics, if Opus Dei is involved, then, obviously, something more sinister is at play here.

John Follain has commented: "Even today, the conspiracy of silence and refusal to admit any responsibility prevails...the Vatican's inquiry remains closed, the files still locked away." The Pope has ultimate control over his archive—this has always been the case—and to this day, no material dated after 1922 and relating to the popes can be examined.

In the case of Estermann and Tornay, as stated, the rumors and theories (all unproven) involving Opus Dei continue, but they provide a case study of how keen commentators are to link Opus Dei to any catastrophe within the Curia. "The Esterman Affair" is a fanciful story, but one that has caused considerable damage to Opus Dei's reputation.

The Walls Came Tumbling Down

Nothing would have been possible without the election of Papa Wojtyla, his travel to Poland, and the continuous obstinate and smart work of the Church. Without the Church, nothing could have happened.

Lech Walesa, leader of the Polish Solidarity movement, in an interview with Oriana Fallaci

On the night of November 9th, 1989, the Berlin Wall—the most potent symbol of the cold war division of Europe—came down. Earlier that day, the Communist authorities of the German Democratic Republic had announced the removal of travel restrictions to democratic West Berlin. Thousands of East Germans streamed into the West, and in the course of the night, celebrants on both sides of the wall began to tear it down. Andreas Ramos, a visitor to Berlin in 1989, remembers the night well:

Over 20,000 East and West Germans were gathered there in a huge party: as each Trabi came through, people cheered and clapped. East Germans drove through the applause, grinning, dazed, as thousands of flashbulbs went off. We met people from Belgium, France, Sweden, Spain, England: they had all left their homes and come to see the wall be torn down. Germans were drunk with joy. Everyone spoke in all sorts of languages and half languages. French spoke German and Spaniards spoke French and everyone spoke a bit of German... Along with everyone else headed towards Berlin were thousands of East Germans; they had been in West Europe for a blitz tour with the kids and grandmother in the back, to look around and drive back again. Without passports, they had simply driven through the borders. Amused West European border guards let them pass. They smiled and waved to everyone. Everything was out of control. Police on horses watched. There was nothing they could do. The crowd had swollen. People were

> blowing long alpine horns, which made a huge noise. There were fireworks, kites, flags and flags and flags, dogs, children. The wall was finally breaking. The cranes lifted slabs aside.

The collapse of the Berlin Wall was part of the revolutionary changes sweeping East Central Europe in 1989. Throughout the Soviet bloc, reformers assumed power and ended over 40 years of dictatorial Communist rule. Elsewhere in Europe, Czechs and Slovaks led demonstrations on the streets to demand political reforms in Czechoslovakia. Leading the protests in Prague was dissident playwright Vaclav Havel, co-founder of the reform group Charter 77. (In January 1977, 230 prominent Czech intellectuals signed and published a manifesto announcing the formation of Charter 77, a "loose, informal, and open association of people" committed to human rights.) The Communist Party of Czechoslovakia quietly and peacefully transferred rule to Havel and the Czechoslovak reformers in what was later known as the "Velvet Revolution". In nearby Romania, the Communist regime of the infamous Nicolae Ceausescu was overthrown by popular protest and force of arms in December 1989. This was swiftly followed by the Communist parties of Bulgaria and Albania also relinquishing their power.

The revolutions of 1989 marked the death knell of Communism in Europe. After Germany reunified in 1990, the revolution spread to the Soviet Union itself, the very symbol of Communism. Mikhail Gorbachev led the country, surviving a *coup* attempt by Communist hardliners in 1991. However, by December 25th, Gorbachev resigned as president of a Soviet Union that had effectively ceased to exist, and ceded power to Boris Yeltsin, who oversaw the dissolution of the Soviet Union.

It was a change most Russians appeared to want and on March 4th, 1992, the *Seattle Times* reported how Mikhail Gorbachev had paid tribute to Pope John Paul II for what he called the pontiff's decisive role in bringing about change in Europe. Gorbachev, the first Kremlin chief to have met with a Pope, wrote that he and the Polish-born John Paul shared a "deep feeling of sympathy and understanding... What has happened in Eastern Europe in these recent years would not have been possible without the presence of this Pope, without the great role, also political, that he knew how to play on the world scene."

During their first meeting at the Vatican, in December 1989, Gorbachev pledged to permit full religious freedom in the Soviet Union, agreed to establish diplomatic ties with the Vatican, and invited the Pope to Moscow. The two men met again at the Vatican the following year. This was a massive step forward for the Vatican, considering the Soviet Union's previous hardline stance towards Catholicism.

Father C. John McCloskey, an Opus Dei priest and former director of the Catholic Information Center in Washington, has praised the Pope's part in the fall of Communism, but there are those who claim that Opus Dei itself played a significant role in the events of the late 1980s and early 1990s. In fact, some theories claim that Opus Dei was actually responsible for the fall of the Communist States. Furthermore, while it is widely accepted that Opus Dei has made inroads across the former Communist countries, further investigations have suggested that the organization has been unofficially present in the Eastern Bloc for considerably longer than the early 1990s.

Robert Hutchison in his book, *Their Kingdom Come*, points out that Opus Dei's first appearance in a Communist country was in Pope John Paul II's Poland back in the early 1970s. "As far as it is known," writes Hutchison, "Poland was Opus Dei's first deep penetration operation." (Note the "as far as it is known".)

Laureano López Rodó, Spain's ambassador to Vienna between 1972 and 1974, is alleged by Hutchison to have been the architect of Opus Dei's Polish operations. However, as López Rodó died in March 2000 it is impossible to discover what activities he was involved in during his time in Austria. Vienna, the Austrian capital, was said to be frequently used by Opus Dei's hard-working members as a vantage point from which to access Eastern Europe, a central European base from which to seek new converts to their cause.

Opus Dei allegedly maintained a strong presence in Vienna and, from the 1980s onwards, the key men, according to Hutchison, were Msgr Juan Bautista Torello; political scientist Martin Kastner; and Dr Ricardo Estarriol, a foreign correspondent for Barcelona's *La Vanguardia* newspaper. All three are indeed confirmed members of Opus Dei, but their status as "key men" has been disputed.

Naturally, Opus Dei's activities in Austria (and through the gateway to Eastern Europe, the Eastern Bloc) have often been treated with suspicion—especially by the likes of Hutchison. Opus Dei was felt to be a rabid critic of Communism, as seen during its "Franco" years in Spain and its actions in South America, and with allegedly historical links to far-right governments, all Opus Dei's actions in Vienna were monitored closely, especially by those with left-wing sympathies. In the eyes of the latter, the Vatican also appeared a menacing force as it was constantly trying to quell the Communists throughout the 20th century. As has been noted before, for Catholics (and indeed Protestants), it was the likes of Franco and other fascist dictators who had saved Christianity from destruction, which in the case of the Eastern Bloc came in the form of the "heathen" Communists.

In 1992, the anti-fascist magazine *Searchlight* claimed that Ricardo Estarriol had taken on an assistant—Jorge Eduardo Rosza Flores. When *Searchlight* started digging, it was discovered that Flores commanded the so-called International Brigade (PIV), a group of mercenaries (including British ones) based in Osijek, in Croatia. Flores' name also frequently cropped up in journalistic investigations into the deaths of British photographer Paul Jenks and Swiss reporter Christian Wurtenberg.

This is hardly the kind of image or reputation that Opus Dei would want within the organization, or even linked with Opus Dei, especially as Flores and Estarriol were reportedly spending a lot of time at the Opus Dei headquarters in Vienna. However, there is no indication *whatsoever* that Estarriol had any involvement in Flores' alleged crimes. This is just another example of further conspiracies, criminals, and criminal activities being linked with Opus Dei, without the organization actually being involved. Indeed, Opus Dei often appears to be a magnet for far-fetched myths and allegations.

Despite the spread of these negative setbacks, Opus Dei has worked hard to establish a foothold in the former Communist states, and was helped by John Paul II's first papal visit to Poland in June 1979 for the 900th anniversary of the martyrdom of St Stanislaus— Cracow's first bishop. The Pope was accompanied by members of his staff, including his personal secretary, Father Stanislaw Dziwisz. As stated in an earlier chapter, Dziwisz has been accused of being a member of Opus Dei but the organization categorically denies that he belongs to it.

The Pope's pilgrimage was seen as epic, and some historians view it as a turning point in the history of the 20th century. Throughout the Pope's many sermons, addresses, lectures, and impromptu remarks, his message to his fellow countrymen was simple: "You are not who they say you are. Let me remind you who you are."

The pontiff reminded the Poles of their history and culture in order to create a revolution of conscience and, 14 months later, some inspired Poles had formed the non-violent Solidarity resistance movement, Solidarnosc. With Lech Walesa at its core, this was a unique hybrid of workers and intellectuals—a "forest planed by aroused consciences", as the Pope's friend, the philosopher Jozef Tischner, once put it. Walesa worked hard to protest vehemently against the Communist restraints, and one of his first, exclusive, interviews was with Estarriol for La Vanguardia—from this point on, it has been alleged that Opus Dei was, then, at the very heart of the anti-Communist revolution.

"The Pope started this chain of events that led to the end of Communism," Walesa said to the press. "Before his pontificate, the world was divided into blocs. Nobody knew how to get rid of Communism. He simply said: 'Don't be afraid, change the image of this land'." While Walesa's affection towards the Opus is well known, it should be noted that he appeared to acknowledge his debt to Opus Dei when he witnessed Josemaría Escrivá's canonization in 2002. Walesa attended the event in Rome and stated: "At last we have a saint for the workers."

Following the Pope's visit to Poland, Opus Dei became active in organizing training courses, conferences, and debates among Polish intellectuals. In 1986, it arranged the first student exchange program between Poland and the West. It was a success.

Reports state that Estarriol and Walesa became close friends. When Walesa visited Rome in 1981, Estarriol travelled with him. According to Hutchison, Walesa was worried about the Soviets trying to destroy Solidarity, and met with senior Opus Dei members as well as some CIA strategists in Rome. Opus Dei denies these claims. As the organization does not see itself as a political power, it says it would not organize meetings as "Opus Dei" with the CIA. Furthermore, according to Andrew Soane, from the London communications office of Opus Dei: "Walesa did not meet with Opus Dei in Rome in 1981, or at any other time, in order to plan against a Soviet takeover of Poland."

Was Opus Dei involved in helping to "liberate" Poland? "Yes", according to Hutchison, who reports that Opus Dei *and* the Vatican had been sending vast amounts of money to Poland to assist Walesa's work. According to David Yallop in his book *In God's Name*, the total amount donated to Solidarity via the Vatican was in excess of $100 million. Naturally, Opus Dei has become increasingly frustrated with these allegations. The organization continues to make the point that it has not, and cannot, engage in financial enterprises, and that there is no truth to the claim that it gave money to Poland. Yet, the myth continues.

"The story about Opus Dei giving money to Soldarity," says Andrew Soane "is not only false, but actually impossible. Opus Dei *cannot* give contributions to political parties. Members of Opus Dei could do what they liked, of course, but I doubt they were responsible for much (if anything) in this area."

According to other sources, mainly Hutchison, the money came from United Trading, the Banco Ambrosiano's offshore network. But, after the bank realized that this could mean funding the entire Polish economy, Hutchison brings another twist into the tale—Opus Dei (and Poland) turned to Washington. Hutchison's theory is that Opus Dei was trying to ingratiate itself with William Casey, the director of the CIA under President Reagan, who was responsible for Washington's response to the Polish crisis. Casey then appointed General Walters to work with him, and it was Walters who paved the way for a meeting between Reagan and John Paul II.

To many, this meeting between the Pope and Reagan illustrated the growth of Opus Dei's influence in Washington in terms of policy and, furthermore, that Opus Dei had, in fact, played a "determining role in shaping the Vatican's reaction to Poland". This, according to Hutchison, was thanks to the number of Opus Dei sympathizers and members within the Polish-born Pope's staff. The theorists alleged that with Opus Dei supposedly at the core of these discussions, not only did Opus Dei have the Vatican's ear but was also at the core of Washington politics. Opus Dei continues to contest these allegations, once again arguing that the Work does not have political intentions and has had no part in playing a "determining role" in the Vatican's view of Poland.

Following the elections in Poland in June 1989, when the Polish

Communist party was defeated in the country's first free elections since World War II, democracy returned to the nation and signalled the end of Communism throughout Eastern Europe. By July 1989 Warsaw had re-established diplomatic relations with the Vatican and Opus Dei launched its apostolic and educational activities in Poland, opening pastoral centers for men and women, and cultural associations.

Seven years after the visit by Alvaro del Portillo, Escrivá's successor, to Poland in 1991, Opus Dei provided funds and personnel, including priests, to help establish an effective Roman Catholic Church in the newly independent Kazakhstan (part of the former Soviet Union). In Kazakhstan, besides the priests and laity of the Prelature who have gone there, members of the Priestly Society of the Holy Cross from the diocesan clergy have begun working in a corner of the country far from the capital. This is just one of many activities taking place across the former Soviet Bloc.

The fall of Communism was, naturally, a cause for great celebration for the Catholic Church, as it had previously been persecuted during the Communist regime. Joseph Stalin had virtually annihilated Catholicism in Russia, demonstrating the historically harsh animosities between atheist Communism and Catholicism. In turn, to show their displeasure, books written by Karl Marx were on the "forbidden list" of books for Opus Dei followers.

In an article in Opus Dei's official journal *Romana*, its Prelate, Bishop Echevarría, was asked about economics and Catholic teaching: "The fall of Communism and Marxism has opened a path for a greater influence of the market economy, at least in theory," the interviewer's question began. "The Church, which was one of the principal rivals of Communism, and in the pontificate of Pope John Paul II also one of the determining factors in its collapse, appears uncertain. It condemns the 'excesses' of capitalism in the name of solidarity, but one does not see an economic model being held up as an alternative. Does such an alternative exist? Is it the task of the Church to intervene in these matters? If so, how, and to what extent?"

Bishop Echevarría responded: "The Church, although it will never cease to condemn errors, does not consider itself anyone's rival. The Church announces the truth of Christ and defends it for the good of humanity. For this reason it does not have an economic model of its own, just as it does not have one in any other field that God has left to man's freedom and responsibility. The Magisterium's interventions in this area are directed towards guiding men and women, fostering justice, defending the dignity of the person, exhorting all to charity and solidarity, rejecting and combating theoretical and practical errors, etc. It is not its role to give specific solutions or provide technical criteria."

While the Magisterium [the Pope's divinely appointed authority, in place to make sure the teachings of the bishops are carried out] provides a formal arm of the Church, it could be said that Opus Dei, with its strict adherence to traditional rules, works on a more practical day-to-day level across the globe. It is a useful tool for the Vatican, which had "fresh" lands to conquer across the former Soviet bloc, and during the 1990s Opus Dei wasted little time in getting across its message (as well as that of the Vatican).

As stated, Opus Dei's first "official" mission was to Poland, but with the barriers down, by 1990 Hungary and the Czech Republic were the next two countries on the list. By 1994, Lithuania was another target and two years later, Estonia and Slovakia also received members of Opus Dei. By the millennium, Opus Dei gave its worldwide figures as 81,854 lay members of the Prelature and 17,534 priests within the movement. So what is the next step? According to Opus Dei:

> In addition to the consolidation of the apostolate everywhere, especially where we have recently arrived, a great desire motivates all the faithful of Opus Dei. It comes down to spreading this spirit of sanctification of daily work and the fulfilment of the ordinary duties of a Christian. When going to new countries in Asia and Africa, where Catholics are still very few, the idea is to collaborate there in the evangelizing mission of the Church. With regards to enculturation, it should be noted that the faithful Opus Dei are already in the same environment as the other citizens, their peers. Like them, they contribute to the conception and the development of changes of their own society, each of which has its own characteristics.

As Opus Dei states, its works in various countries is meant to help "contribute" to the "development of changes". It continues to deny that it has any political motives or aspirations. However, there is one theory—again maintained by Robert Hutchison—that claims that Opus Dei played a significant part in the war for independence between Serbia and Croatia. Naturally, the Vatican feared Serbia—as a predominantly Muslim nation, its threat was far greater than "Christian" Croatia. Hutchison would argue that with the rise of Islam, a group such as Opus Dei, with its strong emphasis on gaining new recruits to the Catholic cause, would be an ideal partner in the war against Islam, especially with the later anti-Muslim feelings following 9/11. Again, the claims are denied by Opus Dei.

The M+G+R Foundation, a previously mentioned website that specializes in extreme conspiracy theories, raises questions of the Vatican's mission in Russia. Its theories query the Russians allowing a Church that is "controlled" by Opus Dei to make inroads in Russia. Furthermore, it wants to know why the Vatican isn't working as hard to spread the word in places like Asia. Finally, it claims that the Russian authorities would be "insane" to allow the Church to proselytize across the country due to the Church's "Opus Dei agenda". The idea that the Vatican is an "Opus Dei-controlled" Church contends that the Vatican is masterminded by the organization—something that both the organization and the Papal State deny, and that both find mildly insulting.

Still, Russia has "allowed" Opus Dei in (there are no centres of Opus Dei in Russia, but its first activities there took place in the late 1990s), and the movement has made impressive strides across the former Eastern Bloc. By the late 1990s, the publisher Kontakt Plus of Bratislava, Slovakia, had published *Rozhovor o Zakladatelovi Opus Dei*, the first Slovak edition of *Immersed in God*, featuring an in-depth interview by Cesare Cavalleri with Bishop Alvaro del Portillo, Escrivá's successor.

Opus Dei works hard within countries to assist charity organizations. Not only does this aid the organization's reputation, but it makes sure that Opus Dei reaches out to as many people as possible. In 1997 in Tallin, Estonia, Opus Dei founded "Alfa Klupi"—two years after its inception, there were 40 active members working with almost 100 boys, between the ages of 10 and 16, who take part in regular and special activities. According to Opus Dei: "Pluralism is a special characteristic of this initiative aimed at the formation of young boys."

"The regular activities of the club are classes in languages and computers," say the organizers of the club. "Weekends have been used for soccer training, which is done indoors given the harsh climate and the scarcity of daylight during the winter. At the same time each member has a tutor with whom he develops a systematic plan of academic counselling and personal development." Again, as other Catholic or religious groups have found through the years, building strong bonds through counselling or personal development is a key way to find potential Opus Dei members, while at the same time ensuring good works for the local population.

June 26th is designated as the feast of "Saint Josemaría" and June 26th, 2002, was an important date for Opus Dei, as 2002 marked the 100th anniversary of Josemaría Escrivá's birth, a celebratory event that demonstrated how far the organization had come on the worldwide stage. It was celebrated in churches throughout the world, from Asia to Australia to North and South America. As if to prove Opus Dei's strength and depth, it was possible to attend a Mass in honor of the founder of Opus Dei in or around June 26th in almost any country in Europe—in many cases, the diocesan bishop or the Vatican's nuncio presided over the Eucharist ceremonies.

In Poland, Masses were celebrated in various dioceses including Warsaw-Praga (a suffragan diocese of Warsaw), Cracow, and Lublin. Bishop Kazimierz Romaniuk, the bishop of Warsaw-Praga, was the principal celebrant in Warsaw.

Some 350 people participated in the Mass in honour of Escrivá in Zagreb, the capital of Croatia—Archbishop Josip Bozanic celebrated with a large number of priests in the Church of St Peter. Like Romaniuk, Bozanic's presence at the Mass was an example of another high-powered papal envoy endorsing Escrivá in the former Eastern Bloc. Bozanic, the Archbishop of Zagreb, was also the president of the Bishops' Conference of Croatia.

There were celebrations in Kazakhstan, where Almaty's Apostolic Administrator, Bishop Henry Howaniec, was the main celebrant at the Mass in honour of Escrivá. Speaking to the congregation in the cathedral of the Most Holy Trinity, Howaniec's homily dwelt on the sense of divine filiation in Escrivá's life and preaching, before encouraging the faithful to imitate his life of prayer. Among the participants were people with Kazakh, Russian, German, and Polish backgrounds.

Lithuania held a Mass in the Basilica cathedral of Vilnius. The apostolic nuncio for the three Baltic countries, Bishop Erwin Josef Ender, was the primary celebrant, assisted by the Regional Vicar of the Opus Dei Prelature and other priests. Ender had been present at Escrivá's beatification in Rome and expressed gratitude for the Prelature's work of both priests and lay people in the Baltic nations. Ender also pointed out that in Estonia, where the Church is still small and developing, he was grateful to see a number of conversions being made. Meanwhile, Prague's auxiliary Bishop Vaclav Maly was the main celebrant at the Eucharistic celebration in the church of Our Lady of Tyn, while Budapest saw Bishop Karl Josef Rauber, the Holy See's nuncio, as the main celebrant. Opus Dei's founder's Mass appeared to be a point of celebration across Eastern Europe and indicates a growing and vibrant Church across the former Eastern Bloc.

As Opus Dei enjoys its Personal Prelature status, it is one of the few Catholic organizations within the Eastern Bloc, which, with the Pope's approval, actively proselytizes with a large amount of success. With centers across Eastern Europe, Opus Dei has paved a strong path to ensure Catholics will always be able to find them.

European Unions and Opus Dei

Highly organized secular humanists in the UN and European governments are "the enemy".

A Vatican official

In December 2004, British newspapers were in uproar about the appointment of Ruth Kelly as the government's new Education Secretary. At 36, Kelly was the youngest cabinet minister by ten years and had been in Parliament only since 1997. A mother of four, Kelly had not been involved in a sex scandal, or any kind of financial mis-appropriation; instead it transpired that Kelly had close links with Opus Dei.

In the first public comments from Opus Dei since Kelly's appoint-ment to the cabinet in December 2004, Andrew Soane, Opus Dei's London communications officer, said: "She has attended meetings." Other sources within the organization also confirmed that Kelly attended meetings of Opus Dei while at Oxford with her brother Ronan Kelly, a hospital doctor in Singapore, who researches herbal medicines and who is a supernumerary within Opus Dei.

Though Kelly's private beliefs are her business, it does seem jus-tifiable to find out just how far her faith pervades into her politics. "People are rightly interested in how it's possible to have a person with a faith at the center of politics," said Kelly in an interview with *The Spectator* in February 2005.

Kelly has declared an affiliation with Opus Dei and it is known that she is a staunch Roman Catholic, who opposes abortion and euthanasia. She also once, reportedly, told the prime minister, Tony Blair, that she could never support stem cell research. According to the *Sunday Times* in England in a report in December 2004: "Some MPs fear her religion may cloud her judgment on issues such as sex education. She was last week excused the three-line whip vote on living wills."

However, in *The Spectator* interview Kelly refuted the claims that she had told Tony Blair that her views on abortion and other medical ethics issues would prevent her taking any jobs in the Health Department. "It's been written but it's wrong," said Kelly. "I've never been offered it...and if I had been offered it I wouldn't have said no."

Secular groups in England reacted with alarm to Kelly's appointment to Tony Blair's cabinet, arguing that someone with such conservative Catholic views on the family, abortion, and contraception should not be in charge of education policy. They were not alone in their complaints, following the Opus Dei "revelations". Leading British scientists expressed concern that the new Education Secretary's conservative views on stem cell research and cloning could affect vital science developments and research grants in Britain. The scientists justified their fears by pointing out that Kelly is responsible for a £1 billion research budget and has opposed motions on embryo research in Parliament.

When the media started digging further, they discovered that the DfES (Department for Education and Skills) refused to comment on Kelly's affiliation with Opus Dei. A spokeswoman merely said: "I am not going to discuss Ruth Kelly's faith." Elsewhere, a senior Catholic source told London's *The Times* newspaper: "There is no doubt whatsoever that Ruth Kelly is a fully paid-up member...on contraception, abortion, euthanasia, and other issues such as stem cell research, Ruth is very straight down the line."

A senior columnist at *The Times* was one of the only journalists who took it upon himself to defend Kelly against all the allegations and hysteria that surrounded her Opus Dei affiliations. "Of all the stories one could not have predicted to hover around the fringes of the news in early 2005," wrote Matthew Parris, "what the newspapers characterize as a shadowy cadre of elite Roman Catholic ultras certainly takes the biscuit. What next?...Will the Lord Chancellor be exposed as a Freemason, or the Children's Minister as a Satanist? And much of the report, Ruth Kelly, must feel, has been unfair. Opus Dei, it is true, can be linked to the Francoist establishment in 20th-century Spain; but some of its members opposed Franco bravely. And so far as they were a political force at all in Madrid, they were in many ways a modernizing influence—nothing like the sinister and murderous organization depicted in *The Da Vinci Code*, a work of pure fiction. Opus Dei in Spain consisted of clever and clubable achievers, not secret torturers. Nor are they today. There is no fair-minded reason for the Education Secretary to feel embarrassed about her association with Opus Dei in 21st-century Britain." Parris was a lone voice, as other papers chose to follow the conspiracy theory route and play on the Dan Brown/*Da Vinci Code* stories—it made better copy.

Kelly has certainly shown her support for Opus Dei—she was listed as one of the guest speakers at Netherhall House, an Opus Dei center near London's Hampstead Heath. Other speakers have included writer and historian William Dalrymple, hotelier Rocco Forte, and Member of Parliament (MP) Stephen Pound. Pound, the Labor MP for Ealing, has not been named as a member of Opus Dei, but during a British parliamentary discussion over amendments to the Northern Irish Police, Pound showed that he had some issues when it came to discussing Opus Dei.

During the discussion, William Thompson, MP for West Tyrone, wanted to amend a bill, which would result in the Knights of St Columbanus [an order of Catholic laymen]; Opus Dei; the Irish National Foresters; and the Jesuits being added to the list of associations required to register with the police. At this point in the debate, Pound interrupted the chairman Henry Malins: "On a point of order, Mr Malins. I would welcome your guidance. If one were a member of one of the four organizations—possibly more, but in my case only one, in amendment No. 254—should one not participate in the vote?" The chair replied: "I can say that there is no difficulty in participating in the vote, whatever organization one belongs to."

This leads to the conclusion that Pound could be a Knight of St Columbanus, or a member of Opus Dei, the Irish National Foresters, or the Jesuits. Opus Dei claims he is not a member of the organization, but the fact that he has spoken at Netherhall House has, as in Kelly's case, led to fears that he too is somehow being guided by an invisible Opus Dei hand. The conspiracy theories continue...

Kelly's association with Opus Dei appears to be a major issue not only for fellow government officials but for various members of the Civil Service, who feel that Opus Dei members are taught that their work must encapsulate their faith at all times, which would mean that the newly appointed minister would not be able to carry out her job to the best of her abilities.

Soane says such fears are overplayed, although he admits that members are encouraged not to separate their faith from their careers. "One message of Opus Dei is that your faith is relevant to everything you do," Soane said in an interview with the *Observer*. "You don't change persona when you go into the office. Everything is done in the sight of God and has to be arrived at following one's conscience. It's useful for people to try to find meaning in their work by relating it to their faith, not setting it aside from their faith."

For some commentators, Kelly's appointment became fodder for ridicule as people began to play on Opus Dei conspiracy fears, discussing ridiculous Opus Dei "plots" to infiltrate the government. Many came in the wake of the resignation of Britain's Home Secretary David Blunkett following his affair with Kimberly Quinn. One columnist, Stephen Moss, satirically wrote in the *Guardian* on the Kelly affair: "It began at Wheelers restaurant in London's St James's, where Opus Dei supporter Petronella Wyatt introduced Quinn (codename "Bimberly") to the unsuspecting Blunkett. Thus began the torrid affair, which—as the west London cell of Opus Dei had planned—was to bring the Home Secretary down and lead to Kelly's elevation. Fellow Opus Dei sympathizer Cherie Blair has been pressing Kelly's claims, and the organization now believes Kelly can become PM at the 2009 election."

An amusing idea but the thought of Opus Dei sympathizer Kelly as a future prime minister is something that worries many, especially those who view Opus Dei as a cultish power-broking organization with the ability to make policy decisions as it conquers Europe. Others question this theory, believing Opus Dei when it continues to plead the fact that it subscribes to individual freedom.

"Opus Dei gives only principles," explains Soane, "which are the same as those in the teachings of the Catholic Church. But lay people have to have complete freedom as to how they apply them or not, as the case may be. For example, stem cell research which involves the death of unborn children is seen by the Catholic Church as immoral. But as to how to apply this, Opus Dei does not tell members how to do this: it is a matter of conscience for the individual. Freedom is very important in Opus Dei."

Despite Soane's explanation, for many British Opus Dei watchers, the movement is still something to be feared. One ex-member, John Roche, wrote in the *Mail on Sunday* in January 2005 about his fears of Opus Dei's attitudes and activities in Europe while he was still involved in the organization: "I kept a diary of events and carefully studied the internal documents of Opus Dei at my disposal. It gradually dawned on me that the ethos of Opus Dei was entirely self-centered, sectarian, and totalitarian, and that it was misleading the Church about important aspects of its character. In the summer of 1973...[I] was requested to resign from Opus Dei. This I did in November 1973."

Despite Roche's suspicions, in terms of "conquering" Britain and gaining more "self-centered, sectarian, and totalitarian" believers, Opus Dei has a long journey if it is to progress. The actual number of UK members is comparatively small. At present, Britain boasts only a meager 500 members and a similar number of supporters, with two colleges in London, four in Manchester and three in Glasgow. Considering that, as of 2003, the UK's population was only 59.6 million, the number of Opus Dei members represents a miniscule percentage.

The movement is beginning to make some strides, however. At the beginning of 2005, Opus Dei was given its first parish in Britain since the movement arrived in the UK in 1946. Cardinal Cormac Murphy-O'Connor, the Archbishop of Westminster, handed over pastoral care of St Thomas More church in London's Swiss Cottage, to Father Gerard Sheehan, an Opus Dei priest.

As of 2005, Father Sheehan is one of 17 priests in Britain who work for the organization, and while none of the other 16 are parish priests, Sheehan is local deanery secretary for the Westminster archdiocese and regularly hears confessions at Westminster Cathedral and St James's Spanish Place.

"Father Sheehan's appointment is a further sign of that commitment and a natural development of his long-standing engagement in the parish," Murphy-O'Connor told journalists. "It reflects, too, the commitment of all of us in the Diocese to maintain the vigorous spiritual and pastoral life of our parishes."

In an interview with *The Times* in London, Sheehan denied that he would be on an Opus Dei recruitment drive but stated: "I will certainly want through the ministry of a parish priest—the proclamation of the gospel and the exercise of the sacraments—to encourage the lay people in the parish to take adult decisions about where God is leading them. If for some of them that means Opus Dei, I won't stop them. I also hope we will have vocations to the priesthood and the religious life."

"The decision by Cardinal Murphy-O'Connor to entrust the parish of 500 souls and their 1968 red-brick church to Opus Dei partly indicates that the organization has 'come of age'," wrote Ruth Gledhill in *The Times*, "and is achieving mainstream respectability within the Catholic Church in Britain."

Up until this point, Britain was the only country in the world where a bishop, in this case, the late Cardinal Basil Hume, issued guidelines to regulate Opus Dei's activities (see Chapter Nine). These guidelines were (and still are) carried out by Opus Dei.

Following Hume's death in 1999, Cardinal Murphy-O'Connor has a more relaxed view towards the organization. Interviewed by John L. Allen Jr in *The National Catholic Reporter*, the cardinal said: "I'm very content to have Opus Dei in the diocese. The Catholics I've met in Opus Dei have clearly been very dedicated Catholics, very committed to the particular path that is prescribed by Escrivá, which is the mission of the lay people in their professional fields."

In the late 1990s, Opus Dei established itself in Belfast. It runs a youth club called Citywise, and has links with schools in Northern Ireland. A similar club exists in Dublin; both have secured European Union support under the Youth for Europe program. For Britain, with Murphy-O'Connor giving the organization his blessing, the numbers of members should rise dramatically in the new millennium.

Despite Murphy-O'Connor's support, there are other Europeans who value Hume's stance on the organization. In 1997, a Belgian parliamentary commission placed the organization on a list of dangerous religious sects, alongside 188 other religious groups from the obscure "Knights of the Gold Lotus" to the more famous movement of the Jehovah's Witnesses, proposing legislation to bring all 189 of them under stricter control.

One European country where Opus Dei has flourished is Ireland. The organization was first set up in Ireland in 1947, headed by a young Spanish engineer, José Ramón Madurga Lacalle, who found a property just off St Stephen's Green in Dublin and began a concerted drive to recruit members into the movement from the nearby University College Dublin (UCD), the College of Surgeons, and other prominent institutions around Dublin.

José Ramón Madurga was born in Zaragoza, Spain, on November 10th, 1922 and studied engineering at the Special School of Industrial Engineering in Madrid and Bilbao before becoming a member of Opus Dei in 1940. In 1947 he began his apostolic work of Opus Dei in Ireland before being ordained a priest in 1951. At that time, Opus Dei was a popular organization, as members were attracted to the movement's idealism and what seemed to be a new and pertinent message regarding the roles of Catholics in their everyday work and society.

According to the Irish newspaper, the *Sunday Business Post*, Opus Dei's first Irish member was Cormac Burke from Sligo town. A UCD graduate in modern languages, Burke was later called to the Bar and was ordained in 1955, becoming the first Irish priest of Opus Dei. Other early vocations included Father Dick Mulcahy (son of former chief-of-staff General Patrick Mulcahy) and Professor Seamus Timoney of Timoney Technology. Burke's sister, Nora, also a modern languages student at UCD, was the first Irish woman to join Opus Dei.

According to Paul Harman, Opus Dei's Irish spokesman: "One of the first apostolic undertakings of Opus Dei in Ireland was Nullamore University Residence in Dartry, Dublin. The official opening in 1954 was attended by the Taoiseach (Prime Minister) of the time, John A. Costello; the Leader of the Opposition, Eamon de Valera; the President of UCD, Professor Michael Tierney; the Lord Mayor of Dublin, Alfie Byrne; and the Archbishop of Dublin, Dr John Charles McQuaid."

Harman also pointed out Escrivá's love of Ireland: "He [Escrivá] used to recall how, as a young boy, he prayed especially for religious freedom for Irish Catholics as he read about the Easter Rising and the War of Independence. In 1959 he spent some days in Dublin and Galway, encouraging the development of apostolic undertakings. While in Dublin he stayed in Ely University Centre on Hume Street, just off St Stephen's Green."

Following Nullamore, other student halls of residence were set up. For men, these were: Gort Ard (Salthill, Galway) in 1958; Ely (Hume Street, Dublin) in 1959; Cleraun (Mount Merrion) in 1982; Castleville (Castletroy, Limerick) in 1985. For women, there were Glenard (Clonskeagh, Dublin) in 1962, and Ros Geal (University Road, Galway) in 1972. Activities for students in Dublin are also held in study centres such as Carraigburn (Donnybrook).

Over the years, with the help of others, Opus Dei members have also set up a variety of youth-clubs. These include, in Dublin, Glenbeag Youth Club for girls and, for boys, Nullamore Youth Club in Milltown, and the Anchor Youth Centre (started in 1966) in Artane on the city's northside. These clubs offer a wide range of activities for young people. Catering and educational centres such as the Lismullin Hospitality Services Centre (Navan) offer courses in catering and household administration.

The *Sunday Business Post* reported in 2002: "Today there are about 700 members of Opus Dei in Ireland, half of them men and half women. There are also around 1,000 cooperators, who assist the organization with prayer, work and financial backing." Furthermore, Opus Dei members have also set up a number of youth clubs across Ireland and have established two secondary schools in Dublin— Rosemont Park School (for girls) in Blackrock, and Rockbrook Park School (for boys) in Rathfarnham.

By the early 1970s, Opus Dei began to develop an involvement in secondary education in Ireland and founded the Educational Development Trust to establish secondary schools for girls and boys around the country. Another important aspect of Opus Dei, not only in Ireland but worldwide, started out in Dublin. Scepter Publishers Ltd was founded in Ireland in 1959 and among the founding directors were Henry Cavanna, a Spanish lay member of Opus Dei living in Dublin, and Wilfrid Cantwell, a Dublin architect (also a member of Opus Dei). The main aim of Scepter was to publish literature on Opus Dei for distribution in Ireland. Scepter is now dormant, but another house, under the same name and also founded by Opus Dei members, now exists in New York.

As with every other country where Opus Dei has made an impression, the organization has met with a mixed reaction from the Irish clergy. The late Archbishop of Galway, Dr Michael Browne, gave it his enthusiastic support, while the late Bishop of Cork, Dr Cornelius Lucey, provided Opus Dei with some stiff opposition, but there are still retreats for Opus Dei members in Cork on a regular basis.

A theory perpetuated by Robert Hutchison in his book *Their Kingdom Come* is that Opus Dei made its biggest breakthrough into the upper echelons of European society via Belgium, when the former Queen (Fabiola) introduced the Catholic aristocracy of Europe to Opus Dei. It appears that when it comes to political conspiracies, Hutchison places Opus Dei at the forefront of European endeavors. He puts members of the organization in highly placed commercial and central banking sectors, as well as within the government bureaucracy across western Europe. Opus Dei again refutes Hutchison's claims.

'Catholics For Choice', an organization founded in 1972, which is pro-abortion and claims around 8,000 members, supports Hutchison in his claims. Catholics For Choice's goal is to preserve the right of women's choices in childbearing and child rearing. It also advocates social and economic programs for women, families, and children, by engaging in public education on being Catholic and pro-choice—not a branch of the Catholic Church that would mix well with Opus Dei. Catholics For Choice said of Opus Dei: "Opus Dei's influence is out of all proportion to the number of its members, thanks to its strategy of recruiting and working in academic circles to nurture a highly educated elite. Through its members and sympathizers, Opus Dei is strongest in the media, medicine, the judiciary, university education, finance, and politics. Its strength is greatest in Europe and South America."

"In Europe," continues Catholics For Choice, "Opus Dei has concentrated with strategic precision on vital activities: opinion forming among academics through frequent conferences and the operation of institutions of higher education; the foundation of bioethics and other research institutes across the continent; involvement with the medical community, including construction of two hospitals; grassroots activities against legal abortion; and a political presence at the highest levels of governments and European political institutions, completing a direct line from the Vatican to the secular heart of Europe."

Throughout Europe, critics and conspiracy theorists continue to allege that Opus Dei members work individually and together to gain political power in order to enshrine the organization's views in public policy and legislation. Opus Dei continues to deny the allegations—the issue of freedom and individuality coming into play again. Yet the critics allege that members and sympathizers serve in national parliaments—including those of Austria, Germany, Portugal, and Spain—with France and Italy being perhaps the relative "strongholds". Opus Dei members and sympathizers are said to include French parliamentarians Raymond Barre, Christine Boutin (a consultant to the

Pontifical Council for the Family who frequently proposes legislation against legal abortion), Hervé Gaymard, and Prince Michel Poniatowski; Italian parliamentarians Adriana Poli Bortoni, Ombretta Fumagalli Carulli, and Alberto Michelini. Yet, with the exception of Michelini, who is a member of Opus Dei, none of the others mentioned above are proven members of Opus Dei. This looks like yet another spin on the organization in order to perpetuate the conspiracy that Opus Dei is a shadowy force looking to take over the world.

According to a report in the *Guardian*: "The Vatican and its political allies have implacably opposed moves throughout Europe to give legal recognition to gay relationships. In France, the struggle against a law supporting civil unions was led by deputy Christine Boutin, a member of the Vatican's Council for the Family, who has been entrusted personally by John Paul II with 'the re-Christianization of France'. Her efforts were backed by the French branch of Opus Dei, although it all came to nothing when the national assembly passed a law permitting civil unions earlier this year."

With Hutchison still convinced that Opus Dei is part of a political revolution, he continues to name alleged Opus Dei members or sympathizers who are trying to "help" Opus Dei to power. Supposedly, President Chirac's wife, Bernadette Chodron de Courcel is sympathetic to Opus Dei's "cause", as well as Italian lawyer Carlo Casini, who chairs the European Parliament Committee on Legal Affairs and Citizen's Rights, a post from which he advocates anti-abortion positions. Rocco Buttiglione, a Catholic who held the title of European Union (EU) commissioner for justice and home affairs, has also been linked with Opus Dei. Again, *none* of the above are actually proven Opus Dei members, but the myth of "power" continues.

Accusations against Opus Dei contend that members are able to advance their philosophies and beliefs through the various international development organizations, which are run by members. These groups allow Opus Dei members to attend discussions at intergovernmental conferences, and give Opus Dei the chance to express its opinions and lobby international institutions such as the European Union (EU) or even the United Nations.

According to journalist Gordon Urquhart, the most significant Opus Dei-linked organizations involved in international development are: the Istituto per la Cooperazione Universitaria (ICU), with offices in Rome and Brussels and a budget of $4.8 million in 1993, of which 85 percent came from public sources; the Association for Cultural, Technical, and Educational Cooperation, a Belgian organization, 70 percent of whose 1993 budget of $867,000 came from public funds; the Limmat Foundation, a Swiss organization accredited to the European Union; and the Hanns-Seidel Foundation, based in Germany, which channels EU and other funding to extensive operations in the Philippines, including the Center for Research and Communication whose goal is to form the country's economic and political elite.

In the above-mentioned cases the ICU does social development work, as does the Limmat Foundation, while the Belgian organization runs youth projects. As for the Hanns-Seidel Foundation, it is possible that the chairman or someone on the staff might be a member of Opus Dei but does this mean that sinister activities are taking place here? Presumably the charity gives to acknowledged good causes, keeps records, and files accounts—there is, surely, no need to assume that anything untoward is being carried out within these charities? However, if a member of Opus Dei is linked to the charity, the worst is usually assumed.

The exception in the list is a genuine corporate work—but then it is not a giver of grants. The Center for Research and Communication is the former name of the University of South-East Asia and the Pacific, a university in Manila that is a corporate work of Opus Dei (much like the University of Navarre in Spain). To say its goal is to form the country's economic and political elite is over-dramatizing: it is a statement that could be made of any university.

As Soane also points out: "Opus Dei itself *does not* handle money. However, some of the vast number of charities in the world among the huge number that exist, have (are bound to have, in fact) members of Opus Dei working for them—maybe even running them." In "normal" circumstances, one would usually never know the religious affiliation of a charity work, but in the case of Opus Dei and when trying to slot the organization into a conspiracy theory, it is immediately branded (unfairly) as "sinister" when, in fact, it is carrying out good works in a community.

Opus Dei watchers are afraid that the organization is growing in both activity and influence, and that it has the wealth to support its aims. The reason for the fear behind much of Opus Dei's work is that the membership of the organization is usually undisclosed. As a result, no one can really confirm exactly who is and who is not an Opus Dei member or sympathizer. Thus, there is a fear that with the growing number of academics, parliamentarians, government ministers, judges, and journalists within its swelling ranks, the organization will soon become large enough to build a powerful, hidden force, which can influence world events.

Opus Dei continues to contend these conspiracy theories—it comes down to one's belief in what Opus Dei is trying to achieve. For Opus Dei, freedom is the key point: without it conspiracy theories flourish. Members of Opus Dei are free, and they represent only themselves. This is Opus Dei's key issue, and without that belief in its aims then, naturally, these tales of power, world domination, and "invisible guiding hands" continue to be perpetuated.

Making a Mark at Home

The situation in Spain with respect to our corporate apostolates has not been particularly favorable either. The governments of countries where Catholics are a minority have helped the educational and welfare activities founded by the members of Opus Dei far more generously than the Spanish government. The aid that those governments grant the corporate activities of Opus Dei, like that they usually give other similar centers, is not a privilege, but a just recognition of their social function and of the money they save the taxpayers... I would not like you to think that I do not love my country or that I am not extremely pleased with the activity the Work carries on there. But it is a shame that falsehoods are occasionally disseminated about Opus Dei and Spain.

Josemaría Escrivá

While "Octopus Dei" continues to spread across the world, Spain, Opus Dei's homeland, is still one of the organization's strongholds. From its humble beginnings in 1928, Opus Dei members have worked alongside world leaders, at high levels within the Vatican, within universities, banks, law courts, and governments. Their success is neatly encapsulated by their strength in Spain, as Opus Dei has been a constant presence within Spanish politics, even after Franco's Republic came to an end.

It is this "success" that has led to further allegations against the organization. It appears that if any scandal, usually within the world of business, involves a member of Opus Dei, then conspiracy theorists choose to involve Opus Dei as an entity. Rarely does this happen to other groups—a believing Catholic arrested for fraud, for example, does not then invoke visions of a papist attack on the world's economy with the Pope holding the strings of his Catholic puppets. Yet, in the case of Opus Dei members, any scandal is seen to reflect on the entire organization—none more so than in Spain, where some individual members of Opus Dei have been involved in some high-profile financial scandals.

Opus Dei, for many Spaniards, has become entrenched as a way of life. Just as Josemaría Escrivá intended, his practises have been put to use by devotees in the business environment. In October 2004, Luis Valls, the 78-year-old executive chairman of Banco Popular, Spain's fourth largest commercial bank, retired. Valls, a lifelong member of Opus Dei, had instilled his work ethos throughout Banco Popular, which now prides itself on being one of the most profitable and efficient retail banks in Europe. The executive pay is modest, while the bank shuns big marketing campaigns. Thanks to its honest, hardworking ethos, the bank has a faithful client base among Spain's small and medium-sized businesses.

Banco Popular has had a long history with Opus Dei—it was the organization's first major financial base. Founded in 1926, just two years before Opus Dei, its founder and first president was Emilio Gonzalez. By 1947, a change of administration had shifted power into the hands of two Opus Dei supporters, Fanyul Sedeno and Felix Millet Maristany. With these two Opus Dei men at the helm, other Opus Dei members began to flood into the bank. Though Banco Popular has not been involved in any scandals during its history, when some Opus Dei members became involved in a financial scandal, it was the Opus Dei link and the scandal that were picked up on, rather than the good works carried out by Opus Dei.

Like the Banco Ambrosiano incident in Italy (see Chapter Eight), Opus Dei was said to be part of a huge banking scandal in Spain involving a textile company called Matesa. Again, this is one of the stories that surrounds Opus Dei—but what actually happened? There seems to be some debate as to the events in question. Some commentators on the affair (including Robert Hutchison) insist that Opus Dei was directly involved, whereas others feel that Opus Dei's involvement in the scandal has been taken out of proportion as part of a smear campaign against the organization.

The story goes as follows. In 1969, some members of Opus Dei were financially involved in a major company, Matesa, which manufactured textile machinery. The company was discovered to have used $150 million in official credits to finance fictitious exports and, on the basis of these fraudulent returns on export sales, Matesa had been receiving large credits from the Banco de Credito Industrial. The main bulk of the money was, ultimately, invested privately abroad.

The managing director of Matesa was Juan Vilá Reyes, who was found guilty of currency offences and obtaining official credits to finance fictitious exports. However, he was not alone in his complicity—members of Franco's cabinet, who were members of Opus Dei, aided him.

The fraud was disclosed in 1969 by customs inspectors, and publicized by liberal and Falangist journalists, critical of the men in charge of Spain's economic ministries who had links with Opus Dei. Those linked to the scandal included García Moncó, the Spanish Minister of Commerce; Vilá Reyes' close friend, the Minister for Development Laureano López Rodó (another known member of Opus Dei); the Finance Minister Espinosa San Martin; as well as the Industrial Minister López Bravo. Vilá Reyes was not only a member of Opus Dei but said to be one of the organization's most generous contributors. As for the cabinet ministers, they were spared from further embarrassment by Franco himself, after he declared an amnesty in 1971. Vilá Reyes, however, had to face the ignominy of a trial.

One of the criticisms raised against Vilá Reyes was that he had taken money to fund Opus Dei. Opus Dei disputes this and points out that Vilá Reyes' donations to the University of Navarre and to Barcelona's IESE (Instituto de Estudios Superiores de la Emresa) amounted to 2,450,000 pesetas (about £12,000) over six years. This was often the level of contribution that many Catalan businessmen gave to help establish a prestigious business school in their capital. In various press interviews Vilá Reyes spoke about this matter and said that the charge that he donated 2,400 million pesetas was totally without foundation; still it has been allowed to continue.

Vilá Reyes was brought to trial in April 1975 and defended by Gil Robles, a veteran conservative Catholic politician. Ultimately, Vilá Reyes was fined and sentenced to three years in prison for his involvement in the scandal. Apparently, it could have been worse—he might have been jailed for 1,290 years if the court had upheld all the charges against him. On December 2nd, 1975, King Juan Carlos I freed Vilá Reyes under amnesty.

This "scandal", however, did not blemish Opus Dei in Spain as no one, at the time, held Opus Dei as an organization responsible for the problems of Matesa, and members of the organization continued to hold prominent positions within the Spanish government. Despite this, the myth now perpetuated is that Opus Dei was at the center of this affair due to Vilá Reyes' Opus Dei membership—it proved a useful conspiracy for those looking to discredit Opus Dei, even though the courts made no reference to the organization.

Some time after the Vilá Reyes affair, commentators have sought to involve Opus Dei in another financial scandal, which involved José María Ruiz Mateos, an Opus Dei member and one of Spain's richest men. Ruiz Mateos was also the founder of Rumasa, one of Spain's largest conglomerates, whose corporate umbrella sheltered some 245 companies, including 18 banks and a number of major chain stores.

It has been alleged that Ruiz Mateos precipitated the bankruptcy of the holding company of Rumasa by donating tens of millions of dollars to Opus Dei. The company had enjoyed over 20 years of success, but in 1983, fearing the company's collapse, the elected socialist government nationalized, split, and defused the capitalist mini-empire. Rumasa was a diversified conglomerate, and expanded due to the acquisition of small Spanish regional banks that were absorbed into the Rumasa structure and managed by family (or friends of the family). Many of the banks lent over 70% of their total credit exposure to Rumasa group companies (nearly 300 subsidiaries) —this substantial bank lending led to the company's nationalization in a bid designed to head off its collapse. As the scandal hit home, Ruiz Mateos felt abandoned. No one wanted to know him, and he complained that he lost his powerful Opus Dei support network. He felt he deserved better—after all, he had paid his dues. Ruiz Mateos later claimed to have contributed some $30 million (in today's US currency) to Opus Dei during Rumasa's existence. The fugitive expressed his bitter disappointment towards Opus Dei as he fled the country to avoid arrest. Furthermore, alleges David Yallop, a "considerable amount of money came from illegal deals with [Roberto] Calvi" (see Chapter Eight).

Since 1985, when Ruiz Mateos left Opus Dei, he has criticized the organization (apparently for not helping him against his enemies) and the conspiracy continues that Opus Dei illegally siphoned capital out of Rumasa to support its corporate works, and the resulting financial hole left Rumasa bankrupt. This is a rather thin allegation, as the company books were opened to the Spanish government after its expropriation, and the alleged illegal transfers were not found—although Rumasa was indeed said to be bankrupt.

Furthermore, Ruiz Mateos' testimony denies that Rumasa was bankrupt—so in his book, Hutchison modifies his theory, agreeing that Rumasa was *not* bankrupt, but that the reason it refused to submit financial information to the government (the trigger for its takeover) was that Opus Dei refused to allow it to do so, for fear of embarrassment at relevations of the illegal transfers. Thus Rumasa was protecting Opus Dei. Obviously, this theory fails for exactly the same reason as the first supposition; there is no evidence.

It is worth pointing out at this stage that scandals like those involving Banco Ambrosiano, or indeed Rumasa or Matesa, were formally investigated by criminal courts, as well as by responsible government agencies in highly publicized and drawn-out court cases, giving rise to indictments, trials, and convictions. At no time in the course of these public investigations was Opus Dei implicated, or even mentioned. Neither the Prelature nor any of its directors were ever accused, charged, or brought to trial, because there were no grounds for doing so. Instead of taking note of serious official investigations and legal proceedings, critics continually surround Opus Dei with a pot-pourri of gossip and speculation. Despite these rumors and supposed scandals, Opus Dei continued to be accepted in Spain.

In July 1969, Franco appointed Prince Juan Carlos de Borbón as his heir, no doubt hoping for a continuation of an authoritarian administration; in terms of the internal power struggles, Opus Dei was flourishing. Members of Opus Dei held positions within the government, but the number of Opus Dei members who held cabinet positions was comparatively small (see Chapter Three). Despite these small numbers (which was across a 20-year period), it was still believed that Opus Dei sought political power. As a result, a story began circulating that one of its own was about to be placed in a prime position.

In 1972 Franco decreed, in the event of his untimely death or sudden incapacitation, that Admiral Luis Carrero Blanco, an alleged political ally and patron of Opus Dei, should immediately become prime minister. No theorist has actually declared the admiral a member of Opus Dei, yet he is often quoted as being an integral supporter, both politically and spiritually as a key member.

With Carrero Blanco at the helm, many felt this meant that Opus Dei had truly arrived in Spain—it would have a key man in power, leading the country and able to dictate reforms, implement educational policies, and put the Opus Dei stamp on Spain—if, again, you subscribe to the theory that Opus Dei seeks power. However, it was not to be, as Carrero Blanco was assassinated in December 1973.

Carrero Blanco had embodied hard-line Francoism and was seen as the main candidate to carry on Franco's policies—it was due to this that Euskadi Ta Askatasuna (or ETA), the Basque paramilitary group that continues to seek an independent socialist state for the Basque people, took it upon themselves to assassinate Carrero Blanco.

"Luis Carrero Blanco, a hard man, violent in his repressive attitudes, was the key which guaranteed the continuity and stability of the Francoist system," said ETA in an official statement issued following the assassination. "It is certain that, without him, the tensions between the different tendencies loyal to General Franco's fascist regime—Opus Dei, Falanga, etc.—will be dangerously sharpened. We therefore consider our action against the president of the Spanish government to be indisputably an advance of the most fundamental kind in the struggle against national oppression and for the cause of socialism in Euskadi and for the freedom of all those who are exploited and oppressed within the Spanish state." Carrero Blanco's assassination precipitated the regime's most serious governmental crisis, and was seen by critics as the start of Opus Dei's declining influence in Spain. Yet, note in ETA's statement that the group links the admiral to both Opus Dei and the Falangist movement—traditional political enemies of each other.

Compared with the 1950s and 1960s, it was considered that with the assassination of Carrero Blanco, Opus Dei had fallen from being one of the country's main political presences within the cabinet to being one among many groups competing for power in an open and pluralist society.

Following Carrero Blanco's death, the new successor was named as Carlos Arias Navarro, who proclaimed a policy of opening the country towards full democracy; Franco was too ill to interfere in the changes. The new premier also promptly ousted all Opus Dei members from the cabinet, replacing them with tough law-and-order men, many of them Falangists. Foreign Minister Laureano López Rodó was replaced by Pedro Cortina y Mauri, while other newcomers included Torcuato Fernandez Miranda and Gonzalo Fernandez de la Mora. Meanwhile, well-known rivals of Opus Dei, such as José García Hernández, were promoted to impressive positions within the cabinet—Hernández himself became the deputy premier.

Aware that Spain's prosperity was at stake, Navarro and his new government continued to press for closer ties with western Europe, aiming for eventual full membership in the Common Market. But Spain's politics remained suspect, especially since the cabinet seemed united only in its fidelity to Franco and his former authoritarian principles. Following Franco's death in the mid-1970s the country was divided and during this era Spain lacked an extreme right-wing party. As a result, it was proving harder to gauge just what percentage of the Cortes' members had extremist leanings. It was at this stage that Opus Dei was linked with a parliamentary *coup d'etat* attempt in 1981.

On February 23rd, 1981, at 6.21pm, a group of 200 armed Guardia Civil officers, led by Lieutenant-Colonel Antonio Tejero and accompanied by Major Ricardo Saenz Ynestrillas, stormed into the Spanish Congress of Deputies, the lower house of the Cortes. When they entered, the Congress was about to confirm the new prime minister, Leopoldo Calvo Sotelo, to replace Adolfo Suárez. The military men attempted to take over the cabinet and lower house, and told 350 deputies that they were to await news of the installation of a military government.

At the same time, many military leaders close to Tejero, led by General Miláns del Bosch, declared a state of emergency and ordered tanks out on to the street in Valencia.

The King (Juan Carlos) assessed whether enough military support could be guaranteed to confront the insurgents. Then, at 1.15am, wearing the uniform of a captain-general, he went on television to appeal for serenity and public confidence. King Juan Carlos said that he had issued orders that all necessary measures should be taken to maintain constitutional order: "The Crown cannot tolerate in any form any act which tries to interfere with the constitution which has been approved by the Spanish people."

Shortly before the broadcast, the deputy-chief of the army, General Alfonso Armada, entered the occupied Parliament accompanied by the head of the civil guard and the chief of national police, apparently to negotiate a solution to the siege. The occupants of the Congress surrendered the following morning without harming anyone, having held Spain's parliament and cabinet hostage for 18 hours.

Tejero was arrested outside the Congress building, and both he and Miláns del Bosch were sentenced to 30 years in prison, although Bosch was released on December 24th, 1988, insisting that he had been a victim of a conspiracy set up by Tejero. Armada was arrested February 28th, 1981. In all, 30 of the 33 suspects tried for the attempted *coup* were convicted.

Armada was released July 1st, 1990, claiming he never did anything illegal. Tejero, the last of the *coup* leaders left in jail, was released after 15 years in a military prison, on December 2nd, 1996. Later it was made known that the *coup* plans originated with Bosch. According to these plans, General Alfonso Armada was supposed to be prime minister if the *coup* succeeded.

It is at this stage, in later reports, that Opus Dei is brought into the equation. Armada, often viewed as one of the masterminds of the *coup*, was said to be linked with Opus Dei. Armada had been King Juan Carlos's tutor, remaining as secretary of the royal house until 1978 when Prime Minister Adolfo Suárez called for his resignation because of his reactionary behaviour. Debates still rage in Spain as to whether Armada and King Juan Carlos reunited during the *coup*, as a number of phonecalls were said to have taken place between them. Whatever the nature of Armada's involvement in the attempted *coup*, Opus Dei denies that Armada was a member of its organization.

This has not stopped conspiracy theories building. Presuming, and indeed believing, that Armada was a member of Opus Dei has led to accusations that there was an Opus Dei tutor in charge of the King—no doubt influencing him to the Opus Dei way of thinking. Then, to further the idea that Opus Dei seeks political power, it was said that an attempted *coup* would have put an Opus Dei man (Armada) in a strong political position. Was this a case of Opus Dei trying to force its way to the top of the democratic tree and take control? That was the later allegation against Opus Dei. It seems an unlikely course of action for the organization. Again, Opus Dei completely denies these claims; once again, others continue to adhere to the "political power" belief of Opus Dei, rather than the "political freedom" that the organization insists it follows.

Although it denies the political power allegations, it is true to state that Opus Dei continues to work in the field of education, which is also seen as the organization's key source of recruitment and influence. According to one commentator: "[Opus Dei] is helped by the fact that the national university system is severely stretched in Spain. In an effort to decrease pressure on places, Spain's former socialist government issued a decree in 1991 setting out regulations for the creation of 'a new generation of private universities'."

The four private HEIs (Higher Education Institutions) in existence in 1991 were all run by the Catholic Church (three by the Jesuits and one by Opus Dei), and accounted for less than three percent of the total number of students. The thought was that any new education initiatives would be secular, like the Ramon Llúll University in Barcelona. However, when José María Aznar's political party, Partido Popular, was elected in 1996, his new Education Minister, Esperanza Aguirre y Gil de Biedma, was alleged to have Opus Dei links. Although the minister has never actually been named as a member of Opus Dei, it appears that, once again, anyone connected with education is always linked with Opus Dei. It was felt that hopes of a secular educational force would prove fruitless as religious institutions would be given preferential treatment, due to Aznar's strong religious beliefs.

It took time for Aznar's party to gain an absolute majority in the Spanish parliament, but once Partido Popular was in, it was felt that Opus Dei directors would be able to rise again in Spain, though this again assumes that Opus Dei, the organization, is a political force.

Aznar was born in Madrid in 1953; and in 1989 he became the presidential candidate of the Partido Popular before becoming Spain's prime minister. Allegedly, two of Aznar's three children attended Opus-run schools and his wife, a devout Catholic, has also been linked with Opus Dei. Again, these links are tendentious—Aznar, and his family, have never claimed to be Opus Dei members. Also, despite all these conspiracy theories, it should be noted that not one Opus Dei member was appointed to a ministry that was deemed important. Political commentators have noted that "some leaders of the *Partido Popular* become uneasy when they are accused of being subject to Opus Dei influence... Opus Dei has also inherited the bad reputation for political maneuvering that the Jesuits had in past times."

Religious conspiracy theories have been around for centuries, but it appears that Opus Dei has become the new "evil" religion in European politics. In the past, the Jesuits have been accused of being behind the French Revolution, or of being part of a crypto-Catholic (Catholics disguised as Protestants) plot myth. It was widely circulated in the German-speaking world in the 1780s that the Jesuits and their confederates, the crypto-Catholics, had infiltrated Freemasonry and were plotting to destroy the Enlightenment and restore papal rule to northern Europe. In September 1678, Titus Oates touched off a reign of terror that swept through London when he testified that there was a vast Jesuit conspiracy to assassinate Charles II and to place his Roman Catholic brother James, Duke of York, on the throne.

Europe is not alone in its anti-Jesuit fervor. It was alleged that John Wilkes Booth, a secret convert to Roman Catholicism, killed President Abraham Lincoln on the order of the Jesuits, who wanted to weaken American institutions for a Catholic takeover. It appears a tradition throughout history to lampoon and denigrate religious groups and assume these "powers" are seeking power in order to propagate their beliefs.

An article by author Robert Hutchison that appeared in the *Guardian* in September 1997 continues to perpetuate the Opus Dei conspiracy theory. Hutchison wrote: "Prime Minister Aznar's government is laced with Opus Dei dignitaries." He goes on to say: "Opus Dei's political ideology has changed little since the 1950s, when two of its leading strategists, Rafael Calvo Serer, a former Director of the Spanish Institute in London, and Florentino Pérez-Embid, published their treatises on Opus Dei as a Catholic regenerator with worldwide reach. Calvo Serer and Pérez-Embid reasoned that with galloping secularism overtaking the Western world, the only way to revitalize Christianity was to resume the Catholic crusade of Charles V—not this time with the resources of a single nation, but through a powerful and vital trans-national Catholic movement, headed by Opus Dei. Like the Spanish empire of old, Opus Dei's new-look Holy League was to have large-spectrum antennae in Latin America and the United States." Opus Dei denies these allegations, too.

By 2000, Opus Dei's success could be noted by the fact that every Spanish city or Latin American capital had at least one Opus Dei school for boys and another for girls—coeducation is not encouraged. Some cities have three or more—an impressive tally for an organization that started out on the back streets of Madrid, during a period of Spain's history when Catholics were being persecuted for their beliefs.

Within these schools, Opus Dei takes responsibility for "all that relates to their Christian orientation" and, apart from secondary schools and universities, Opus Dei also includes vocational training centers, medical clinics in underdeveloped areas, schools for farmers, institutes for professional education, and student residences among its corporate works. Some have seen these works as dangerous and a means to take young, vulnerable, and impressionable potential candidates and then brainwash them. Opus Dei takes umbrage at such theories, as members feel that they provide a valuable service across the globe in providing education, especially for those who can't afford it.

"In every country in which it works, Opus Dei carries out social, educational and welfare projects," said Escrivá. "Its corporate works are all directly apostolic activities: training centers for farm workers, medical clinics in developing countries, schools for children from underprivileged families."

In terms of corporate and apostolic works, Opus Dei says that its chief activity is providing spiritual formation to people through retreats, recollections, prayer and study groups, workshops, classes, and spiritual direction. One of the things Opus Dei emphasizes in this spiritual work is the importance of addressing social needs. As a result, Opus Dei's members often undertake social initiatives. In the case of corporate works, the organizers of an initiative often entrust the spiritual components of the initiative to Opus Dei, and Opus Dei in turn ensures the Christian orientation of the undertaking.

"Apostolic work is not limited to specific fields such as education, care for the sick, or other forms of direct social aid," says Opus Dei on its official website. "The Prelature seeks to remind people that all Christians, whatever their background or situation, must cooperate in solving the problems of society in a Christian way, and bear constant witness to their faith."

One of Opus Dei's major apostolic works is the University of Navarre, which Escrivá founded in 1952, and its main campus is in Pamplona. According to a report in the (London) *Guardian*'s education pages: "Few people in Spain would dispute that the University of

Navarre offers some of the best university education in the country. Yet the fees it charges are roughly half those levied in the public system. Pamplona's state-run university, which has only half as many students, has a similar budget." As a result, Opus Dei provides generous funding towards the university to ensure not only its academic reputation, but that it remains an attractive financial proposition for future students to come and attend.

"Opus Dei's aim is to do things well," explained Luis Gordon, Opus Dei's chief spokesman in Spain. "So, if Opus Dei sets up a university, the most important thing is for it to be a good university. If, as a result, people get closer to Opus Dei, well, fine. But that shouldn't be the primary aim."

Nearly 20 percent of the lecturers and professors at the university are said to be members of Opus Dei—numeraries, associates, or supernumeraries. Only about ten percent of the students attending the university come from Opus Dei families. It is felt by many Spanish that the University of Navarre offers a solution to parents who want their children to have a higher education but wish to shield them from the dangers and temptations found in ordinary universities.

Opus Dei's success at the University of Navarre can also be measured in the world of journalism in Spain. The university's journalism faculty is widely recognized as the best in the country. Its ex-alumni include the editors of El País, El Mundo (at one stage there were 17 ex-Navarre graduates working on the paper), and at least one former editor of Diario 16, as well as the presenters of two of Spain's three current affairs morning radio programs.

In 1958, the IESE (Instituto de Estudios Superiores de la Emresa), which has become one of the nation's leading business schools, was set up in Barcelona as the graduate business school of the University of Navarre. The school was created thanks to some impressive support and advice from the professors of the Harvard University Graduate School of Business Administration. Due to Harvard's involvement, IESE was virtually grafted from the American university's model. Another success for Opus Dei, the university proved to be the training ground of many of the Opus Dei technocrats, who had their heyday in the late 1960s and early 1970s. With branches in Latin America, IESE has carefully trained selected students in US management techniques to become managers and executives.

"The proof of our success is the 23,000 alumni of IESE programs working in more than 91 countries around the world," says Jordi Canals, the dean at IESE as of 2004. "They are known for their professional excellence, integrity, and broad vision of life. Moreover, IESE is normally ranked among the leading business schools of the world."

In 1999, nearly 90 percent of IESE students had at least two years of work experience, compared with ten years ago, when 70 percent had spent less than a year in the working world. The geographical mix is also fast changing. IESE's goal is a student body of 60 percent non-Spaniards, 40 percent Spaniards. The ratio now stands at about half and half. Applications for the autumn term in 1999 were 48 percent above the previous year's tally. The most popular countries of origin, after Spain, include the US, Germany, the UK, Mexico, and the Netherlands. Despite its changing profile, IESE's view of business has not wavered. "To that extent, the [Opus Dei] affiliation probably helps," Carlos Cavallé, a dean of IESE back in 1999, told the *Wall Street Journal*. "It keeps us focused."

IESE and Navarre, perhaps rightly, feel that their Opus Dei foundations are something to be proud of, as the official website of the university states:

IESE is an initiative of Opus Dei, a Personal Prelature of the Roman Catholic Church with activities on every continent. IESE believes that companies are communities of people and management should be centered around people: how to deal with people, how to create a context for professional and personal development, how to create powerful teams, and how to develop and sustain trust in personal relationships. The ethical and moral values the School draws from are based on the Christian tradition, a perspective that has been at the roots of social and human progress all over the world. These values emphasize the intrinsic rights and dignity of every person, and constitute the linchpin of any successful organization and society at large.

As proof of IESE's success, several international banks and industrial companies regularly visit the graduate school to recruit bright candidates for their companies. In 1982 alone, according to Juan Antonio Pérez López, who worked at IESE at this time, job opportunities outnumbered graduates by three to one—and this in a country with one of the highest unemployment rates in western Europe. Looking back at the first MBA graduation list of 1966, the majority of IESE's graduates in that year became high-flying business men in their companies while others have become political players. At one stage, there were five IESE graduates in the Cortes.

Proud of their Opus Dei roots, IESE and Navarre continue to flourish and, following the millennium, Opus Dei members are also beginning to return to key government posts. In 2002, the cover story of the Spanish magazine *Tempo* ran a feature on "The Real Power of the Opus" and identified key individuals of the Spanish government as members of Opus Dei. They named Luis Valls, the co-president of Banco Popular; Jesús Cardenal, the attorney-general; Federico Trillo, the Minister of Defense; Juan Cotino, the former national police chief; and Isabel Tocino, a former minister and then current representative in the Spanish legislative chamber. Valls and Trillo are certainly members, and have said so publicly, but not every name on the list has been formally identified as a member of Opus Dei.

Opus Dei's chief prelate in Spain, Monsignor Tomás Gutiérrez, has replied to criticisms of the movement in an interview with Associated Press, rejecting all claims that members secretly conspire to influence government or the professional world. Those in public office "are exclusively subject to the norms and guidelines" of their government, he said, notwithstanding Opus Dei's strict adherence to Vatican doctrine on issues such as abortion and birth control, which are legal in Spain. He also maintained the organization's financial assets were "scarce"—no more than necessary to cover education and salaries of its 1,800 priests and sponsored activities. He declined to give figures.

Relations between Spain's government and its clerics took a hostile turn in September 2004. As reported on Reuters by Emma Ross-Thomas: "Socialists swept to power earlier this year with a pro-gay, feminist agenda, and the Church is putting up a fight. Spain is a non-denominational country, according to its 1978 Constitution, but the state still funds the Roman Catholic Church. In September the government, which took power after a surprise election victory in March, plans to start legalizing gay marriage. It also plans to ease access to divorce and abortion. Church leaders have spent the summer warming up for a fight. Spain's leading bishops issued a statement saying that gay marriage was dangerous."

Clerics have responded by saying they could not watch the "moral degradation of legislation" and the country's "general apostasy". According to a recent poll, however, nearly 70 percent of Spaniards are in favor of the law to legalize gay marriage, while only 12 percent said they were strongly opposed to it.

"The former right-of-center government," continues Ross-Thomas, "which included at least one member of the conservative Catholic group Opus Dei, approved a law that made religious education, or the alternative subject 'ethics', count academically as much as mathematics. Religious education in public schools is Catholic based unless there are at least five students in a school of another religion or denomination who ask for separate classes." The new government quickly overturned the attempt to make religious education compulsory.

In 2003, Opus Dei members were still seen as targets for the Basque terrorists. As reported by Jonathan Luxmoore in the *National Catholic Reporter*: "Basque terrorists have threatened to target members of the Catholic Opus Dei movement during the current Spanish election campaign because of their links with the country's political establishment."

Although the threat was initially dismissed by a Spanish bishops' conference spokeswoman, who insisted the country's Catholic Church had "never taken sides" on political issues, it still shows that Opus Dei members are seen as legitimate targets. Among the estimated 28,000 Spanish Opus Dei members, the terrorists believed that some of them were members of Aznar's government.

Today, Opus Dei is more or less an accepted feature of the Spanish cultural landscape, and with more and more candidates graduating from its universities and taking senior positions across Spain the movement can only get stronger. Yet the general understanding of Opus Dei and its work still appears to be one of confusion. Despite corporate works across Spain, it is seen as a strong, dominant political force. Terrorist organizations name it as a target, and Opus Dei is still seen as a malevolent power when conspiracy theories are brought to the fore. This may yet change in time.

The Dei Today

The novel moves rapidly from cliché to cliché, is full of logical and psychological improbabilities and culminates in a saccharine denouement. The business with codes is quite disappointing... It seems that the reason for the success of this book is neither the sophistication of the riddles in it, nor the very modest quality of the writing. What thrills many of the readers is its pretension to a revealing and daring interpretation of authentic materials from Christian history and the Christian religion. *The Da Vinci Code* purports to reveal a Catholic conspiracy and show us its underpinnings. The author does not, of course, claim that his book is not a novel, but he does say that the novel is based on genuine materials that at least give rise to questions.

Aviad Kleinberg, Haaretz Daily *(Jerusalem), November 7th, 2003*

At the turn of the millennium, hardly anyone had heard of Opus Dei, apart from those with some knowledge of either Latin American politics, Spanish economic policies, or Vatican intrigues. The organization had a cloistered anonymity to such an extent that many committed Christians and even Catholics were unaware of the existence of the ultraconservative Roman Catholic movement. But that was before Dan Brown's *The Da Vinci Code.* Published in March 2003, *The Da Vinci Code* sold more than 20 million copies worldwide (as of April 2005), topping the *New York Times* bestseller list and conquering Europe. It also won the UK's "Book of the Year" award in 2005.

The frantic plot of Brown's blockbuster novel centers on a ruthless Opus Dei monk who commits murder to protect the secrets of the Holy Grail. The book reinforces enduring conspiracy theories that the movement is a shadowy, powerful elite, with tentacles stretching up to the highest echelons of society.

How much truth is contained in the book? Very little, according to many leading academics. Experts continue to reject much of the research throughout the novel, which cleverly links stories of the

Knights Templar, Leonardo da Vinci, the Priory of Sion, the Holy Grail, and Mary Magdalene into a murder mystery. The novel's elaborate claim that Mary Magdalene gave birth to Jesus's offspring after their marriage pushes the boundaries of belief just too far.

The feeling is that Brown's main contentions come from a series of forgeries that were invented in France during the 1930s and 1940s by a group of believers in esoteric doctrines, anti-Semites, and supporters of Henri-Philippe Petain, the Nazi-accommodating leader of "Vichy" France from 1940 to 1944. The theories invented in these forgeries were then picked up and used in a number of books, including the forerunner (and these days grossly overlooked) *Holy Blood, Holy Grail*, which was published in the 1980s and was hugely successful. These forgeries (involving the Priory of Sion and its spurious list of leaders) were exposed long ago—but still the legend, thanks to Brown, lives on.

The Priory of Sion was a club founded in 1956 by four young Frenchmen. Two of its members were André Bonhomme (who was president of the club when it was founded) and Pierre Plantard. The group's name is based on a mountain in France, Col du Mont Sion, not Mount Zion in Jerusalem. It has no connection with the Crusaders, the Templars, or previous movements incorporating "Sion" into their names. The organization broke up after a short time, but in later years Pierre Plantard revived it, claimed he was the "grand master" or leader, and began making outrageous claims regarding its antiquity, prior membership, and true purposes. It was he who claimed that the organization dated from the Crusades, he (in conjunction with later associates) who composed and placed *Les Dossiers Secrets* in the Bibliothèque Nationale, and he who created the story that the organization was guarding a secret royal bloodline that could one day return to political power—hardly the stuff of biblical legend.

While academics dispute Brown's theological and historical theories, the book has left a greater legacy: that of striving to destroy Opus Dei's reputation. While it is considered true that Opus Dei has considerable power and influence around the world (or at least that many of its members have held prominent political and religious roles within certain countries), the image of the organization as one containing murderous monks seeking to kill to protect the "Holy Grail" is one that has not only damaged Opus Dei, but portrays a grossly fictional scenario. There may well be aspects to criticize, as there are within any ultrareligious Catholic groups, especially when discussing issues of homosexuality and abortions; but with Opus Dei, Brown has taken his depiction a step too far.

Writing in *Crisis*, Sandra Miesel, the author of *Dismantling the Da Vinci Code*, notes: "By manipulating his audience through the conventions of romance-writing, Brown invites readers to identify with his smart glamorous characters, who've seen through the impostures of the clerics, who hide the 'truth' about Jesus and his wife. Blasphemy is delivered in a soft voice with a knowing chuckle: 'Every faith in the world is based on fabrication'."

In Meisel's book, the author dismantles Brown's "shoddy" history and delves into the sources Brown cites, scrutinizing his choices in his methodology. In a fascinating, academic read, she explores Brown's version of Christianity, taken from the extra-canonical Gnostic texts, before exploring his misrepresentation of the Knights Templar and Leonardo da Vinci.

Brown, naturally, is keen to defend his work and has stated that there are "thousands of sources to draw from". However, in the front of the book, a page headlined "FACT" offers this description of Opus Dei: "a deeply devout Catholic sect that has been the topic of recent controversy due to reports of brainwashing, coercion, and a dangerous practise known as 'corporal mortification'."

Brown makes no excuse for his "FACT" page and argues that all the documents, rituals, organizations, artwork, and architecture that he refers to in the novel actually exist. Brian Finnerty, Opus Dei's US communications director, said a letter was sent to Doubleday, the book's publishing house, asking it to remove the "FACT" page and to correct claims such as that Opus Dei had drugged college students to recruit them.

"I think people reading the book will be confused as to what's fact and what's fiction," said Finnerty in an interview with US magazine *Newsday*, adding that Opus Dei is simply an organization devoted to helping lay people lead holy lives. Doubleday has turned down Opus Dei, said Finnerty, who would not comment whether the letter was a prelude to legal action. "We hope that they'll still make corrections in it. We'll see what happens in the future."

The Prelature of Opus Dei in the United States has made several statements about Brown's book in its effort to set the record straight. Firstly, the Prelature states: "Many readers are intrigued by the claims about Christian history and theology presented in *The Da Vinci Code*. We would like to remind them that *The Da Vinci Code* is a work of fiction, and it is not a reliable source of information on these matters... We also want to point out that *The Da Vinci Code*'s depiction of Opus Dei is inaccurate, both in the overall impression and in many details, and it would be irresponsible to form any opinion of Opus Dei based on reading *The Da Vinci Code*."

Naturally, Brown is keen to stress that Opus Dei's anger at its depiction in his book is merely because he has "exposed" the organization for what he feels it represents. Brown defends his work, stating that he worked hard to "create a fair and balanced depiction" of the organization.

One journalist, Johann Hari, would no doubt support Brown's claims. Writing in the *Independent*, Hari said: "Brown has performed a valuable service. He has reminded the public about the existence of an authoritarian, ultraconservative cult that will play a key role in picking the next Pope—one of the world's most powerful men—and has been intimately involved with some of the ugliest fascist regimes since World War II. They want to make the Vatican an even more hardline campaigning force, battling the 'evils' of contraception, homosexuality, and divorce. In developing countries, their influence will mean the difference between life and death for thousands of poor people." This is a harsh criticism of Opus Dei—but within the book itself, readers would find it hard to differentiate between fact and fiction.

In *The Da Vinci Code*, Opus Dei members are monks. There are no monks within Opus Dei. The movement is not a monastic order, but "a Catholic institution for lay people and diocesan priests". As Opus Dei itself says: "Numerary members of Opus Dei—a minority—choose a vocation of celibacy in order to be available to organize the activities of Opus Dei. They do not, however, take vows, wear robes, sleep on straw mats, spend all their time in prayer and corporal mortification, or in any other way live like *The Da Vinci Code*'s depiction of its monk character. In contrast to those called to the monastic life, numeraries have regular secular professional work." Within the organization, married couples live in their own homes and attend parishes for worship, just like other Catholics. Centers of Opus Dei are depicted as monasteries in *The Da Vinci Code*, with members praying throughout the day in their cells. In fact, members of Opus Dei, whether single or married, have commonplace jobs and dress like ordinary lay people.

There are continual allegations throughout *The Da Vinci Code* and in the media that Opus Dei members practice bloody mortifications. Brown's detailed descriptions in the book discuss Silas' corporal mortifications with a discipline, as he whips himself over his shoulder until he feels the blood flowing down his back.

The discipline is a cord-like whip, which resembles macramé, used on the buttocks or back once a week. Only a minority of Opus Dei members use it, and they must ask permission. There is a story that Josemaría Escrivá was so zealous in using the discipline that he splattered the bathroom walls with streaks of blood. As part of the mortification process, most numeraries take a cold shower every day, and offer it up for the intentions of the current Prelate.

The cilice, meanwhile, is a spiked chain, worn on the upper thigh for two hours each day, except for feast days, Sundays, and certain times of the year. This is perhaps the most disturbing of the corporal mortifications and, generally, Opus Dei members are extremely hesitant to admit that they use them. The cilice is a mortification which causes discomfort, and if over-used could leave marks in the flesh. With these masochist acts appearing within the movement, does Opus Dei perhaps attract members with warped sexual tendencies? After reading *The Da Vinci Code* this could be the only conclusion or attraction of the organization—there is little else.

Brown constantly litters *The Da Vinci Code* with tales of mortification using the cilice and discipline as his focal points. Silas, the villainous albino monk, seems to wear his cilice regularly as a "perpetual reminder of Christ's suffering". It was also part of the "cleansing ritual of his pain". The description of Opus Dei's "practises" of corporal mortification, as represented by Silas's bloody purging rituals, are at best grossly distorted and at worst fabrications. Following the publication of the book, Opus Dei released a statement, saying:

> The Catholic Church advises people to practice mortification. The mystery of Jesus Christ's Passion shows that voluntary sacrifice

has a transcendent value and can bring spiritual benefit to others. Voluntary sacrifice also brings personal spiritual benefits, enabling one to resist the inclination to sin... In the area of mortification, Opus Dei emphasizes small sacrifices rather than extraordinary ones, in keeping with its spirit of integrating faith with secular life...some Opus Dei members also make limited use of the cilice and discipline, types of mortification that have always had a place in the Catholic tradition because of their symbolic reference to Christ's passion. The Church teaches that people should take reasonable care of their physical health, and anyone with experience in this matter knows that these practises do not injure one's health in any way. *The Da Vinci Code*'s description of the cilice and discipline is greatly exaggerated: it is simply not possible to injure oneself with them as it depicts.

Sharon Clasen, a former member of Opus Dei, who is now one of its harshest critics, says that the bloody whippings Silas gives himself in *The Da Vinci Code* are exaggerated, although less severe than the beatings Escrivá is reported to have given himself.

Clasen reports how her "spiritual director" pointed out a passage from a secret Opus Dei book, which described how Escrivá would tie little pieces of broken glass, razors, and other sharp objects on to his discipline and "beat himself until there was a huge puddle on the bathroom floor, that his assistant Don Alvaro del Portillo had to clean up. Apparently, Escrivá was doing penance for the priests who were being killed during the Civil War in Spain. So I [Clasen] really did adhere sharp objects to my discipline, namely small open safety pins, but I still could not get myself to inflict too much pain on myself."

Andrew Soane, Opus Dei's communications officer in the UK, plays down the importance of the practise. "It's a very minor thing. It's not something that looms large in the life of a member of Opus Dei. It's optional. You could compare it with training for a rowing race or a marathon, or some of the more rigorous slimming regimes. It sounds dramatic, but it isn't."

On Clasen's first day as a numerary, she was given a hand-sewn bag containing her cilice and a small whip. "Before I joined as a numerary," says Clasen, "One day, very soon after I had written 'the letter', I received a little cloth sack covered with flowers with a drawstring. The director opened the bag and took them out and showed them to me. She said, we wear the cilice for two hours every day except for Sunday and we use the discipline once a week and say prayers while we are hitting ourselves with it. She sort of demonstrated the method of how to hit yourself over her shoulder, hitting her back. The whole encounter behind closed doors did not last more than two minutes, so then I was on my own to figure out how to use these things and report every week to my spiritual director whether I had done so."

Allegations such as these lead to cult allegations—claims that are prevalent throughout *The Da Vinci Code*. As Opus Dei continues to assert, the organization is a fully integrated part of the Catholic Church and has no doctrines or practises except those of the Church. Brown's book also casts aspersions on the movement's close relationship with the Vatican. In *The Da Vinci Code*, Brown describes a new pontiff who distrusts Opus Dei and who removes its Personal Prelature status. To clarify this point, *The Da Vinci Code* refers to the organization as a "Personal Prelature of the Pope". Opus Dei is, in fact, a Personal Prelature of the Catholic Church. The term "personal" does not mean that Opus Dei belongs "personally" to the Pope, or to anyone else, but refers to the type of prelature that it is, as distinct from a "territorial" prelature.

Naturally, the book's snide digs regarding Opus Dei's precarious position within the fictional world of Dan Brown's Vatican has upset Opus Dei. Brown implied that when Pope John Paul II died, so would Opus Dei. As yet, with Pope Benedict XVI's election (and his continuation of John Paul II's work) it seems unlikely that Opus Dei will be ostracized. Added to this, Opus Dei members feel that *The Da Vinci Code* makes "melodramatic assertions" that the group engages in "brainwashing", "coercion", and "aggressive recruiting"—Silas is asked in the book to be a "soldier" of God.

Opus Dei's response is simple: "As a manifestation of its beliefs about the importance of freedom, Opus Dei has specific safeguards to ensure that decisions to join are free and fully informed. For example, nobody can make a permanent membership commitment in Opus Dei without first having completed more than six years of systematic and comprehensive instruction as to what membership entails."

Despite these statements from Opus Dei, there has been a growing group of ex-members, who dispute its claims. "I found as I got deeper and deeper that they were more like a cult," said Dennis Dubro, a former member of Opus Dei who lives in California. "The leadership was inner and secret."

Naturally there are many keen to defend the group: "They're devout Catholics who get a bad rap because they're a bit old-fashioned," said Terrence Tilley, a theologian at the University of Dayton in Ohio, who is not a member of Opus Dei. Still, the complaints against the organization continue.

"When you leave, you get a feeling of vertigo because you are used to being told how to act in every circumstance or how to fill every minute of your day," explains Clasen. "When I left, I was afraid that I wouldn't know what to think about, and it took me years to reconstruct my critical thinking skills and my power of concentration. It is a rebuilding of the self that has been almost completely destroyed over a period of years. You have to choose clothes for yourself for the first time, choose a style, choose where to live, find a job, find a boyfriend, discover music (I missed out on the 1980s music). My favorite part of freedom was watching movies. I love movies that deal with oppression of freedom and love of life. I love Iranian films, *It's a Beautiful Life, Butterfly, Osama, A Room with a View*. I also healed myself through reading many books over the years. There is censorship of books in Opus Dei—you are only allowed to read books okayed by your spiritual director—ones that are supposed to help your soul. Isabel Allende has been very healing for me."

According to ODAN (the Opus Dei Awareness Network): "Opus Dei members form 'teams' and develop strategies to attract new members. For example, if the potential recruit is an avid skiier, then the numeraries may plan a weekend ski trip, during which the 'numerary friend' is pressured to tell the recruit that she may have a vocation, after which the numerary must report back to the Director. If the recruit is receptive, then the Director may talk more in depth about the vocation. They discuss 'promising recruits' at their daily get-togethers (for members only) and during spiritual direction with Opus Dei priests and lay members. Opus Dei members often know which recruits are closest to joining, even if the person is hundreds of miles away. Opus Dei members are typically taught to always have

12 to 15 'friends', with at least three or four who are very close to join-ing. This leads to the utilization of friendship as 'bait'. Often, Opus Dei members drop friendships with those who are unlikely to join Opus Dei."

Dianne DiNicola, from Pittsfield, Massachusetts in the US, started ODAN after her daughter Tammi became involved with Opus Dei and she was forced to resort to an intervention expert to get her daugh-ter to leave the group. "They control a person's environment," said DiNicola, "their mail is read, what they watch on TV is monitored."

Following the publication of *The Da Vinci Code*, testimonies from the likes of Clasen, DiNicola, and Dubro are now being heard, and, more importantly in their eyes, investigated. Mistakes may have been made in the past, but Opus Dei has been trying to become more open. They have press officers across the globe who are on call to answer criticisms and the many theories that have multiplied concerning the organization's alleged behavior within the confines of Dan Brown's book. Furthermore, the statement frequently allocated to Opus Dei that it "does not want the rest of the world to know what it is doing" is one that the organization deeply objects to. The mission that the Church has entrusted to Opus Dei can be found by anyone who sin-cerely wants to know it. Opus Dei's Statutes, a public document, spell out exactly how it operates.

Nearly 20 years before the publication of *The Da Vinci Code*, the Prelature filed suit against a German publisher about to issue a book that was deemed libellous. A Munich court ruled in favor of the Prelature and decreed that several statements could not be men-tioned, among them:

- That Opus Dei is a financial enterprise.
- That Opus Dei has indulged in criminal financial activity, illegally moving money for speculative purposes.
- That enterprises of Opus Dei have been involved in arms traf-ficking.
- That Opus Dei has intermixed religious issues and economic interests.

Despite this court ruling, most of the accusations against Opus Dei all appear to concur that at least one of the above statements is true.

Certainly, this is the case in Brown's book, which alludes to the fact that Opus Dei has been involved in criminal financial (and other) activities, but as it is deemed "fiction" (despite Brown's statements of "fact") there is little that can be done.

The Da Vinci Code also depicts Opus Dei as having unenlightened views on women and their role in Church and society. As of 1997, the women's section of Opus Dei accounts for half the membership and half the leadership—a point completely ignored by Brown in his book.

In an interview that appeared in the Chilean paper *El Mercurio* in 1996, the Prelate of Opus Dei, Bishop Javier Echevarría said: "I give thanks to God often on seeing how the women of Opus Dei work in every sector of society: running corporations and hospitals, working in fields and in factories, holding university chairs and teaching in schools; they are judges, politicians, journalists, artists; others dedicate themselves exclusively, and with equal passion and professionalism, to the work of the home. Each one follows her own path, conscious of her dignity, proud of being a woman, and earning the respect of all, day after day."

A further statement, given by Professor Elizabeth Fox-Genovese, professor of history at Emory University and the founding director of the Institute for Women's Studies, said, in January 2004: "Opus Dei has an enviable record of educating the poor and supporting women, whether single or married, in any occupation they choose. In the end, Opus Dei exists to bring dignity and respect, sanctity and purpose, to the work—in all its guises from the humblest to the most prestigious—upon which our world depends."

One former member, the Rev Alvaro de Silva, a Boston priest who left Opus Dei in 1999 after 35 years, said Opus Dei members should be justifiably upset at the group's portrayal in *The Da Vinci Code*. But he told *Newsday* that he hoped the next Pope would be sceptical of Opus Dei. "My hope is that Opus Dei will change and embrace modernity and the modern Catholic Church," he said. "Maybe the next Pope is going to be different, and then Opus Dei will have to change."

The organization has certainly had to make some changes over the last 20 years. In March 1994, Bishop Alvaro del Portillo, the Spanish leader of Opus Dei and disciple of Josemaría Escrivá, died of a heart attack. He had been Opus Dei's leader for nearly 20 years and his successor, Msgr Javier Echevarría, was the Vicar-General before taking his role as spiritual leader. Echevarría had been Escrivá's private secretary from 1953 until 1975. This slow succession—a leader for life—serves to preserve the supposedly sinister personality cult of the founder, and safeguards the ethos of the organization for the future.

The death of several of the first faithful of the Prelature, who knew Escrivá in the early 1930s, has represented the end of an epoch, says Opus Dei. "The example of their life remains as a glowing ember for those still struggling here on earth, along with the example of many others who in these years have also entrusted their soul to God in a holy way. In this regard, another reason for joy since the last Congress has been the opening of the causes of beatification of a number of faithful in the Prelature." Who will take over next? When Echevarría dies, there will be no one left who had known and worked closely with Escrivá and, more importantly, known the founder's desires for Opus Dei. The organization might well modernize, which is something that ex-members have been waiting for.

One of the other issues facing the movement is its massive public presence. Since 2003, hundreds of Americans have visited the now famous Opus Dei headquarters in New York, while others have travelled to England to see Netherhall, Opus Dei's college in London's Hampstead Heath. This intercollegiate hall of residence for men has now become part of the European "The Da Vinci Tour" in the footsteps of Robert Langdon (Brown's hero)—the Louvre Museum in Paris even has a "Da Vinci Code" tour available for tourists.

Jack Valero, a numerary and the head of Opus Dei's PR in Britain, told the *Sunday Times*: "They come in buses with their copies of *The Da Vinci Code*. They look up at the windows, hoping to spot Silas. But there are no albinos here, nor monks. No Holy Grail behind the bookshelves... Transparency's the best policy. I invite them in and tell them we're just a Catholic lay group bringing Christ into our everyday lives and work."

"[The book has] probably done us some harm," says Andrew Soane, "but in some ways it has done us some good. It's certainly raised levels of interest in Opus Dei. It's never as bad as you think. I knew we'd made it when someone removed the sign at the end of our road."

In some respects, Opus Dei certainly has "made it". It continues to spread across the world. With Latin America, the US, and Europe under its belt, Opus Dei has moved into Africa and Asia, and has made progress in both continents.

The Regional Vicar of Opus Dei in the Philippines, Msgr Joseph Duran, points out that there are around 3,000 members in the Philippines alone: "the greater number in Metro Manila, Metro Cebu, Laguna, Iloilo, Bacolod, and Davao. Around 70 percent are married, called supernumeraries. There are politicians, bankers, corporate managers, businessmen, lawyers, and other professionals who are well known in public. The great majority of the faithful are relatively unknown to the public. They are employees, housewives, domestic workers, laborers, farmers, and ordinary professional men and women, struggling to do the best in their daily work."

The number of Filipino priests has also increased since Opus Dei went there in 1964. The first priest was ordained in 1975; there are now more than 40 Filipino priests of the Prelature, both in the Philippines and neighboring South-East Asian countries. Impressive figures, but what next? Will Opus Dei take over the world? Can Opus Dei take over the world? Does Opus Dei want to take over the world? There is no doubt that the organization has plenty of key members in influential positions and now, due to the popularity of *The Da Vinci Code*, people are aware of the group and are starting to ask questions.

One of the possible reasons behind the suspicion felt towards Opus Dei is its doctrinal view of the Church. Within Opus Dei, first and foremost, the main focus of the Church is helping people to achieve and obtain eternal salvation. This is a conservative vision (but not necessarily "right-wing" which is the label so often attached to Opus Dei), whereas a more liberal viewpoint would be that the Church's focus is to make people's lives better or to help the poor. With different views across the spectrum, it is reasonable to expect Opus Dei, like other factions of the Church, to be a subject of criticism—but not to the levels that it has experienced.

The organization continues to deny any political involvement in global politics. However, throughout history, Opus Dei members have been involved in various governments and, according to critics, have attempted to push through Opus Dei agendas (recently issues of abortion and same-sex marriages have been raised by members).

As stated before, however, individual freedom is the key point to bear in mind when considering members of Opus Dei who are in politics. There is no Opus Dei law to follow or a guiding hand, members are Catholics and make their own individual choices when it comes to accepting or rejecting bills or statutes of State. Opus Dei takes no credit for a good politician, and no blame for a bad one. That is one of the main results of its members having freedom.

So, if Opus Dei is not looking to take over the world, what is its mission? Is it targeting an elite? "I don't think we go for the elite," says Soane, "but I don't think we let them go either. We do put a lot of emphasis on academic institutions and we have universities that are run by Opus Dei. I think it's that the apostolate with intellectuals is challenging and difficult, so that's why there is an emphasis in that direction. It's not an overwhelming emphasis but certainly there is one. I think that's true. And I think the reason is that if you work with intellectuals you have a certain say in the way culture develops."

This could be interpreted as a "takeover" in terms of dictating culture. The evangelization of culture could be deemed a threat to everyday life, but it is something that Pope John Paul II spoke about in the past. The idea here is to transform the way people think and make the climate more favorable to Christianity. In light of this, can Opus Dei be branded a "cult"? In a technical sense, the answer is clearly "no": it remains an officially recognized branch of the Roman Catholic Church. Yet some ex-members argue that it has the hallmarks of one, since cults frequently regulate the individual's psychological and spiritual "reality".

"I think if one doesn't understand or accept that members of Opus Dei act independently of each other and are free to do their own things, then of course the whole thing sounds like one big conspiracy," says Soane. "So you might consider that politicians act together, that bankers act together in concert with them, and that they are all acting together with one over-riding end. That's simply *not* the case. The problem is the failure to understand the idea of freedom, which the founder of Opus Dei was very strong on." In light of this, deciding whether or not Opus Dei is indeed an organization that seeks world domination comes down to a question of belief—belief that Opus Dei means it when it *continually* states that it does not seek power. Perhaps as Opus Dei's mission becomes more widely known and understood, the general concern that surrounds it, mainly linked to the fear of the unknown, would be allayed.

Chronology of Opus Dei and Josemaría Escrivá

1902   Jan 9: Josemaría Escrivá is born in Barbastro.
Jan 13: Escrivá is baptized in the parish church of Our Lady of the Assumption, in Barbastro.

1904   Escrivá falls gravely ill, and is suddenly cured through the intercession of our Lady of Torreciudad.

1912   Apr 23: Escrivá receives his First Holy Communion.

1915   Escrivá's father's business fails, and the family moves to Logroño.

1917   Escrivá has inklings of his vocation. In late 1917/early 1918 footprints in the snow of the bare feet of a Carmelite brother stir up in him an intense desire to love God. Escrivá decides to become a priest.

1918   Escrivá begins his ecclesiastical studies as a day student at the seminary of Logroño.

1920   Escrivá moves to Zaragoza to finish his studies for the priesthood at the pontifical university of the archdiocese.

1923   Escrivá begins to study for a Licentiate degree in Law at the University of Zaragoza.

1925   Mar 28: Escrivá is ordained a priest in the church of the Seminary of St Charles.
Mar 30 He celebrates his first Mass in the Basilica of Our Lady of the Pillar, offering it for the repose of his father's soul. The next day he is assigned to substitute for the parish priest in Perdiguera, a village outside Zaragoza.

1927   Jan: Escrivá receives his Licentiate in Law.
Apr 19: Escrivá moves to Madrid to study towards a doctorate in Civil Law.

1928   Oct 2: While on a spiritual retreat in Madrid, Josemaría Escrivá, under divine inspiration, founds Opus Dei as a way of sanctification for people from all walks of life, in their daily work and the fulfilment of their ordinary duties as Christians. (The name "Opus Dei" was not used until the early 1930s. However, from the outset, in his writings and conversations about what God was asking of him, he would talk of the "Work of God.")

1930   Feb 14: While celebrating Mass in Madrid, Escrivá
       understands from God that Opus Dei is also intended
       for women.

1933   The first Opus Dei center is opened in Madrid—the DYA
       Academy, mainly for students of law and architecture.

1934   DYA becomes a residence for college students, from which
       Escrivá and the first members offer Christian formation,
       and spread the message of Opus Dei among young people.
       Consideraciones Espirituales (Spiritual Considerations), the
       forerunner of *Camino (The Way)*, is published in Cuenca,
       Spain.

1936   The Spanish Civil War begins: religious persecution is
       unleashed, and Escrivá is obliged to hide in various
       different places, and temporarily to delay his plans to
       expand the apostolic work of Opus Dei to other countries.

1937   Escrivá and some Opus Dei members complete a harrowing
       escape over the Pyrenees through Andorra, and make
       their way to Burgos, Spain, where Escrivá restarts the
       apostolate work.

1939   Escrivá returns to Madrid. Opus Dei expands to other
       Spanish cities. The beginning of World War II prevents
       expansion to other countries. The first edition of *The Way* is
       published in Valencia.

1941   Mar 19: The Bishop of Madrid, Leopoldo Eijo y Garay, grants
       the first diocesan approval of Opus Dei.

1943   Feb 14: During Mass, God lets Escrivá solve the juridical
       solution that would enable priests to be ordained for Opus
       Dei: the Priestly Society of the Holy Cross.

1944   Jun 25: The Bishop of Madrid ordains three members of
       Opus Dei as priests: Alvaro del Portillo, José María
       Hernández de Garnica, and José Luis Múzquiz.

1946   Escrivá moves to Rome.

1947   Feb 24: The Holy See grants the first pontifical approval.

1948   Jun 29: Escrivá establishes the Roman College of the Holy
       Cross (for men).

1950   Jun 16: Pope Pius XII grants definitive approval to Opus Dei,
       enabling married people to join Opus Dei and secular clergy
       to be admitted to the Priestly Society of the Holy Cross.

1952 The University of Navarre is founded in Pamplona, Spain.

1953 Dec 12: Opus Dei establishes the Roman College of Our Lady (for women).

1957 The Holy See entrusts the prelature of Yauyos, a mountainous region of Peru, to Opus Dei. Escrivá is appointed a member of the Pontifical Academy of Theology and Consultor of the Congregation of Seminaries.

1960 Oct 21: Escrivá receives an honorary doctorate from the University of Zaragoza.

Oct 25: Escrivá inaugurates the University of Navarre.

1961 Pope John XXIII names Escrivá Consultor of the Pontifical Commission for the Authentic Interpretation of the Code of Canon Law.

1962 Oct 11: Vatican II begins. Escrivá asks all his "children" in Opus Dei for prayers for the supernatural effectiveness of the Council.

1965 Nov 21: Pope Paul VI inaugurates the ELIS Center, a vocational training centre for young people in Rome, together with a parish entrusted to Opus Dei by the Holy See.

1967 Publication of *Conversations with Msgr. Josemaría Escrivá*.

1969 A special general congress of Opus Dei meets in Rome to study the change of Opus Dei's legal status in the Church to that of a Personal Prelature, a juridical structure introduced by the Second Vatican Council and ideally suited to the pastoral characteristics of Opus Dei.

1970 Escrivá travels to Mexico. He prays for nine days at the shrine of Our Lady of Guadalupe, and addresses large groups of people on topics affecting their Christian life—the first of what he called his catechetical journeys.

1972 Escrivá travels throughout Spain and Portugal on a catechetical journey lasting two months.

1973 Mar: *Christ Is Passing By* is published. (Another volume of homilies, *Friends of God*, *Furrow*, *The Forge*, and *The Way of the Cross* are published later, after his death.)

1974 Escrivá's catechetical journey to six South American countries: Brazil, Argentina, Chile, Peru, Ecuador, and Venezuela.

1975   Catechetical journey to Venezuela and Guatemala.
        May 25: Escrivá visits Barbastro and Torreciudad.
        June 26: Josemaría Escrivá dies in Rome. (Opus Dei
        membership totals 60,000 people.)
        Jul 7: Inauguration of the shrine of Our Lady of Torreciudad,
        near Barbastro, Escrivá's birthplace.
        Sept 15: Alvaro del Portillo succeeds Escrivá as head of
        Opus Dei.

1981   May 12: The cause of canonization of Josemaría Escrivá
        opens in Rome.

1982   Nov 28: John Paul II establishes Opus Dei as a Personal
        Prelature, and appoints Msgr Alvaro del Portillo as its
        prelate.

1983   Mar 19: Formal execution of the apostolic constitution
        establishing Opus Dei as a Personal Prelature.

1985   Inauguration of the Roman Academic Centre of the Holy
        Cross (which in 1998 would become the Pontifical
        University of the Holy Cross).

1990   Apr 9: Publication of the Decree on the Heroic Virtues of the
        Venerable Servant of God Josemaría Escrivá.

1991   Jan 6: Pope John Paul II ordained Msgr Alvaro del Portillo as
        bishop.
        Jul 6: Publication of the Decree on a Miraculous Cure
        Attributed to Escrivá's Intercession.

1992   May 17: Beatification of Josemaría Escrivá in St Peter's
        Square in Rome.

1994   Mar 23: Death of Bishop Alvaro del Portillo in Rome.
        Apr 20: Msgr Javier Echevarría is appointed as Prelate of
        Opus Dei by Pope John Paul II, confirming his election by the
        general elective congress in Rome.

1995   Jan 6: Msgr Javier Echevarría is ordained bishop by John
        Paul II.

2001   Dec 20: Publication of the Decree on a Second Miraculous
        Cure Attributed to Escrivá's Intercession.

2002   Oct 6: Canonization of Josemaría Escrivá.

Dates on which Opus Dei Began its Work Across the World

1946	Portugal, Italy, Great Britain
1947	France, Ireland
1949	Mexico, United States
1950	Chile, Argentina
1951	Colombia, Venezuela
1952	Germany
1953	Guatemala, Peru
1954	Ecuador
1956	Uruguay, Switzerland
1957	Brazil, Austria, Canada
1958	Japan, Kenya, El Salvador
1959	Costa Rica
1960	Holland
1962	Paraguay
1963	Australia
1964	Philippines
1965	Belgium, Nigeria
1969	Puerto Rico
1978	Bolivia
1980	Congo, Ivory Coast, Honduras
1981	Hong Kong
1982	Singapore
1983	Trinidad and Tobago
1984	Sweden
1985	Taiwan
1987	Finland
1988	Cameroon, Dominican Republic
1989	Macao, New Zealand, Poland
1990	Hungary, Czech Republic
1992	Nicaragua
1993	India, Israel
1994	Lithuania
1996	Estonia, Slovakia, Lebanon, Panama, Uganda
1997	Kazakhstan
1998	South Africa

Bibliography

Aarons, Mark; Loftus, John, *Unholy Trinity: How the Vatican's Nazi Networks Betrayed Western Intelligence to the Soviets*, St Martin's Press, 1992.

Bolaño, Roberto, *By Night in Chile*, trans. Chris Andrews, New Directions Publishing Corporation, 2003.

Bowers, Fergal, *The Work: An Investigation into the History of Opus Dei and How it Operates in Ireland Today*, Poolbeg Press, 1989.

Bramley, William, *The Gods of Eden*, Avon, 1993.

Brenan, Gerald, The Spanish Labyrinth: *An Account of the Social and Political Background of the Spanish Civil War*, Cambridge University Press, 1943.

Bristo, Father Peter, *Opus Dei: Christians in the Midst of the World*, Catholic Truth Society, 2001.

Brown, Dan, *Angels and Demons*, Atria, 2003.

Brown, Dan, *The Da Vinci Code*, Bantam Press, 2003.

del Carmen Tapia, Maria, *Beyond the Threshold: A Life in Opus Dei*, Continuum International Publishing Company, 1997.

Carr, Raymond, *Spain, 1808–1975*, 2nd edn., Oxford University Press, 1982.

Carr, Raymond, *The Civil War in Spain 1936–1939*, Putnam, 1962.

Clark, Michael, *Reason to Believe*, Avon Books, 1997.

Cornwell, Rupert, *God's Banker*, Dodd, Mead & Co., 1983.

Coverdale, John .F, *Uncommon Faith: The Early Years of Opus Dei (1928–1943)*, Scepter Publishing, 2002.

Crozier Brian, *Franco: A Biographical History*, Eyre & Spottiswoode, 1967.

Escrivá, Josemaría, *Conversations with Monsignor Escrivá de Balaguer*, Ecclesia Press, 1972.

Escrivá, Josemaría, *The Way*, Scepter Publishing, 2001.

Estruch, Joan, *Saints and Schemers: Opus Dei and Its Paradoxes* (trans. Elizabeth Ladd Glick), Oxford, 1995

Follain, John, *City of Secrets: The Truth Behind the Murders at the Vatican*, William Morrow, 2003.

García, Ismael, *Justice in Latin American Theology of Liberation*, John Knox Press, 1987.

Gilmour, David, *The Transformation of Spain: From Franco to the Constitutional Monarchy*, Quartet Books, 1985.

Girola, Pier Michele; Mazzini, Gian Luca, *Sopravviverà la Chiesa nel terzo millennio? (Will the Church Survive the Third Millennium?)*, Paoline Editoriale Libri, 2002.

Goñi, Uki, *The Real Odessa*, Granta Books, 2002.

Gurwin, Larry, *The Calvi Affair*, rev. edn., Macmillan, 1984.

Havill, Adrian, *The Spy Who Stayed Out in the Cold*, St Martin's Press, 2001.

Herman, Edward S.; Chomsky, Noam, *Manufacturing Consent: The Political Economy of the Mass Media*, Seven Stories Press, 2001

Hitchcock, James, 'Condoms, Coercion, and Christianity: A Princeton Tale', *Academic Questions*, winter 1990–91; vol. 4, no. 1.

Hutchison, Robert A., *Their Kingdom Come: Inside the Secret World of Opus Dei*, St Martin's Press, 1999.

Ibañez Langlois, José Miguel, *Josemaría Escrivá como escritor*, Ediciones Rialp, 2002.

King, Francis, *Satan and Swastika*, Mayflower, 1976.

Lernoux, Penny, *People of God*, Viking Books, 1989.

Miesel, Sandra; Olson, Carl E., *The Da Vinci Hoax: Exposing the Errors in 'The Da Vinci Code'*, Ignatius Press, 2004.

Mitchell, David, *The Spanish Civil War*, Granada Publishing, 1982.

Moncada, Alberto, 'Catholic Sects: Opus Dei' (trans.), *Revista Internacional de Sociología*, Madrid, 1992.

Payne, Stanley G., *The Franco Regime, 1936–1975*, University of Wisconsin Press, 1987.

Preston, Paul, *Franco*, Basic Books/HarperCollins, 1994.

Preston, Paul, *The Spanish Civil War, 1936–39*, Weidenfeld & Nicholson, 1986.

Rocha, Jan; Branford, Sue, *Cutting the Wire: The Story of the Landless Movement in Brazil*, Latin America Bureau, 2002.

Royal, Robert, *The Catholic Martyrs of the Twentieth Century: A Comprehensive World History*, Crossroad Publishing Co, 2000.

Schwarzwaller, Wulf, *The Unknown Hitler: His Private Life and Fortune*, National Press Books, 1998.

Simpson, Christopher, *Blowback: America's Recruitment of Nazis, and its Disastrous Effect on Our Domestic and Foreign Policy*, Collier/Macmillan, 1988.

Stossel, Scott, *Sarge: The Life and Times of Sargent Shriver*, Smithsonian Books, 2004.

'Third World Congress of Pro-Life Movements, Rome, 2–4 Oct., 1995' in *Familia et Vita: Pontificium Consilium Pro Familia*, Vatican City, March 1996.

Urquhart, Gordon, *The Pope's Armada: Unlocking the Secrets of Mysteries and Powerful New Sects in the Church*, Bantam Press, 1995.

Walsh, Michael, *Opus Dei: An Investigation into the Powerful, Secretive Society Within the Catholic Church*, HarperSanFrancisco, 2004.

Williamson, Edwin, *The Penguin History of Latin America*, Penguin Books, 1993.

Yallop, David, *In God's Name: An Investigation Into the Murder of Pope John Paul I*, Jonathan Cape Ltd, 1984.

Index